Vanishing Acts

Vanishing Acts

THEATER SINCE THE SIXTIES

Gordon Rogoff

YALE UNIVERSITY PRESS

NEW HAVEN AND LONDON

For Morton Lichter

True artist and witness, my better self

Published with the assistance of the Frederick W. Hilles Publications Fund of Yale University.

Designed by Thomas Whitridge and set in Monotype Bembo by Ink, Inc., New York.

Printed in the United States of America by Sheridan Books, Chelsea, Michigan.

Library of Congress Cataloging-in-Publication Data

Rogoff, Gordon, 1931–

Vanishing acts: theater since the sixties/Gordon Rogoff.

p. cm. Includes index. ISBN 0–300–08248–7 (cloth : alk. paper), 0–300–08777–2 (pbk. : alk. paper)

1. Theater–New York (State)–New York–Reviews. I. Title.

√ PN2277.N5 R64 2000

792.9'5'097309045–dc21   00–027527

A catalogue record for this book is available from the British Library.

The paper in this book meets the guidelines for permanence and durability of the Committee on Production Guidelines for Book Longevity of the Council on Library Resources.

10   9   8   7   6   5   4   3   2   1

Contents

Playwriting

Shakespeare and the Brits

Operas and Musicals

Ideas, Obits, and the Critical Act

Endgames

Preface

Beckett's Gogo, reaching for what he hopes will be the most insulting word in the language, suddenly finds it in "Crritic!" And who's to say he's wrong? For too many good reasons, the theater critic is rarely popular and almost never honored. What's popular, instead, is the public image that the critic enjoys being miserable. And once again, who can doubt that several critical reputations have been buttressed by a cruel, arbitrary talent to belittle and denounce?

Yet it ought to be repeated from time to time that real criticism, as opposed to consumer reports, is an act of writing, an effort to meet artists on their own terms. The artists, if they're reading at all, may be looking only for thumbs up or down; for them, reasonably enough, the secondary action of the critic—rendering opinions—is all that matters. Why take trouble over a flashing perception that criticism might emerge from a solitude like their own? Never about shifting tastes or casual enthusiasms, it can be a rigorous discovery of what Robert Lowell used to call "the unmediated fact."

Between the viewer and the maker lies a vision of possibility, ripped from thoughts, impulses, and actions beyond the realm of words yet nonetheless requiring articulation for those actions to be complete. The critic's particular solitude, more than the artist's, shares too much space with history and precedent. Relief, therefore, comes when contemplation dissolves into an act of writing. In that moment is the beginning of clarity: the critic doesn't propose or dispose; he or she is there, more than anything, to report an experience, to tell a story about what one person has witnessed and understood.

No profession with Leigh Hunt, William Hazlitt, Edgar Allan Poe, George Henry Lewes, George Bernard Shaw, and Henry James in its pedigree need apologize to anyone. It might be argued that, for most of them, performance criticism was as marginal as serious theater itself, a matter of marking time before the next painting, haunted tale, biography, play, or novel. Yet surely there can be no surprises about theater's long positioning as an afterthought in the imperium, even before reality turned virtual and space became cyber. What survives is their remarkable legacy to the most fugitive of the arts—Kean's Shylock, an image sketched by Hazlitt, the startling first appearances of Ibsen's Nora Helmer and John Gabriel Borkman freshly minted by Shaw and James.

Thanks to this legacy, and with no illusions above my station, I've been able to "go on" in Beckett's famous sense by accepting a calling. If I keep returning to these writers and to more recent heroes, such as Stark Young, Eric Bentley, Kenneth Tynan, Stanley Kauffmann, and Richard Gilman, it's because they help me to believe in the cardinal importance of whatever is unimportant to those in power. For me, it has always been a privilege to write on a subject that will never change governments or prevent catastrophes. Better still have been the delights, perhaps imperceptible to others more ambitious, in settling for the deliberate austerity of the short form. An epic poem is not preternaturally better than a sonnet, and I take it as axiomatic by now that Henry James, the failed writer of more than a dozen plays, might agree with some of us that his comments on "the scenic art" finally represent a distinguished thing truer to his gifts. The form, whether long or short, gains its authenticity whenever the writing is powered by urgency and need.

Which, not so incidentally, I'm always trying to find in drama and theatrical performance. The pieces collected here, changed only minutely from their originals, are not single-minded about anything but themselves: you won't find obsessive celebrations of an actor or a dramatist—no Kean for me, no Ibsen. But I hope you find a reasonably reliable witness to theatrical events—a witness, by the way, who knows better than anyone that worlds elsewhere have been bypassed in the journey. As a critic of the critic, however, I see a narrative here of achievement and loss, live theater declaring victories over new realms while holding the line against threats from every direction.

I go on, luckily, because I have no choice. A card-carrying pessimist, I want, nonetheless, to believe that even badly behaved theater—traducing intelligence, shunning its natural intimacy—is better than no theater at all. It's an appalling thought, but all the world's a screen, Jaques, not a stage:

even Shakespeare's prophetic soul has been outflanked by our recent century's descent from unprecedented inventiveness to a barbarism beyond the pale. Yet, weirdly, the stage refuses to recognize its own demise, persisting as a metaphor for resistance.

Shaw admired Lewes and even an almost-forgotten critic named John Forster for seeing the stage "really and objectively," for analyzing "what they saw there." Shielded by an accident of birth from the modernist perception that seeing the real is never objective, he was wise, anyway, to signal faith in the eye trained on analysis—or what I should prefer to call "description." Whenever I find the right subjective words—never often enough—I'm suddenly jolted into recalling that, for all my talismanic pessimism, I still trust the theatrical act. By writing about it, including its surrenders to the common bad, I'm reminding myself that theater keeps vanishing, only to return again as a form offering reflective wisdom, relief from the enveloping chaos, and—also not often enough—just plain fun.

Acknowledgments

Not for the first time, my gratitude goes to Eric Bentley for turning argument into a palpable, even loving, instrument. Perhaps it's because he *is* the playwright as thinker, a conversational and writing genius always in perfect pitch. Similarly, I thank Richard Gilman again, this time as guardian of the language: he's kept me alert, prepared to banish myself into a corner should he ever find me "riveted" to my theatrical seat or "stunned" by a performance. Both great writers, in their different and differing ways, have taught me to model myself on myself.

Erika Munk continues to be my favorite and most formidable editor, but many of the reviews published originally in the *Village Voice* have benefited from the incisive editorial wisdom of the late Robert Massa and the late Ross Wetzsteon. Thanks to Marc Robinson and Catherine Sheehy, former Yale students properly transformed into Yale colleagues, I was able to write for *American Theater* in a manner that was as liberating to me as any work I've ever done. I'm amazed at how many students I might cite for helping me to keep the faith, but if I limit myself to naming just two more here, it's not for want of gratitude to the others: James Magruder and Charles McNulty behave dangerously at times like my fans, which in the end never hurts. Magruder's lyrics and translations give me continuing delight, but I'd like them even more if they didn't seem to remove him from the critical scene. McNulty, bless him, is still there, upgraded at last from the "cameo" form to which he was consigned by the mid-nineties *Village Voice*. (I faded from its pages myself, yielding space for younger stalwarts, but less generously, from impatience with what I saw as its headlong rush to render all human experience trivial.) Thanks to McNulty, especially, for helping me to select and shape these pieces into book form: he was the first to spy a narrative in my journey, and I'm hoping that he won't prove to be the last.

Another fan, and the best of demanding friends, is Alan Helms. Offering himself as my personal grammar cop, he hasn't seen all of this work, so must not be held accountable for the dangles and skids to which my writing flesh is always heir.

If I appear to be favoring students over colleagues, it's only because, after nearly forty years, I don't know where to begin. With that in mind, then, I'll confine myself to thanking my latest colleague, James Leverett, a symbolist who could scarcely be more present in the here and now. In Jim, at last, I've discovered a co-mate in my frequent exiles to concert halls and opera houses. I like to think that, together, we're symbols of how theater critics keep themselves honest by loving other arts.

Several of the pieces here appeared in journals other than the *Village Voice,* some in *American Theater* and *Theater Magazine.* "That True Phoenix, da Ponte," was published in the now-defunct *High Fidelity Magazine.* "Emotional Weather: Notes on Alban Berg's Theater" appeared in *Parnassus,* edited by that most elegant of editors, Herbert Leibowitz, for whom I'd like to write more often, though I keep letting myself slip away too easily from his grasp. "E. B. on Acting" was written for *The Play and Its Critic: Essays for Eric Bentley,* edited by Michael Bertin, and published by University Press of America in 1986. "The Management Game" is an expanded version of "The Management of Management," which appeared in my book *Theatre Is Not Safe* (Northwestern University Press, 1987). Two essays, "The Neutral Space" and "The Critic Vanishes," are appearing here for the first time.

I'm grateful, finally, to George M. Nicholson, undaunted agent and true believer in the word; also to Jonathan Brent, behind me on *Theatre Is Not Safe* for Northwestern University Press and still with me at Yale University Press on this latest vanishing act; and to my manuscript editor Susan Laity, perfectly poised for commas and their cousins: her enthusiasm persuades me that this act may not vanish after all. Without the support of the A. Whitney Griswold Fund of the Whitney Humanities Center at Yale, I should not have been able to put together the organizing and finishing touches for this book.

Acting and Directing

The Figure in the Carpet

Great actors are always right. When Erland Josephson's Gaev sniffs the air around him while preparing to leave his sister Ranevskaya's estate during Chekhov's breathless coda to *The Cherry Orchard,* he asks, "What is this smell of herring?" In an instant, recognizing the source—Yasha, Ranevskaya's valet, returned from Paris with half-learned graces—he brandishes a huge white handkerchief, swatting the upstart like an arrant fly. Gaev's done this sort of thing before: Yasha always seems to be trailing cheap scents into the vicinity of his cultivated nose. The estate may be lost, and life has passed him by almost unnoticed, but he never misses intrusions on his gentility.

That handkerchief is Josephson's punctuation; Chekhov suggests only that he "looks at Yasha." Josephson turns that look into a complete, startling action, all of a sudden not so much in a hurry that he can't pause for a swat or two. Like everybody else in the merciless yet loving ode to foolishness, Gaev adores his passionate distractions more than life. Saucer eyes gazing into the inscrutable past, he's been stopping himself and everybody else all along with his unwanted observations. "Ladies and gentlemen, the sun has set." To which, of course, there can be no reply.

Not that it matters: Josephson's Gaev sweeps into conversation with only the most delicate hold on other people's imperatives. For him, the sudden discovery of where he's been, what he's noticing, how he might possibly push on with the life yet to live, is a cue for muted, pseudo-thoughtful oratory. He's a white-haired, bearded baby, scarf askew, fingers quizzically dabbing at his chin as if in half-hearted readiness to shut himself up. Josephson is a master at filling stage space with envisioned personality. He never shouts or insists on his theatricality, he's just there.

If only that were true of all the others in Peter Brook's beautifully staged yet strangely neutral production of Chekhov's great play. Perhaps more than any other dramatist, Chekhov can't be "helped" by ingenious conceptions or directorial whims. Brook has long since made a persuasive case for the magic of virtually empty space, an uncluttered environment signaling the audience's freedom to receive and imagine on its own. Until now, however, the liberation has been on behalf of Shakespeare or of Brook's scenario-texts, which move from one vast exterior to another. Nineteenth-century naturalists such as Chekhov or Ibsen yield less plausibly to a technique offering few places to sit and minimal distinction between one interior and another—or indeed, one interior and the outdoors.

Placing just a few occasional screens, one armchair, Gaev's indispensable bookcase, Ranevskaya's little table, and several scattered straight-back chairs on a vast landscape of oriental rugs is a risk worth taking even when it fails—as in the second act, when the rug-bound "field" remains airless. Given so much spatial freedom, the play adapts easily to the driving, rapid rhythms favored by Brook, his powerful argument against the dangerously languid—and dumb—productions of the past. Moreover, he almost justifies doing the play's four acts without intervals: here, at last, one can't possibly miss Chekhov's architectural integrity, the astounding way in which his echoes, counterpoints, and symmetries are constructed.

Yet the clean slate operates also as precisely that—the perfect production for those who come to it wishing to see the perfect production. This is Brook: humble, offering blanks for us to fill on our own. Against antiquated "mood," he poses postmodernist signals—a play with an international cast that could be taking place almost anywhere. Missing more than anything else is a sense of place, the particular spirituality of Russians overflowing with messy ideas and extravagant need. If anything, the experience here is peculiarly Anglo-Saxon, not in the stern, teacherly manner of the colonialist so much as in the polite, half-withdrawn believer in no ideas at all.

Some of the losses, unfortunately, can also be traced to Brook's directorial obsessions. With actors on their knees or haunches much of the time, Ranevskaya's and Gaev's mock-humble prayer-positioning to Lopakhin —"What are we to do? Teach us."—looks like the actions of everyone else. For the sake of theatrical gesture, Brook is too ready to muddle a reality he's already set up: two paneled screens are established as walls separating ball-from drawing-room, yet Lopakhin's miserable, drunken triumph when he's bought the cherry orchard leads him all too predictably into a lurching stumble, which topples one screen over.

Throughout, Brook's commitments to theatricality too often undermine Chekhov's painstaking instructions, or obstruct those gorgeously suggestive moments in the text when actors can imply whole histories for their characters. Anxious to push energetically to the end, he brings Firs on immediately after everybody leaves, thus missing the emptiness and quiet asked for by Chekhov. Similarly, Natasha Parry's Ranevskaya invariably barrels past any heart-stopping awareness of her beloved walls, objects, and orchards.

These blurs are more than incidental. When a scene change—such as the rolling up of the central carpet between the third and fourth acts—is more tenderly observed and fully realized than dramatic events, then surely some values have gone astray. Good performances here—Josephson's, Linda Hunt's assured and eccentric Charlotta continually surprising herself with pensive laughter, Roberts Blossom's marvelous Firs pushing his pained legs forward with his hands as he settles into the armchair abandoned like himself—seem to be wrenched heroically from the surrounding speed and generalities. Brook's directorial wisdom is increasingly picturesque, less and less about inventive acting.

How else can one explain the drop in acting temperature when Josephson, Hunt, Blossom, David Hyde Pierce (Yasha), Mike Nussbaum (Pishchik), and—to a disappointingly lesser extent—Zeljko Ivanek (Trofimov) are absent from the stage? Most of the voices are pitched to the ample rafters, evidently not noticing, even from Josephson's example, that Chekhov's thought can always carry. Brian Dennehy's Lopakhin stands oafishly at the center of the production's murkiest moments, a hand-slapping football coach sent out to do a job needing hard-earned refinement, elegant restraint, a moment or two—as with all Chekhov's characters—of carefully honored meditation.

Dennehy, at least, makes a statement. Most of the women would fade into the woodwork, if there were any. Perhaps they take their cue from Parry's overly glamorous, sketchy Ranevskaya. Not a hair out of place when arriving from the exhausting six-day journey from Paris, having cried—so she says—all the way, she's more like visiting royalty than a woman torn, joyous, or anguished. Chekhov says that Lopakhin's momentous disclosure finds her breaking her fall by grasping a chair: Parry dutifully does so, but then simply stands hunched over without doing anything else. Stephanie Roth is emphatically peevish as Varya, but rarely gets beyond that initial profile. Rebecca Miller's Anya is heart-shaped pretty as Anya, but she keeps disappearing without trace from her unexplored relationship; Kate Mailer's Dunyasha tries harder, but by the end it's clear that she's more pudding than peasant.

Brook is daring to suggest that his vision and philosophical authority can go it alone, without the continual nourishment offered by superb actors. Happily, the play as text and possibility shines through, moving and often funny, mainly because Brook's miscalculations—casting above all—are never so wildly conceptual that they get in the way of his frequent directness, his clean sense of line and rhythm. But oh how splendid it would be were he to cover his stage with a dozen Josephsons rather than a hundred rugs.

(February 1988)

E. B. on Acting

Eric Bentley has never been swept away by the tidal waves of romantic slush so often reserved for actors and the art of acting. If somebody slighted Uta Hagen's Joan (in Shaw's play) as a performance "pieced together," Bentley caught immediately that behind the pejorative remark was a popular respect for "something vague, sweeping, impressionistic," precisely what he was avoiding in his own performance appraisals. Instantly, he turned it around; "pieced together could mean something else": the selection of "bits of reality . . . the way a peasant girl walks . . . to be rendered step by step." If you notice her "rubbing her shins when the chains are taken off," and if you think a little, then you might also observe—as Bentley does—that "this is not a Rosalind in tights." E. B. can do this not merely because of a reluctance to gush but also because he respects plays as much as acting.

More: he knows plays as few critics ever bother to know them. Not just their pedigree or partial successes but their reason for being, their structured intelligence, all those specific assaults on a specific formal world. What follows then, is that he obtains ideas from the plays about how they might be acted. "It is the others," he says, "not Joan...who grow poetical and chant a litany." Hagen's Joan, he is saying, is not the Joan of mooning enthusiasts, she is "a real girl...genuinely bewildered." Carrying on where Shaw left off, Bentley notices that when Hagen cleans the dust off Joan, she is rescuing Shaw from creaking Shakespeareans of the day. Shaw was addressing himself to "the problem of credibility and knew that the Shakespearean actors would be his arch-enemies." Just for good measure, he adds a suggestion still worth heeding today for both Shaw and Shakespeare: find "the fine Elizabethan woodwork" underneath "the wallpaper and the plaster."

On acting as on plays, Bentley's phrasing glides effortlessly between an austere regard for observable truth and an expansive concern for subliminal ebb and flow. To know text is to honor subtext automatically. Bentley does this free of jargon, never a slave to theory at the expense of practical reality. In the last chapter of In Search of Theater, called "1900–1950," his summation is breathtakingly plain and comprehensive. Here is the playwright's champion acknowledging that "the theater's principal instrument is the actor." If this seems scarcely revolutionary, it isn't meant to be; against the background of feuding academicians viewing Shakespeare only as poet, never as actor, or conceptual directors selling Bright Ideas rather than Live Performance, Bentley's casual claim for the actor's sovereignty still needs to be argued rather than defended. "The purpose of theater," he says as the chapter begins, "is to produce great performances." His ideal critical world would have long ago produced more direct descriptions of "Duse and Bernhardt, Irving and Moissi, Chaliapin and Mei Lan-fang, Louis Jouvet and Laurette Taylor." Lacking such a historical criticism, we can move with him through the twentieth century's movements, ranging from Wagner and Ibsen to Brecht and Jean-Louis Barrault, noticing along the way that Stanislavsky's achievement—the theater's response to realism—could find itself mixed into such diverse figures as Jacques Copeau and Max Reinhardt. Like all great critics, Bentley finds links within links, getting his poetry from the facts.

For a time Barrault was his hero, but never a conquering one. Who but Bentley at the time had more right to notice "an actor as thinker"? Were our directors today to read him on Barrault (but do they read?), how could they possibly refute his reference to "Barrault's sanity," an approach to drama as "an art in which the actor serves the author and in which *the other theater arts and artists serve the actor.*" (My italics because that emphasis screams for a hearing now more than ever.) Bentley's other heroes—Brecht and Shaw—always had advice for the players, either formally or (with Shaw) informally in the shape of letters. Surely Bentley was the first to make uneasy reconciliations with two artists, Brecht and Barrault, so different from one another. Brecht's committed view of life is contrasted with Barrault's less definite nature: on the one hand, distance, light, ironical comment; on the other, magniloquence, ceremony, magical illusion. Lucky enough to see Helene Weigel's Mother Courage, he tells us what she looked like, standing outside the role, "cool, relaxed...with great precision of movement and intonation."

There it is, of course: who could be more precise in movement, more punctiliously aware of tone, than Barrault? Bentley, always ahead of everybody in his reading, found still another authority, now unhappily forgotten, for explaining his embrace of artists who might normally appear antagonists: Louis Jouvet, remarking after the Occupation that Antonin Artaud might not be the answer for everyone, said that "none of the theater's manifestations follows a straight line. None of the gestures or rites of genuine theater comes from a 'tendency.'" Bentley was tirelessly pulling all of them into his circle of research and discontent. Stanislavsky, Shaw, Ibsen, Barrault, Artaud, Copeau, Charles Dullin, Etienne Decroux would drop into his pages like the most natural companions, friends, at least, for a day. Hovering behind them in the mists of recent theatrical history were the cantankerous ghosts of Wagner and Edward Gordon Craig. It's easy to forget that nobody—not James Agate in England nor even Bentley's beloved Stark Young in America—was interested in, let alone capable of, these remarkable duos, trios, and sextets. E. B. was conducting a new opera all his own.

Young, however, had to be a daunting model for his disciples, especially when writing about actors and the art of acting. Sculpting actors' images with a molded, jeweled prose, Young meant to freeze their most ephemeral moments in an hourglass. He was—and shifting metaphors may be the only way to keep up with Young's mercurial, descriptive imagination—like a delicately poised hunter of butterflies sweeping them into his net only to give them swift release after noting the way a stripe or color caught the sun. Bentley has always been steadier, less susceptible to the mix *and* the metaphor. But Young's example had to be inspiring. Young, for him, was "a critic in the fullest sense—one who *judges* by *standards* that are not imposed from without but prompted and checked by his own first-rate sensibility."

His jewels, pro and con, may not have glowed, like Young's, in the pervasive critical darkness surrounding him. (The daily newspapers rarely see and describe; they sell and explode.) Bentley could honor any performance with appreciative detail, but he didn't simply collapse in awe or anger. For him, context—stress on *text*—was just about everything. More than anyone, he sees the whole performance in the whole play, never patronizing the actor with dithering flattery. He couldn't be intimidated— and how refreshing this continues to be—by what Shakespeare called "bubble reputation." Brando, for example, may have been an amazing young actor, but for Bentley, he was destabilizing *Streetcar:*

Brando has muscular arms, but his eyes give them the lie.

Here he is on some of the others.
Katharine Cornell:

She can neither raise herself to the semblance of greatness nor lower herself to the semblance of baseness, and acting Cleopatra involves both.

On Maurice Evans:

The perpetual "poetic" singsong! The laborious explanatory manner....Evans' Tanner is simply Evans got up to look as pretty as possible. And the whole play is transposed accordingly into a key of good-looking idiocy.

On Lee J. Cobb:

One of our finest actors. I do not mean we have no misgivings about him. His besetting temptation is sentimentality. When in doubt, he thumps the table, screams his head off, or wallows in a fit of weeping. Like most actors of his school, he sometimes seems to mistake the jitters for creative energy.

And on Viveca Lindfors he allows himself at the end a positively Youngian vocabulary:

> Miss Lindfors' hands and arms perform large gestures: one watches them perhaps with surprise, perhaps with incredulity, but hardly with pleasure. Passion, with her, is never convincing. She suddenly yells. She uses a sweeping movement of hand or arm. But we hear the yell and see the movement in isolation from the context. There is no connection, no cohesion, let alone liquefaction and flow.

If anything, however, he is even better when transported by those rare moments when performance slips with apparent inevitability into the textures of the play.
On Godfrey Tearle's Antony:

> I had no idea that the many sides of this Shakespearean hero could all be enacted by a single artist. Dignity and indignity, courage and self-indulgence, astuteness and apathy, swift practicality and amorous abandonment—all those are equally well suggested.

On Ina Claire:

> Such precise timing, such delicate underlining, such subtle modulations from phrase to phrase and word to word are almost unknown to our stage today. Our younger actresses, whose hands creep so nervously about in so many directions, might watch the fewer but righter paths travelled by Miss Claire's. Our light comedians, who so regularly practice the double take and other tricks of the eye and turning head, might profitably watch the quickness of muscle and attention by which Miss Claire avoids having her devices identified as tricks at all.

On John Gielgud as Clarence in the recording of *Richard III:*

> A model of Shakespearean speaking. The assignment was a very hard

one: to tell the story of a dream, keeping all the values of the story itself, though the teller of it is a man distraught and near death. Perhaps none of our actors but Sir John could realize both sets of values so fully: he gives all the flamboyance of the narrative plus all the inwardness of the character. Here is a great actor who has much that Olivier has and much that Olivier has not, including warmth, richness, and grandeur of utterance.

Even allowing for the moderately cranky, corrective reminder that Gielgud has been acting for a half-century with an extraordinary, if flawed, competitor getting most of the glamorous notice, only Bentley would be so quick to place Gielgud's achievement within the framework of the story itself. Great acting for him is never technique or display alone; rather, it is a meeting of textual complexity with acting complexity, the latter in touch with realms where there are no subordinations: Gielgud, master of shape, nuance, rhythm, rubato, and crescendo, all of these giving sway to momentary reality, the sudden call of inner voices, lifelike spontaneity sweeping all before it. Soberly, calmly, using a vocabulary and phrasing that keep transforming feeling into thought, E. B. tells us not merely what he knows, but what he adores. A rare, generous critical gift.

When he wants to be plain, he's plain, whether describing Charles Laughton as "sublime" when reading Bottom in a living room, or viewing Martha Graham and Charlie Chaplin not only as performers but as actors who just happen to be writing plays. Bentley is especially good—unique, in fact—in finding good or great acting where nobody is looking for it. Could anybody else so audaciously link Graham's "projection" with Mae West's? Yet why not? Such a showstopping allusion keeps the imagination crackling with images supportive of one another. One might even say that E. B.'s greatest gift when dealing with acting is his continual release into discreet illuminations—quite simply, ideas and images fielded modestly for the first time.

Perhaps the best summation of his enveloping appreciative powers has been his lonely championship not of Brecht, Pirandello, or even Shaw but of that solitary Neapolitan genius Eduardo De Filippo. It is literally crazy that references to naturalism or any theatrical version of reality are usually subsumed under the Stanislavsky or Brecht headings, as if there haven't been others, sometimes equally graced, pursuing similar inspirations. Italian theater—what there is of it—has not in this century been the sum of its conceptual directors' decorative dreams but the singular, unaggressive, maverick work of Eduardo—a "commedia" fugitive, living out of time yet rooted in specific place, a dialect comic totally (in Stark Young's famous phrase about Martha Graham) scraped back to the image.

"It is no slur on his playwriting," says Bentley,

> to say that he is first and foremost an actor, perhaps the finest actor in Italy today!... For five minutes or so he may be a complete letdown. This is not acting at all, we cry; above all, it is not Italian acting! Voice and body are so quiet. *Pianissimo*. No glamour, no effusion of brilliance. No attempt to lift the role off the ground by oratory and stylization, no attempt to thrust it at us by force of personality.... A series of statements, vocal and corporeal... beautiful in themselves—beautiful in their clean economy, their precise rightness—and beautiful in relation to shifting, between one speech and the next; there is a carefully gauged relationship between beginning, middle, and end.

But isn't this, however unintended, a description of Bentley himself as critic, not least of Bentley as critic of actors and acting? There he stands—a pensive observer, melancholy at times, wishing for something better from life, aware of his pedigree yet never playing on it, more complete than his predecessors, an unswerving explorer, the best possible theatergoer teaching the rest of us because he's such an adventurous student. It is no slur on the playwriting that he has been doing in later years to say that he is first and foremost an actor playing seriously and delightfully with the critical possibilities of theater.

How lucky we have been to know him, read him, follow him. He taught us tradition, enthusiasm without delirium, scholarship without pedantry, the love of plays coupled to the love of players. Special, he has not been isolated. Years ago, Henry James wrote of Benoît-Constant Coquelin in terms that reflect Bentley's lessons: "If... the American spectator... learns, or even shows an aptitude for learning, the lesson conveyed in his finest creations, the lesson that acting is an art, and that the application of an art is style, and that style is expression, and that expression is the salt of life, the gain will have been something more than the sensation of the moment—it will be a new wisdom."

Mining wisdom, new or old, in journalism's quarries is never completely satisfying: editors don't want meditative intelligence or, indeed, anything new, only whatever momentary fancy they can see as news. Meanwhile, somebody like E.B. sets standards because, luckily, he doesn't know how to do anything else. Writing of Eduardo again, he asks if we "understand what it means to live in a tradition—as against merely believing in tradition, professional traditionalism?" For Bentley, Eduardo stood "in direct contrast to that dissipation of energy by which talents elsewhere are frittered away." Those gifts—and once again he could be writing about the great E.B. himself—"took him across...the threshold of great theater...and it is thus that one of the most traditional artists of our time became one of the most original."

(1986)

The Low Points

How quickly the Avant falls behind its guard. The Wooster Group's *The Road to Immortality*—revised from their 1982 *L.S.D.*—fights battles already won and is showing unmistakable signs of visual exhaustion: that table stretched across the raised platform covered with microphones, a typewriter, some audio equipment, a telephone, and the obligatory T.V. monitor. In this context, one monitor may constitute a strategic retreat and, therefore, a revolution: Peter Hall is currently framing the proscenium of the Lyttelton at the National Theater with sixteen monitors and accompanying soundtrack noise for Stephen Poliakoff's *Coming in to Land*. And was it only two years ago when the Jack Abbott play did much the same?

Familiar territory, then, promising more of the same, still another work repeating what is already sufficiently known, in a theatrical vocabulary that has no new place to go. What's worse, time and events keep catching up with the group's scattershot political intentions. The racism charge, for example, already played out in the *Village Voice*, still stands when *The Road to Immortality* presents Kate Valk in blackface as Tituba in what ought to be called "Not *The Crucible*." Can't they get it through their collective head that theater is not about intentions but about what is seen? And what is seen here is a white actor rolling her eyes and airing her skirts in a cruel caricature of those desperate Hollywood Jemimas caught in the horror of their own survival. Begging the question even further, however, Valk switches to the role of white Marie Washington, still wearing blackface since she hasn't time to wipe it off—thus playing a white woman no longer pretending to be black even though her teeny-tiny voice still echoes Butterfly McQueen.

Yes, I know the answer: they are daring us not to interpret. In that case, my departure before the second half must not be interpreted as outrage at the perceived racism or dissatisfaction with what had already been seen. Like the work itself, I had many reasons and I don't have to tell you what they were. Even so, I'm willing to be known by these random signs no longer trying to be a review.

Entering the Performing Garage is not easy on this occasion. Walk two flights to get your tickets, wait with the crowd, and then climb downstairs again, only to meet traffic coming the other way with others stuffed in the two doorways to the performing space. My press packet offers hints and expectations, several reprints of articles painstakingly rehearsing issues raised by the Group's earlier deconstructions of American plays, the *L.S.D. Manifesto* of 1984—"No! No! No!"—and Stephen Holden's *Times* defense (January 2, 1987) in which he says that *Route 1 & 9* "has itself been accused unfairly of racism."

I hadn't known before that a fairness doctrine had a right to accompany me to the theater, monitoring and controlling my response. When some of those nice white people in the audience giggle at Tituba's cartoon funniness, or when others guffaw at the nude photo of Allen Ginsberg and Peter Orlovsky held up during Act 1, it isn't fair if I feel discomfort edging toward fury. So, of course, I'll try not to feel what I'm feeling. Meanwhile, I can always read my packet to make my own map of the semiotic signs and landmines ahead.

The *Manifesto* tells me that any Resistance I might have to this work is Sentimental. Against my experience of 1986 as the year of *Challenger*, Chernobyl, and numberless Scamgates, or even the shock the other day of reading anti-Reagan and pro-Gorbachev editorials in the same edition of the *Times,* I am expected to concur with the group's claim that these "Times...are neither Better nor Worse, neither more Reactionary nor more Revolutionary than other Times." Why don't I feel reassured? I remember when I used to think how lucky I was to be living in a medically sophisticated age when Black Plagues are no longer possible. Now, however, I'm watching friends die, not a little concerned for my own life, and morbidly fascinated with the story in today's *Times* with the headline, "AIDS May Dwarf the Plague." Pardon me, Group, I'm not amused.

I go home early, preferring my own deconstruction to anything the Group may offer in the second half. Evidently, "the performers took a collective LSD trip, videotaped the experience, watched it and reproduced as closely as possible every detail." Once upon a time, artists used their imaginations, but no doubt my reservation is Sentimental, a Diversion, linking me with the "dodos" denounced in the *Manifesto* for confusing postmodernism with impressionist realization.

Semioticians don't refer to "intentions," rather to "intentionality," a sign that, far from trusting direct response, they can't place faith in language used with clarity and grace. Reading fragments from Ginsberg, Timothy Leary, Aldous Huxley, Jack Kerouac, William S. Burroughs, and Alan Watts, the Group may have the "intentionality" of presenting a document about the failure of the drug experience, but it may also be that they want to demonstrate their Superior Intelligence. Out of the muddle, they're making more muddle.

At home, I was able to put on a tape of Luchino Visconti's *Conversation Piece* dubbed in English with Japanese subtitles; while waiting for the tape to start, my monitor showed Laurence Olivier dying in J. B. Priestley's *Lost Empires*—a deconstruction of Archie Rice—and Lesley Stahl in a T.V. show where experts were lined up on a stretched table to discuss what they would do in a hypothetical terrorist attack. It wasn't difficult to surround myself with fragmentary madness in my living room. Outside, I knew the world was burning, but I also knew that the Wooster Group was at peace with itself, saying No! No! No! to everybody's world but their own.

(February 1986)

Buzz Words

Ping Chong's *Kindness* begins with a slide lecture in which we are asked to note the similarities and differences found in two images or words. How, for example, are two geometric shapes alike and unalike? Answer: both are green, but one is on the left, the other on the right. Two other shapes might show a hot color next to a cool. Meanwhile, there is Quran on one side, Torah on the other, Think Tank and Tank Top, Chimera and Camera. For some of these, the voice-over offers no comment; for others, he records either what is obvious or, in some cases, what is wrong. (*Chimera* is not the word for camera in Italian.) Message received: mistakes notwithstanding, note the differences and respect them.

Another message, perhaps, is that *Kindness* itself will be a cool work on a hot subject. The slide lecture sets the matter-of-fact tone. Earlier, however, with the houselights up, the audience heard pop songs and blues, with occasional sounds of a growling gorilla behind them. By the time the play proper begins it's clear that Ping Chong has been warning us to watch and listen with special attention, as casually woven images and sounds tiptoe in and out of his near-conventional narrative. He is using mixed media and a nonlinear technique to produce, of all things, a didactic play.

In other hands, his story could have been turned into a nostalgic teenage musical. Six high school friends during the Vietnam period play, dance, and study together, sometimes on the edge of romance, at other times pulling away from each other. Submitting to the voice-over's question, they record their backgrounds and feelings. Daphne is the richest girl in town, hotly pursued by Alvin, the poorest and most vulgar boy. Against his pop tastes, she prefers Mozart. Meanwhile, Rudy is a real card who can't resist a solemn joke. Dot is a blind Jewish girl from Scarsdale who sees herself as a soul singer, and Lulu is an Irish blonde giddily in love with Buzz, the kindest of them all but in love with opera. Buzz is different from the rest of them in one other significant way, only barely noticed most of the time: Buzz is a gorilla.

Accepted by the others as just another student, Buzz communicates with sounds and gestures that are instantly clear to his classmates while being translated over the loudspeaker to us. Buzz is the only one who declares that he is never angry and does not fear death. When he sits down to look at his book of family photographs, he listens to Cavaradossi's aria from *Tosca* sung in German. Lulu delights in his picture book, noting his tan when he surfed in California, overjoyed to see him standing in front of La Scala (as who wouldn't be?), and suffused with warmth when reminded of a trip over Mardi Gras with their pals. When Daphne gets the news that her favorite brother has been killed, everybody except Buzz turns into a screaming, cursing monster, denouncing gooks, commies, Jew-bastards, niggers, and everybody else except themselves and the U.S. Buzz is left alone, looking up at the rain while the lushly melancholy strains of the slow movement from Schubert's C-Major Quintet are heard underneath. From above, a group of cards descends, many saying "Rain" on them, others "Autumn," "El Salvador," "Winter," Afghanistan," and—unaccountably—"Norway." Buzz is possibility, the rest are what we are.

That all this goes down so smoothly, yet finally with so little satisfaction, may be part of a special set of problems set up by Ping Chong's unorthodox techniques. On the one hand, there is predictable comedy and romance; on the other, there is an unusual protagonist placed in theatrical circumstances that keep suggesting astonishment and revelation. Yet despite his good intentions and the gentle, loving atmosphere, Ping Chong is able to deliver only what is already known. Nudging its way into characterization, his text keeps behaving like a crafted play when it most wants to leap into realms belonging to his more sharply crafted visual imagination. As requested in the slide show, we can't help noticing similarities crashing into differences. The most fatal similarity, however, is to plays that patronize their characters: Buzz may not be able to speak directly for himself, but he is manipulated and over-voiced by his creator.

It can't be enough to tell us that humans are beastly while beasts are not. Ping Chong is a reliable reporter of associative images, a less reliable spokesman for ideas. When the kids dash on- and offstage backward, windswept and antic, the image hops into memory unmatched by all the words. How odd that *Kindness* can be so pleasingly self-possessed and unstrident yet can't resist the mind-stopping notion that all would be well if we could be kind as a gorilla. Ping Chong knows how to gather momentum, he can mix charm into his media, and he is endearingly not above a vaudeville turn in which Buzz keeps moving chairs without being noticed by a baffled chum. But for all his theatrical clarity, he is viewing modern life through tear-stained glasses.

When Buzz joins the others in autobiography, he says that he was born in Rwanda and that his father was decapitated, his hands and feet sold to a European. Now they're on display in a German apartment next to a samovar from Kiev. Yet Buzz is not angry. Assuming that none of those fragments is arbitrary—the German allusion inserted so graphically next to last week's news from the Soviet Union—then why in the name of complicating human kindness can't Buzz find anger in his heart? In the last moments, he is seen as Daphne's husband, wheeling a stroller past a desultory gorilla on all fours in a zoo. Yet moments before he appeared to have deserted her while gazing at the stars, both of them momentarily convinced that there must be life out there. Ping Chong, laboring under Buzz's cool and sentimental spell, can't seem to make up his mind: he can make fun and feel sorrow, but he never raises his voice. Having taken so many risks already, placing so much tender beauty and bitter meditation on his liberated stage, he has left his indignation in the wings.

(May 1986)

Directorially Bound

Florence and Milan. With Ingmar Bergman finding unpredictable sexuality and violence in almost every scene of *Hamlet,* Robert Wilson turning Strauss's *Salome* into an erotically charged masque for singers and mimes, and Klaus Michael Grüber presenting Aeschylus's *Prometheus* in a translation by Peter Handke that actually binds the god to the astonishingly high brick wall of the Piccolo Teatro, it can be said that, for one weekend, theater in Italy was refusing to be dead. No matter that Italian was to be heard only in the usual round of public discussions in both cities, where professors of theater history, art, and music climbed over each other's aching brains to prove they had done their homework. Moribund and unoriginal as theater may be in Italy, it remains the playground of the richly pedantic, always reliable for provoking ideas and debate. As Wilson found out, audiences in Italy still boo vociferously, especially when the press has prepared the way for (much beloved) scandal.

The headlines after Bergman's *Hamlet* in Florence were about a scandal that didn't happen: the Swedish critics had been outraged by Bergman's authorial rearrangements, and the Florentines were poised for the kill. In the event, they surprised themselves by liking it. How could it be otherwise? Perhaps Stockholm has been spared auteurs at their worst, plundering texts for glossy meanings. Or—and this is a strong possibility—Swedes are uncomfortable with Bergman's conceptual openness, his refusal to lock the play into one period or another, his effortless, graceful decision to let the story tell itself within the framework of theater as theater. While he never stops springing surprises, he allows them to appear logical, part of a scheme that pitches ordinary, natural behavior into a background of the extraordinary. The Ghost appears unexpectedly throughout and shockingly at the end when he grips Claudius's arms so that Hamlet has to deliver the final thrust; Ophelia is also seen throughout as a hovering, disturbed presence, even after her death.

Bergman's Hamlet is a furious graduate student enraged at first by public responsibility and subdued finally by the discovery that he, too, can kill. Peter Stormare enters dragging a black Thonet chair behind him, wearing shades and sprawling his lanky legs as he sulks, weeps, and retches over the disgusting events. To make matters plain, Bergman first shows a drunken Claudius chasing an equally besotted Gertrude down his vast, open stage, bold shafts of light marking the space where he finally slams her to the floor, turns her over, raises her skirts, and starts to fuck her. For this pair, court duties are unwelcome interruptions to their festive game. Claudius is seen after the shock of *The Mousetrap* in a wildly demeaning encounter with a blowsy woman who could be a dead ringer for Gertrude, both of them smeared with lipstick and stains. Moments later, having torn off his undershirt (Claudius as a rotund Kowalski?), he beats his chest, finds his hands suddenly in front of him, and descends to the floor in prayer.

Hamlet's sensual life is something else again. An immensely physical man, his arms and hands can't resist a touch or embrace. With Horatio, he is comfortably at peace with body and soul, a perpetual schoolboy, tucking Horatio's spectacles into his coat pocket when telling him of the limits to his philosophy, or lying against his chest, relaxed in his fisherman's sweater and boots, after the English voyage. Delighted with his advice to the players, having delivered "To be or not to be" to them as he finds a mock dagger in his hands, he turns to Horatio, kissing him—as surely they have done before—passionately on the mouth.

For Bergman, none of this is reducible to concept or shock. These are natural events in a play about action and reaction. Hamlet, his family, and his friends are always responding to momentary, passing impulses. The nunnery scene, consequently, is more terrible than anything in the play; Hamlet knows he's being spied upon, yet he can't help hugging Ophelia, holding her legs while on his knees, then beating her, spitting in her face, and just as quickly kissing her.

Bergman's balancing act—this wholly physical world, played against the bleakness of the play's political and spiritual worlds—is a remarkable achievement, the most eloquent reading of Shakespeare since Brook's *Lear.* Beginning with the sounds of a player piano playing the *Merry Widow* waltz and ending with a blast of rock music as Fortinbras and his modern army descend upon the Danish dead, gunning down Horatio and taking a photo opportunity over Hamlet's body, Shakespeare is presented with a paradoxical respect, making intelligent sense out of episodes that usually hang back in unexplored shadows. Bergman makes theater look more flexible and resonant than film. *Hamlet,* for once, emerges like a painting scrubbed back to its original colors.

If Robert Wilson's *Salome* doesn't turn the same trick, it is partly because the challenge is so different. You wouldn't know it in Milan, but neither Wilde's nor Strauss's *Salome* can be viewed comfortably as a sacred icon. Greater kitsch has never been more proudly flaunted.

Wilson's solution—partly induced by La Scala's management, which had planned only enough rehearsal time for a concert version—is to make it into the quintessential Wilson pageant, offering the density of a Jackson Pollock painting on three levels of the stage while placing the singers on a platform over the orchestra pit. Beginning and ending in silence, Wilson's version suggests a way of coping with singers who can scarcely sing and move at the same time; also, it makes a case for allowing ears and eyes to have separate sovereignty—what is heard does not necessarily have to be matched directly with what is seen.

Has any opera been more beautifully lit (Beverly Emmons) and more magisterially staged? Wilson places perhaps too many Salomes and other configurational characters onstage. Strangely, however, the eye can return to the singers' platform, where Montserrat Caballé—more at ease and consequently more musical than ever—can be watched, making her black veil stand in for Jochanaan's severed head, concentrating on the intensity of her musical experience, reacting visibly to what she, too, sees on Wilson's stage. The effect, finally, is of a more sensuous, lyrical Salome, an event about the confrontation of obsessive personalities detached from each other and from visible reality.

The Scala audience was incredibly rude to the talented NYU students —late of Wilson's *Hamletmachine*—who were imported to mime much of the action on the stage. Later, Caballé let it be known that she wants to work with Wilson again. His ideas will continue to rejuvenate the theatrical possibilities of opera suitable for myth and multiple visions—*Tristan* and *Parsifal* certainly, and maybe *Pelléas*.

Finally, the sober truth of Grüber and Handke's *Prometheus Bound* came as a refreshing reminder that the theater can still play it straight. In the vast space of the Piccolo Teatro's Studio, Aeschylus's drama plays itself as quiet music. Bruno Ganz confronts only one other actress—Tina Engel—as both Chorus and Io. Broodingly they talk, quietly they fade from one another. In whitened face, standing on a high platform, trailing a huge scarf down his front and below his feet, Ganz is tied by rope to the distant wall, a figure trusting in the power of the word and the splendor of acting. Ancient tragedy had other points to make, but there is no vision more honorably lonely than the actor's art and the theatrical act in command of themselves as if no other world could possibly exist.

(February 1987)

Post-Neo-Vaudeville

Bill Irwin may be made of silly putty, but he'll never be putty in the hands of critics. Clown, so-called new vaudevillian, he's the best gadfly we have, buzzing away at hoity-toity theatrical conceits fussily presenting themselves as the bearers of the Word. Nobody escapes his wickedly inventive gaze in *The Regard of Flight*. Using body—more than word—English, Irwin mocks postmodern pretensions, proving once again that the most telling "image" in theater is the actor triumphant.

His trump card is himself—dreamer, baffled fugitive, a running-walking-fleeing distress signal in search of something truly pure. Instead, he meets M. C. O'Connor, playing the artist's paranoid nightmare, that intrepid wrecker of dreams, always in hot pursuit of whatever Irwin is trying to do or be, a relentless, literal purveyor of mean questions and horrific doubts. On Irwin's other side is Doug Skinner at the upright, like a silent-movie accompanist, lecturing on the evils of the proscenium arch and other obsessions, translating critical rubbish—"new theater calls for a commitment to the affective mode"—into equally goitered French.

Irwin is an instinctive ironist, profoundly skeptical about the uses of metaphor while soundly permitting his besieged soul to look like the battered theater image it has every right to be. *The Regard of Flight* is the ideal arrangement for his antic gifts. In *The Courtroom,* two years ago, he tried unsuccessfully to organize a thematic evening that had to do double duty as some kind of half-imagined, half-linear story—in that case, an appraisal of the law. With *Flight* he's on more familiar ground. He's looking at the liberations of an unassuming imagination, asserting in the most humble way that theater can't be wished into existence, that it never hurts to be talented as well.

O'Connor chases him all over the joint, leading him for one terrifying moment to insist that he'll fly from the balcony. Fortunately, he returns to—where? The proscenium arch and its convenient apron, struggling as always for territorial rights over his actor's costume trunk, one of those bottomless pits where angelic clowns retreat whenever under unreasonable assault. Irwin is always on the run, sometimes caught in the powerful draft of an offstage vacuum pulling him into the oblivion he may finally be seeking. Whether standing shyly at the lectern on behalf of plausibly dopey ideas or dashing away from O'Connor's critical or directorial pursuits, he's always the best judge of his own fears. The pleasure he offers is not the loud guffaw: he's too droll for that; give him the chance and he might slip away, find a better job, gently telling most of us that we're more dangerous than a clown could ever be.

Even so, he's funnier than those exhausting stand-up jokesters who think that laughs are the measure of everything. Unashamed of visual and verbal puns—he tells O'Connor that the jump into new theater isn't easily made; O'Connor pulls out a trampoline and jumps right into it—he never claims to be a prophet, only a "nonprofit." The show may be labeled "new vaudeville"—he knows how desperate critics are for categories and "isms"—but Skinner's dummy, Eddie Gray, says it's "not that new," he saw it on Channel 13. The audience sighs with unabashed relief at the sight of the rabbit out of the hat, only to be demolished by Irwin's whiplash observation that it's not real. Skinner announces dance segments, free association segments, and even an obscene monologue, yet only by the end is it clear that Irwin has no intention of showing any of them.

Irwin adds something like an encore to *The Regard of Flight's* loosely organized fancies, calling it "The Clown Bagatelles." In fifteen minutes, he revives the red nose, the fright wig, and the giant spectacles, offering a foolish continental waiter wrestling with restless pasta, a rock dancer caught in the loose rhythms of a loony song, and a one-minute summary performance of *Lear* where the "common people died like flies"—lest we forget. Irwin is no more pretentious about his conscience than he is about his art. Even so, he can't help being a critic of an uncritical, boring establishment so full of itself that it can't recognize how empty good brains can be.

My own regard of theater this year tells me there's no show business like old business: the lone—or almost lone—performer is the only dependable force we have. Barbara Cook's return to theater may be marred by the souped-up amplification that her clear, sweet, soaring soprano doesn't need—no better moment in her concert than the unmiked singing of Michael Leonard and Herbert Martin's quietly voluptuous "Why Did I Choose You?" from *The Yearling*—but it's one of those astonishing evenings, like Irwin's, in which confident talent is a reminder that the gift for the simple is what theater does better than anything. Cook's chat between numbers isn't thrilling, but it's better than the stormy drainage of personal confession offered by Lena Horne. Where have Cook and unpretentious musicals like *The Yearling* been anyway? Must Broadway

invest millions in no-talent, high-tech operettas forever? How long before
we're rescued from the machine that can't dance, clown, think, or sing?

(April 1987)

Cinderella Double Take

Like so many conceptual directors recently–Peter Brook, Peter Sellars,
and Robert Wilson–Anne Bogart evidently wants to rescue traditions
she views as boring. That her peculiar reduction of Massenet's *Cendrillon*
manages to invent new boredoms may well be her point: opera, for her,
is an opportunity not to tell a story with clarity but to overwhelm its sim-
plifications with hints that she knows something even deeper than music.

What Bogart presents, however, is a fussy textual gloss on the music
coupled with a restless series of gestures meant to illustrate every thought
and line. When I say "meant to," I can be accused, accurately, of begging
some questions, since Bogart's intentions have a way of slipping casually
from their decorative moorings. Still, it's safe to make guesses based on
the overload.

Does she want us to understand? Probably not: Massenet's arias and
ensembles are sung in French, while Eve Ensler's textual interpolations
are spoken in English. The effect is not unlike Galina Vishnevskaya's first
appearance as Aida at the Met, when she sang in Russian to a cast singing
in Italian, as much as to say that words don't matter or that characters in
opera are in such an unreal tradition anyway that it's enough for them to
make recognizable vowel sounds. Ensler's English ranges from the all-
too-clear–the sisters' mother counseling one of them to "suck in that
fat"–to strange chants ("dead mother, good mother") and neurasthenic
reflections ("I am a pumpkin splitting in two"). If Bogart and her colleagues are saying anything, it's about their right to speak in two languages at once. More: that opera from those languages can't be trusted to
tell us much about Bogart's theatrical gifts.

Which would be all very well if the means were any more articulate.
Bogart might be assuming that Cinderella's tale is so well known that she
can easily bypass obvious details. The program's synopsis refers to the
famous glass slipper and the clock striking midnight, but Bogart can't be

bothered with either. Or if they were there I missed them: they take second place to "effects" such as smoke slithering from under a platform and a Prince—sweetly sung by Jeffrey Reynolds—dressed unaccountably in a West Point cadet's uniform.

Added to the obscurities are not one, but two Cinderellas, the first called Lucette, looking like the usual chimney waif in most productions, and the second a more mature woman called Cendrillon, decked in a blowsy red gown. They sing and doze together in what the program describes as Lucette's "lapses into reverie." Lucette is also supposed to be "amazed at the vision of Cendrillon," imagining that "she is looking in a mirror," but she must have poor eyesight indeed, since no attempt is made, either with masks or hairstyles, to have them look alike to the rest of us.

Bogart's pugnacious imprecisions go further than these disparities between synopsis and action. Using Victoria Petrovich's handsomely designed series of four increasingly smaller proscenium arches, Bogart appears to be making distinctions between "real" events and Lucette's various "reveries" and "nightmares." Yet it's impossible to locate the difference. Perhaps she's committed only to abstract prettiness, Massenet's silken score taken as her license to evade detail. This is impressionism with a vengeance, wallowing in its own self-conscious lyricism.

Why Cinderella, anyway? By now, is there anything left to feel about the romantic victim who finally triumphs over her disgusting oppressors, all of them the most insufferable caricatures of women ever invented by— no doubt—a furiously disturbed man? Bogart's version is no less misogynist than Sondheim's. From Joyce Castle's Mother, she coaxes an arch, heavily pointed performance that might embarrass a drag queen, all smirking teeth and wagging tail. One Ugly Sister attacks the other for her flat chest, though the flat one looks bigger; moments like these lead me back longingly to Prokofiev's ballet, with its solidly based storytelling and its merciful freedom from words.

The sisters' ugliness isn't half as annoying as the spectacle of pseudomodern theater presenting itself as superior to all its sources. Bogart's seriousness is not in question, only her unwillingness to let us in on her passion. Gestures are never enough, especially now, when most of them have been taken up by fashion photographers and cosmetic firms.

Massenet's text has the mother instruct her daughters to be neither banal nor too original ("Ne soyez pas banales ni trop originales"), advice that Bogart mixes up just as she clouds most issues. Trying stressfully to be original in every breathing moment, she hasn't yet noticed that there's nothing more banal than busy images wedded to lazy thought.

(January 1988)

Future Lieder

Tears make flowers, sighs turn into a choir of nightingales, the soul sinks into a lily's cup, and those flowers whisper and speak: imagine the lieder singer's life, everlastingly condemned to yearn for impossible, dreamy, unrequitable love. This, at any rate, is the special mission of Schumann in his setting for sixteen of Heinrich Heine's 1827 lyrics, the *Dichterliebe* (Poet's love), a cycle that makes only the vaguest pretension to a narrative line. Between them, Heine and Schumann follow the path of a neurasthenic young man in love with love—with the precious, delectable images he can find as his affair heaves itself into exquisite failure.

If the great, authoritative singers of the lied in this century are to be believed, even the interior narrative of the song must be conveyed through a minimalist actor's art: the flash of an eye, the slow descent of a hand, and, more than anything, a steady gaze into past or future as the singer listens intently to the piano's ironic or decisive conclusions. Nothing is done to upset the balancing act of the emphatic words, the vocal line, and the piano's quicksilver shifts from support to dispassionate comment. Schumann's songs may offer temptations for heart-in-mouth display, but Dietrich Fischer-Dieskau, Hermann Prey, and Peter Schreier give us the facts as intimations. Not for them the literal reenactment of the lied's bad dream.

Nor did I ever think I would see one. For years, I've done my own bathtub renderings of Schubert, Schumann, and Brahms, gagging on high notes but compensating for technical lapses with a repertoire of grand, illustrative gesture that would surely make Sarah Bernhardt and rock singers look like masters of restraint. Devout cowardice my religion, I never thought that what I was urging myself to do was performance art.

Now, however, thanks to the droll good humor of dauntless John Kelly, the least solemn and most lyrical of our performance artists, I have seen my future—and it works!

Kelly's version of the poet's dream is set magically in what may be the most original theater space in New York, Kelly himself more like a found object than an actor protected by the usual illusions. The room is on the second floor of the Battery Maritime Building overlooking a part of the harbor where ferries crisscross one another with magnificent indifference to the poet's despair. Against the calming, amplified sound of water lapping at the building, and surrounded by lavender drapes, a mound of dark sand, and a huge bucket of dried autumn flowers underneath a giant, gnarled tree trunk, Kelly at first sleeps through Fernando Torm-Tohá's graceful, meandering, Schumannesque fragments on the upright as a black-and-white silent movie plays on the drape above his narrow, ineffably lonely bed. He's dreaming of a girl in a secret garden, always yards behind her as she sweeps into a cave or drops the largest handkerchief in the world on the forest lawn; inevitably, he meets Death, heavily shrouded while digging a grave. When poet and girl finally find themselves on either side of a bench, they glance shyly at one another, each nudging a ball in the other's direction—evidently the best they can manage.

When Kelly awakens, Schumann's song cycle and its delicious deconstruction begins. First seen in his nightshirt, he actually envisions the nightingale that is never far from any romantic song cycle, chasing it as he did the girl, his gestures far-flung pleas to the air, the moon, the stars. Then, at his writing table, he flips the dial of his radio—Wouldn't Heine have done the same?—never satisfied by the arias he's hearing, preferring instead to write a little, drop his pen, and let his hand fly to one side as he copes with deliquescent pain.

And so it goes, with infinite variations on the crack-brained yet delightfully free vocabulary of gesture available to our self-pitying hero. He weeps during a song's postlude, or stops suddenly at the piano, catching his accompanist's eye, but like all such threats to the intoxicating misery, he slips past the opportunity like those ferries in the night, submitting to the call of the next song. His nightshirt discarded, he disappears into the outside darkness with the pair of scissors found in the sand, returning after a movie interlude with what looks alarmingly like shorter hair. Whether pacing, climbing the ladder, gazing out a window, soaking his head, or falling on the mound, Kelly is always the perfect sufferer, gloriously ascetic, deliriously in thrall to a power greater than love—music and words.

For the most part, he sings in German, Michael Feingold's graceful translation flashed as supertitles on the drape above the bed. Fischer-Dieskau need not tremble: Kelly sings in two plaintive registers, suffering momentary pitch problems when pushed to the top. His phrasing, however, is as musical as his dark, uncovered alto, and he makes the words seem palpable—like the pear Torm-Tohá bites into at one point, or the piece of cheese Kelly himself munches as he listens gravely to Schumann's final comments.

"Fast zu Erns" (Almost too serious) is the title of a *Kinderszenen* piece played by Torm-Tohá, a warning heeded throughout by Kelly. Only once does he lapse into caricature, singing "Ein Jüngling liebt ein Mädchen" (A young man had a sweetheart) in a shrieking cackle that suddenly refuses to let the poor soul off the hook. Kelly is Lord Byron, not Robin Williams, at his best when he gives sway to the true poet shining through his baleful gaze. His quiet beauty is the strongest argument against easy-come silliness.

The cheese and the pear are comment enough in what is finally a heroic tribute to Schumann, Heine, the wonderful intimacy of lieder, and the unrecoverable romantic spirit. Kelly is that choir of nightingales, both the singer and the song.

(October 1990)

Power to the Actor

Faced so consistently with actors maneuvered by auteur-directors who disdain them almost as much as they loathe the transparency of good playwriting, I'm prepared, at last, to confess that Donald Wolfit was one of the greatest actors I ever saw. By which I mean to indicate, quixotically perhaps, that great actors in the full sway of their passions, eccentricities, and startling ideas are likely to be more persuasive conduits to the interior of plays than postmodernist directors with their terrifying grip on arbitrary, decorative conception.

Confession is called for in Wolfit's case because he would appear to be the worst argument on behalf of actors versus directors. As a student in London, I joined my classmates at his performances in order to be astonished by an antediluvian display of actor-manager tricks; we knew him as the last survivor of a thoroughly discredited fashion – the actor as organizer of Great Moments featuring Himself. In Gielgud and Olivier, we recognized not rivals so much as complementary actor-visionaries in touch, albeit from different directions, with tradition and possibility, willing to serve the directorial quirks of Tyrone Guthrie and Peter Brook even as they were preserving the granitic truths embedded in their own talents. Wolfit, by contrast, was letting the century pass him by without giving a pass to what had been learned about acting. Not for him the reflective intelligence of Chekhov: more than pre-Freudian, his acting was positively biblical in its hortatory, insistent presence. The role may have been Lear, Oedipus, or even Volpone, but Wolfit was always Job.

Surely that was what we thought we were seeing. How could we look ahead to a time when such gigantic individuality would be missed? Instead, our dismissive laughs helped us to overlook what was splendid amid the ruins. There he stood toward the end of a long evening as Oedipus in both parts of Sophocles' tragedy, alone center stage on a raised platform, surrounded by a company that would have disgraced Crummles's troupe in *Nicholas Nickleby*. Preparing himself for his final declamation by paying absolutely no attention to the buzz and bustle of his hapless colleagues, he was blind Oedipus in search of his follow spot. Meanwhile, he was also uncomfortable with his hat, pulling it forward, nudging it back or side saddle, intent on making it sit squarely over his great white pudding face. And considering that it was more like a Dalí-designed chapeau than a hat, a cross between a futuristic schooner and a hero sandwich, this was quite an achievement. When the fuss was over, his blind eyes silenced the others with a gaze so baleful that it might have burned through steel. The speech – and speech it was – could now begin.

But this too was excavation rather than acting – a voice heard unaccountably after the lava had frozen the dead city. The first sound, a primordial wheeze, was the signal for experienced Wolfitians that the organist was merely pumping air into the pipes. This was baby breath, the early, tentative statement of a fugue that would soon gather a second, third, and even fourth voice into its complex weave, striding finally into an outburst of sunshine on a storm-swept sea—Wolfit as reckless mixed metaphor, not likely to be ruled by manners or restraint. Had we known better about such distinctions forty years ago, we should have seen not "ham," but a porcine Olympian defying the other gods: I may be a falling star, he was saying, but don't take any wagers on what the cosmos will be like without me.

That it hasn't done so well isn't exactly news, though truth to tell, a multitude of Wolfits would not have much effect on our sorry situation in all its particulars. Most American directors have long since turned from the pressure of the text and presence of the actor to Smart Moments featuring Themselves. At the New York Shakespeare Festival recently, Anne Bogart's version of Brecht's *In the Jungle of the Cities* was obsessed by a private agenda involving faces made up in differing colors. (Greg Mehrten's Worm, for example, was a sickly sea green that did nothing to conceal his own discomfort as an actor required to stand ramrod-stiff while shouting his lines.) Brecht's journey into blasted souls—Garga and Shlink, especially, on a strange slow-motion trajectory into each other's sexuality—was nowhere in evidence, not out of prurient indifference but simply because the actors were programmed to do something else, most of it having to do with postures, gestures, and positionings. Two actors going literally nose-to-nose in an argument are not automatically a howl, at least to those of us who haven't yet called a truce with canned laughter.

Similarly, the festival's *Pericles,* under Michael Greif's rambunctious commands, slips in and out of styles as strenuously as it moves from one century to another, much as JoAnne Akalaitis's *Henry IV* did last year. I suspect these same directors are exhausted by rising expectations about their inventiveness, every production an apparent test of their capacity to float Big Ideas about Existence. Now that fashion tells us the universe is indifferent or that we're mere pawns on a chessboard or fragmented chemical compounds, the directors are avoiding time displacements and the singular metaphor in favor of warps and woofs that cut through Concept altogether.

Instructive to watch Campbell Scott as he takes Pericles on a tour all his own, despite the surrounding mix of vaudeville and cartoon. No barnstormer he, yet he is a throwback to simpler times when an actor was expected to carry the narrative on his back, listening well and talking even better while giving arc and architecture to the emotional pressure points that count the most. Acting is a discretionary art in which the actor seizes rehearsal surprise for information no director can ever give him. For Scott's Pericles, this means holding on to his fundamental quietness even as he's tempest-tossed: he must stay vocally on top of the real shower Greif pours down upon him, but he does so without losing his grip on stoic wonder, that firmly drawn outline of a man sustained by a life inside himself so pensive and confident that it never bends to passing defeats. His guard slips only once, when compelled by Greif to dance a tango at Simonides' court in Pentapolis. As if saying, "Don't cry for me, Pentapolis," his astonishment sails right out of the play's situation into Greif's wrenching joke, and for one flashing moment he looks as if he'd rather be light years from the giddy stage. He's too good to be anything but true.

Actors don't always escape so gracefully from their directors' whims. The cast of John Patrick Shanley's *Beggars in the House of Plenty* at the Manhattan Theatre Club was directed by Shanley himself in what must qualify as the noisiest slam-bang shouting match of the season, all the more strange in a space small enough to pick up the sound of a sneezing mouse. Shanley can hardly be blamed for wanting theater to make a more mythic statement than the movies he's been writing, but hollering lungs and arms thrust out accusingly do not heroic tragedy make. It's an odd reflection on Shanley's misconstruction of his domestic fable that an actor such as Wolfit, when finally cast in a movie—*A Room at the Top,* in 1958—is more plausible than Shanley's stage actors without shedding a pound of his bulky extravagance for the camera. ("A sledgehammer performance," wrote Kenneth Tynan.) Wolfit's mythic force turns out to have been his naturalism; Shanley, on the other hand, denatures his actors.

If a finger must be pointed, it could aim not for the usual directorial suspects, but for Wolfit's predecessor, Edward Gordon Craig, inventing his dream of the actor as *über-marionette* after a youth spent in ambivalent relation to Henry Irving and his mother, Ellen Terry. (Imagine what it must be like to have actor-managers as your literal and spiritual parents!) By the time we were encountering Wolfit, the stage was indeed looking more magically beautiful under director-designers than it had ever looked under actor-managers. Yet, as usual with shifts in power, something's been lost. "The director's role," says Ariane Mnouchkine, no slouch in the visionary sweepstakes, "is to liberate the space in front of the actor and to help him reach the level of metaphor, that is, not to be realist." She looks to the East for inspiration: "For thousands of years they have understood that acting is a series of rituals. Even Brecht was looking for the same thing: for the actor to accede to the responsibility of the artist."

But that can't happen if, unlike Mnouchkine, you're ripping metaphor from every source except the text and the actor. Too often, the images on stage reveal a director at work who has lost the memory of how an actor moves from one point in his discoveries to another. Just as instrumentalists such as Vladimir Ashkenazy and Daniel Barenboim travel from solo performance to podium, actors might seize the day for themselves, not necessarily assuming they're better than our best directors, only that—like their musical counterparts—they have vital messages to deliver about an ancient art. Let the auteur be the author, even when, in Shanley's case, he stumbles over his own words. Better that miscalculation than the pretense that live theater is about amplified voices, moving scenery and airtight grouping of bloodless, semi-paralyzed actor-marionettes. "An actor," says Mnouchkine, "is not paid to conceal but to show," although you wouldn't always recognize that truth when directors work so hard to conceal what actors can show.

Wolfit surely courted status as an endangered species, but he dominated the stage, as Tynan said, "by a mighty exercise of talent, thrust, and will," qualities available to actors that needn't be buried yet. It's not the actor who's endangered, anyway, it's the audience. But I doubt if anything's to be done except to revive our faith in the primeval ritual of the living performance.

Let a director have the last word. Mnouchkine again: "Each time, the path toward beauty in the theater seems harder and the precipice steeper. I feel this fragility more and more. I think that theater is eternal, although when I watch the television, I sometimes think that it might die. I'm afraid that soon we will no longer know what an actor is."

(February 1992)

The Neutral Space

London theater, once and for all, is not the best in the world, but it does offer good actors a chance to do what is best for actors, and what they can't do in the movies: complex roles under their own command. Too often, London neglects the polishing details. Four staircases keep lumbering on and off for the Royal Shakespeare Company's *Hamlet* (with Roger Rees), revealing their masking; even more absurdly, an actor climbs grandly up the steps only to be seen climbing down the (supposedly) offstage side. Similarly, the RSC's *Mother Courage* last winter gave Judi Dench a wagon only an elephant could hope to push. Stagehands kept running like mock-Kabuki shadows whenever Dench was forced to give up her heroic efforts. Unlike the Kabuki, unfortunately, theirs were unscheduled entrances. Poor Dench, thinking she was in a Brecht play of epic simplicity about the Thirty Years' War, was, instead, trapped in a war against modern stage design.

If my two 1985 visits to London reveal any one thing, it is that a week can satisfy a collector's appetite for provocative theater: good plays, old or new, conceived and acted with intelligence, passion, and—yes—epic simplicity. Like New York, musicals outnumber plays in the West End. Even the RSC has recently dropped its repertory system for nine weeks in deference to a money-spinning long run for *Les Misérables,* a musical version that Trevor Nunn hopes to make into a subsidizing annuity, quite frankly banking on a success comparable to *A Chorus Line's* beneficence to the New York Shakespeare Festival. Half of the sixteen or eighteen musicals running in London are likely to be recyclings from New York. A second week in London would be a sentence to nostalgic imprisonment in the blood-sucking worlds of *Barnum, Evita, 42nd Street, On Your Toes, Pump Boys and Dinettes,* and *Singin' in the Rain.* Plays running in London are dominated by titles such as *Daisy Pulls It Off, Run for Your Wife, A State of Affairs, Stepping Out, Two into One,* and *Up 'n' Under,* suggesting that the British are even more light-headedly sex-crazed than we are.

In spite of such burdens, the British tradition of the actor ascendant, proud image of a stalwart, hard-working, stiff-upper-something nation, continues to make itself felt. In England actors work on stage more than they wait on tables. Stars keep returning to theater even when it might be

more practical to pursue Oscars and Emmys. What is even more important, the work many of them do on stage is usually worth doing.

Judi Dench, for example, is neither nature's nor Brecht's perfect choice
for Mother Courage. Breathing practicality, hers is a secretarial intelligence far from the shrewd, animal maneuvers of Brecht's jaunty survivor.
Her thick, heavy-blanket clothes seem to be wearing her rather than the
other way around, not unlike the pipe shoved into her mouth: she's not
only pushing that ridiculously over-stuffed wagon, she's urging herself to
be grim and tough. Yet despite the mountain-climbing effort, she also
breathes free and honest air; her actor's sensibility leads directly into plain,
unfussy emotional responses. Expansive and giving, she never seems to be
asking for sympathy or help from anyone, least of all from the audience.

The stage in this production may have been her enemy, but that doesn't
stop her from standing up to it, pound for pound its equal in determination,
sheer spaciousness, guts. For her, clearly, the stage is the best place to live.

Acting onstage can always hold its own as an image of free will and conscious choice. British actors, playing to a nation that doesn't believe in
interior life, can't find it easy to the touch. By acting so much on the
stage, however, they come in contact with real pressures and demands
that can be met only by releasing all the real life that's in them. English
reviewers, everlastingly vigilant about externals, like to notice makeup
and business. For years, Olivier seduced them with putty noses. Yet all
those funny face-paintings would have emerged as Still Lifes if they had-
n't been put there by those quirky, personal gestural creations that rise to
the surface from Olivier's bubbling subterranean lakes.

Acting for the camera is something else. Lillian Gish reports that
D. W. Griffith "taught that you must not be caught acting. The audience
won't believe you," in short, that the camera never lies. Its merciless eye
is kind to the small—Bogart's fingers caressing an earlobe, Bette Davis's
lemon-pursed mouth—but it doesn't always know what to do with the
tremendous and the bold. When Ralph Richardson had the nerve to
adopt Jehovah as his character image in Carol Reed's film of Conrad's *An
Outcast of the Islands,* many reviewers found him over-sized and eccentric.
But "eccentric" is his middle name. Richardson is always large, auda-

ciously weird. Onstage, his extravagant individuality is at home unques-
tioned; onscreen, in this instance, it looks precariously like a lie. The
camera can't resist corridors, streets, even refrigerator doors; the stage, on
the other hand, is the emptiest space in the world, begging for sizable
actors to shock it into submission.

The movie version of *Kiss of the Spider Woman* opens with a wandering camera gazing in passing at Molina's film memorabilia on the walls of
the cell he's sharing with Valentin. For several minutes, he isn't seen at all
while his voice is heard telling the sordid little twopenny plot of a
favorite film. The camera, always restless with most directors, wants to
move, not that much interested in William Hurt. When it finally alights
upon him, he's bathed in colored light and shadows, head swathed in a
Marlene-turban, floating through what looks like luxurious confinement;
an ideal space for the jumped-up camera, a less convincing one for the
chamber play about to be enacted by Molina and Valentin. With movement so desirable for a movie, it's inevitable that Molina's remembered
plots will be enacted during various interludes. These sepia melodramas
turn out to be seductively interesting, not merely pulling the two men
out of sight but making the camera's return to their story feel like an
afterthought. The camera's betraying truth is that it wants to show the
more colorful story, while Manuel Puig's novel wants to tell another.

In London, Puig's adaptation of *Spider Woman* to the stage reveals a
different game entirely. Lights up on a tiny cell, no posters on the walls
because in this literal chamber version, played in a small theater above a
pub, there's only one wall anyway. Simon Callow's Molina is sitting on a
cot, legs crossed with one foot in ballerina pointe position while he stares
ahead, telling the movie plot. Callow is undecorated: no turban, no luxury, just himself in shorts and a shirt worn with its tails tied around his
ample, stuffed-turkey abdomen. The territory could scarcely be more
radically distant from Hurt's in the film. These stage characters are truly
confined; more important, they are there in the fullness of acting, the
only source of energy, the only feasts for the eye.

Commerce dictates differences, too: Callow's succulently chubby
Molina would never happen in movies, at least not in American films;
Hurt's quiet, standard, square-jawed handsomeness is what the movie is

buying—and selling. Callow, not so incidentally, outed himself some time before his *Spider Woman* appearance. Hollywood flacks and relieved reviewers congratulated Hurt because he's straight, doing a brave gay job. Not that those realities automatically make a difference. A bad gay actor in a gay role is not going to be more persuasive than a good straight actor in the same role. The difference here is in the actors themselves—what they're willing to do—and in their mediating circumstances.

Bravery, anyway, is what actors' agents argue against. Good acting thrives on impulse and perception, however unpopular the personal revelations may prove to be: the actor, after all, is using himself, not being himself. Theater, moreover, urges the actor to use most of himself all of the time. Film says less is plenty most of the time. And this plays comfortably into the hands of an actor like Hurt, who, on stage and screen, seems to be in perpetual retreat from his character, even—as in this case—when he is assuming mannerisms and gestures new to him. Callow's Molina, no less quiet in its intensity, would be just as much at home in film, but on stage that intensity can rise and subside with architectural generosity.

In the end, of course, Callow is simply better, more convincing, more there. Gently caressing his knee or primping his pepper-and-salt curls, he is always digging deeper into parts of himself that seem to be lying in wait for discovery. Hurt's technique is naturally more passive. He doesn't dig, he resists, knowing that his steamed sensuality can occupy much of the space he's otherwise refusing to fill. Callow loves words, finding light and weight in syllables and consonants, his voice an instrument for etching differences, making distinctions. Hurt gets caught in an easy-come, easy-go undertow common in movie acting. The monotonous buzz of his voice gives him away, one word no more or less important than another. When he rises out of his studious torpor, it often feels arbitrary, forced, even though it's always a relief. He's tentative and unassuming, which may be part of his attractiveness, but Molina has driving energy—intent on changing his life in that cell, finding someone to love despite the odds. Callow's alertness fixes everything: like any good stage actor, he's constructing opportunities, seizing the day. Hurt impersonates, Callow acts.

Maybe it's just that London is (relatively) kind to actors. Anthony Hopkins returned from Hollywood last year, performing in Arthur Schnitzler's *The Lonely Road* and in David Hare and Howard Brenton's *Pravda* (not playing, unfortunately, during my September visit). In Schnitzler's play, he has a scene with Colin Firth in which he must withhold himself from admitting what Firth has come to realize—that they are father and son. Both actors stand away from one another with a still breathlessness that would do justice to a Mahlerian pause. Eternity is only seconds away, giving them time to reflect and absorb while permitting the audience to visualize their histories—what has been lost and can never be recovered. Hopkins's stare, like Callow's in the beginning of *Spider Woman,* sails into theatrical space, filling it with knowledge and rarefied grief. Film would confine it, all tension focused on the dappled, crystalline tears rather than the world behind them. Moments like these are more suggestive than the most startling close-ups: more of the actor can be seen when there's less skin tone.

The stage is especially user-friendly to Hamlets. (Well, there are exceptions.) For a start, young Hamlet's story can be told without cuts; better still, it doesn't need to roam through castle corridors (as Olivier's Hamlet did) or prepare the way by showing Hamlet racing thrillingly on horseback to his father's funeral (as in Grigori Kozintzev's film). Stage limits are opportunities for both economy and completeness. No need to waste time with seascapes, beaches, and horses. The play's the thing.

Roger Rees's Hamlet is whole, vibrant, and, more than anything else, amazingly lucid. Partly this is because Ron Daniels's production is so modest, so deliberately unclever; no voracious concepts consume the play's oxygen. Especially touching and illuminating is Rees's relationship to Nicholas Farrell's Horatio, the two of them clearly prepared for discussions about falling trees making or not making noise when no one's around—perpetual students, Hamlet not yet prepared for life. When did you last see a memorable Horatio? Certainly not Norman Wooland's traditionally sturdy oak in Olivier's movie. Farrell is the quintessential Cambridge school chum, not much less self-absorbed than Hamlet but quicker to jump through hoops.

In this production, all the men have sharp, distinctive behavioral profiles: Kenneth Branagh's tough bantam Laertes, a spunky chip off the pompous Polonius block, quite simply not as bright as Hamlet or Hora-tio; Christopher Benjamin's Polonius, as thick in body as in brain, every inch the modern diplomat who hears everything and understands noth-ing; and John Stride's superbly authoritative Claudius, whose resonating power makes Hamlet's hesitations all the more credible. Only the Ghost and the Player King talk in rhetorical flourishes; the rest simply converse and think. Suddenly, those words sound newly coined, natural parts of speech, logically derived from thought pressured by experience. Even Rees's soliloquies emerge without cliché or pumped-iron passion: here they stand as Hamlet's efforts to feel what he sees the Player King feel. They are summaries of what he knows, Hamlet's private, experimental dramas, launching him circuitously into action.

Best of all, Rees's Hamlet returns fresh and newly minted from the long voyage to England and his pleasing betrayal of Rosencrantz and Guildenstern. Again, the textual clarity is suddenly vivid: Hamlet is more decisive in crisis than anyone else in the play. Faced with death, he too can kill. Confronted as he was earlier by doubt and thought alone, he's simply more humane than the others – not paralyzed, just kinder, gentler, smarter. He's not cursed with intelligence; rather, he's weighted by other people (Sartre's Hell before its time), not least that vengeful, unsubtle, bullying, dubious Ghost. When Rees comes back to Denmark, he's liv-ing in white-shirted liberty, no longer cramped, halting, and vocally misty but hearty and full-voiced, not just a Sunday swordsman, but a grown-up for all seasons. A lovely performance that builds and connects through actor's techniques in a space that uses them well.

The National Theatre is now offering a double bill of Tom Stoppard's *The Real Inspector Hound* and Sheridan's *The Critic* by the Ian McKel-len–Edward Petherbridge company: a more cohesive, witty pairing would be difficult to imagine, let alone find. Neither play is comfortable in the brutal, convention-hall reaches of the Olivier Theatre, but within minutes they declare their theatrical sunniness, casting those stormy cloud-thoughts to one side. Stoppard, in his first fling at directing, has found a measured, stately rhythm in his marvelous demolition of jaded theater critics and boring plays. He doesn't rush or push, giving his gifted company (Petherbridge, Eleanor Bron, Roy Kinnear, Selina Cadell, and McKellen) time to enjoy the development of their caricatures. Without such providential carelessness with time, they would be mere pencil sketches. Here, instead, they expand, contract, and repeat, always deepening the texture, loading the canvas with more squiggles and tics. Result: laughs earned, payoffs from setups, wondrous silliness loved for its own sake and consequently lovable to watch. Cadell's Mrs. Drudge limps across the stage for what seems a thousand times, delivering hors d'oeuvres to the guests who can't believe any more than the audience can that she's going to make the long journey again. Stoppard's faith in Cadell and in the repeated action is like his faith in wordplay. He seems to know that theater respects tenacity and visible conviction, responding joyously to the release of ideas into action.

One theater comment deserves another, so *The Critic* turns out to be a natural partner for Stoppard's dotty vision. Directed by an actor, Sheila Hancock, it becomes an actor's dream even when Sheridan's wordplay gets stuffy and clotted. Ian McKellan, often clotted by wordplay, too fancifully aware of who and where he is, plays Mr. Puff with a goofy, spontaneous sweetness. Petherbridge is his customary, relaxed, vaguely snooty self as Sir Fretful Plagiary, sniffing the air as if other people were intrusive mosquitoes, a performance in keeping with the vagrant humors of the entire production. By the end, when the play self-destructs in an explosion of flying flats and floating flags, Petherbridge and Cadell are playing delicately dancing shepherdesses, he cuckoo-calm and oblivious, she cuckoo-crazy and paranoid. Sheridan's double message is alive and well in this double bill: theater is at once the screwiest and most noble delirium of all.

This would be understood, too, by Peter O'Toole, whose natural theater techniques have been so long in exile in unaccommodating films. His Henry Higgins in Shaw's *Pygmalion* is flawed only by his ravaged voice. Otherwise, the rest is simple revelation, an entirely new view of a character rigidly embalmed in the movie images of Leslie Howard and Rex Harrison. O'Toole's Higgins is a bewilderingly restless wanderer in the first act, never coming to a halt for an instant, always moving, reaching for fruit, biting into it, discarding it, circling the room again only to fall upon a grape. At first it seems like carelessness, as if he doesn't want to be there. He's searching for something, but what? Could it be peace, happiness, love, fulfillment of an elusive kind, or just a movie sound stage? The mystery continues into the second act, when suddenly all is revealed: waiting for Eliza to appear in his mother's drawing room, his perpetual motion has by now taken on heroic proportions; this is too much for his aged mother, who says in a lightning-bolt reprimand, "Henry, will you please stop fidgeting?"

So that's what it has been about: an actor's preparation, a characteristic buried in dialogue previously ignored, a behavioral truth that reveals Higgins, finally, as a mother's boy who will never be able to settle upon an agreeable wife. Insecure, never more at peace than when he is spread out on the floor at his mother's feet, head leaning on her legs, he is an eternally wounded lover, condemned never to make love. Shaw doesn't often inspire such dimensions. But then again, neither does film.

(October 1985)

Carnal Knowledge

Montreal. It takes only an instant to realize that small talk plays no part in Ariane Mnouchkine's repertoire. Her lion-maned shock of speckled gray hair recalls Beethoven, almost as if she had stumbled on the visible signs of her anachronistic identity—an eighteenth-century purist defying this most vulgar and indifferent century to stay out of her way. Which means, by analogy, that whatever she directs with her Théâtre du Soleil in Paris— and for the past two years it has been *Les Atrides,* a titanic unearthing of Aeschylus's *Oresteia* trilogy preceded by Euripides' *Iphigenia in Aulis*—she does with a Beethovenesque obsessiveness that points to a daily life in which she eats choral odes for breakfast, fractured myths for lunch, and divine interventions for dinner.

That she doesn't claw and spit out critic-interviewers is still another— and different—sign, a clue to her essential discretion with text and her undoubted courtesy to actors. We agree quickly that both of us would run cheerfully in opposite directions if we could, interviews not exactly our style. Yet with earth-mother instinct, always the director, and using gently inflected English perfected when she studied at Oxford, she leads me from our appointed meeting ground, the netherworld of Montreal's Arena Maurice-Richard, built years ago for Olympic wrestling, to a windswept park bench, where, of all strange declensions, other voices compete with decidedly undivine interventions, most of them lifted from life, yes, but too absurdly close to the conventional background trappings of realistic theater: children playing, dogs barking, and even the insinuating appearance of a young beggar whose gambit is that he wants to know when the next performance begins.

Small talk, after all. In this situation, at any rate, Mnouchkine welcomes interruptions, whether from assistants warning her that time is running out on *The Libation Bearers* inside the arena, or from another would-be interviewer asking politely to listen in on our conversation, or indeed from the beggar, eliciting the warmest response of all. For a fleeting moment, the greatest traversal through ancient retributive murders takes a backseat to one young man's primal need, reminding me suddenly that Mnouchkine began her career in the sixties with plays by Gorky and Wesker. Since then, her "collective creations" (*Les Clowns, 1789, 1793,* and *L'Age d'or*) have given way to Molière's *Don Juan,* an adaptation of Klaus Mann's *Mephisto,* several Shakespeares, and in the mid-1980s, Hélène Cixous's *11 septembre: L'Histoire terrible mais inachevée de Norodom Sihanouk, roi du Cambodge,* and *30 septembre: L'Indiade ou l'Inde de leurs rêves.* In between, whether from direct desire or momentary need, she's made some films, most notably her astounding *Molière* (1977), a dramatic biography that dares to con me, at least, into suspending all my usual disbelief, pulling me through labyrinthine, mud-soaked streets, backstage upheavals, and finally into the dark recesses of a cosmically comic imagination: Charles Foster Kane meets Groucho Marx.

But now, at last, it's the most daunting challenge of all, what we foolishly persist in calling "the Greeks," as if the surviving shards had ever set out to call across the centuries in one conclusive yawp. I had already seen the Euripides prologue and two of the Aeschylean trilogy, looking forward to what little dramatic relief might be offered by the meditations on peace and justice in *The Eumenides.* Mistaking my quarry, I thought I might begin some distance from the looming question of tragedy, history, and the way she works by urging her to share her enthusiasms—favorite painters, composers, actors. But she'll have none of it. Like her theater, the interview had better be about something: "I don't see how to enumerate," she says, putting full stop to my effort on behalf of easeful indirection.

So there we are—in the middle of my own obsessive enthusiasms, most of them having to do with theatrical losses and corruptions. I ask about what it is she seeks from the actors, and what she thinks may have been lost in our knowledge and experience of theatrical possibility in the wake of what actors actually perform.

"Every time I look at television or even at certain types of film," she says, "I think that if it goes on like this, in fifty years we will have forgotten the art of acting as we've forgotten the art of silk. What's going on very often has nothing to do with the poetry of acting—the transformation of an emotion into a form. And then there's nothing to be emotional about."

She doesn't know how to describe the way she works with the Armenian, Brazilian, Indian, and even French actors who will be performing *Les Atrides* for the Brooklyn Academy of Music at the Park Slope Armory in October. "I always say that the only method I know is that I don't know," an echo for me of remarks made years ago by Peter Brook, but meant then to describe a challenge to the actor rather than a modest attempt—Mnouchkine's—to point the way to company exploration, an archaeological dig rather than a theatrical ploy. And sure enough, her next reference, perhaps not meant to be taken as a wrist slap to Brook, the director of Paris's Center for Theatrical Research, is about her conviction that "it seems a bit pretentious to use 'research' to describe her process," though she's discovered that scientists claim "they don't know either—they don't find what they're looking for, they find something else."

She knows, however, what she doesn't want, thus putting the beggar and Gorky out of the frame, and that is "falsity, realism, psychology—ideas imposed on the text." She wants "to understand what Aeschylus and Euripides mean, how these mysterious texts can be put on stage...so difficult at the beginning." For her, the dig is about being "humble enough to believe what they're saying, to believe that what each character is saying is true, even if it is a lie." Nothing, therefore, is ornamental: "Everything is essential, useful. Nothing is there to make it seem pretty or seem deep, because then it would look so stupid."

Which, I assure you, it never does, even when she makes *les bêtises*—the mistakes—as she puts it, that any explorer makes on the way to surprise and discovery. Even at that, they're surely few and far between, more like tonal miscalculations, particularly (as I was finding out that evening) in *The Eumenides,* where Aeschylus, too, invites a shift from the stately jagged edges surrounding earlier encounters into a more courtly and even cozy charm in the final scenes. Mnouchkine, in her fidelity to laying out the text as if charting the unregenerate human heart, is apt to fall back on routine borrowings from French classical theater—the occasional trembling voice or high-pitched plaintive whine, the young actor assuming a bony, geriatric walk coupled with an extended gaze into some abstracted middle distance. In short, she—even she—is not above confusing ritual with trance.

That said, she's in command of amazing forces on behalf of dramas that continue to elude convincing theatrical scrutiny by others. (Thirty years ago, Elia Kazan gave up on *The Oresteia* after staging twenty minutes at the Actors Studio!) Without a tunic in sight, she achieves an improbable resurrection of a tradition that, at bottom, is unknowable, or at least as elusive as certainties about fifth-century Athenian meals and personal hygiene. Mnouchkine, her father Russian-Jewish, her travels and interests extensively Asian, simply sets up a huge, timbered stage, 80 feet wide, flanked by a 200-piece gamelan orchestra under the direction of Jean-Jacques Lemêtre, the prodigious composer-performer, who, along with one or two assistants alternately playing, singing, and mopping his brow, manages to sound and look like an octopus that has suddenly acquired musical genius. For more than eight hours, he and his friends undulate swiftly from timpanis to strings and winds, sometimes playing all at once, taking pause only when pressing the button for prerecorded, massed orchestral interludes. For me, the continual underscoring of every phrase, every action, seems like a series of emotional cues for actors and for the audience, not unlike unstoppable Wagner or even silent film with the busiest pianists who ever lived.

Mnouchkine, however, calculates that the actors are listening more "with their skin than their ears," an observation that slides smoothly into her rehearsal experience, with the ways in which Euripides emerges so differently from Aeschylus, while the "carnal differences"—as she puts it—in Aeschylus's three plays "come out when one works theatrically on them." Aristophanes referred to Aeschylus's style as "pegged, wedged, and dovetailed." And that can stand accurately for Mnouchkine's conversation and, almost certainly, for her awesome mix of theatrical vocabularies.

The list is as infinite as the tragic implications: actors in startling white makeup, gorgeous oversize costumes, the repeated use of mirror images—Electra, for example, appearing in the costume last worn by Clytemnestra—the Kathakali choral dances, the whistling wind, the wondrous blue ramp that keeps pouring out of the "vomitorium" to bring on still another Kabukiesque character, ecstatic tribal dances in one play giving way to exhausted individual sarabands in another, and the ominous reappearance throughout of a huge moving platform—a Macy's float, if you like, carrying the latest bearer of bad new and prophecies.

"It's not only Kathakali," says Mnouchkine, and of course that's the point. The sources, as she says, "are also imaginary," because they are "trying to find a civilization which is"—and here she pauses—"of course, Greek." But since "nobody knows," then why not assert, albeit with a throwaway smile, that she's "sure it was like that"? What counts, surely, is not the game of tag she's playing with history or tradition but rather her liberation of collective imagination into theatrical legacies that otherwise slumber within the text as we struggle with centuries of translation and professorial aridity. As I try to tell her, these hours spent with her company release me into recesses and associations that themselves dance around my future grave. Do I take responsibility for the vengeance in my soul? Or, in a not truly lighter vein, do I give the young beggar a dollar?

But lightly, almost gaily, she gives him two. Just as she finds sardonic humor in *The Libation Bearers* or a more piquant, childlike amusement in *The Eumenides,* so does she lead me into unlikely associative memories: Guy-Claude François's set as a sliced-in-half fort from a John Ford Western, the shock in *The Eumenides* that the Erinyes look like Mother Courage meeting her destiny on a chalk circle, the image of Cassandra as a white-robed geisha stepping out of Kurosawa, Simon Abkarian's Agamemnon moving backward as if caught in a rewinding film, and Lemêtre's score suddenly breaking out in shtetl celebration...or is it an

Irish jig? Yet none of this is foreign, arbitrary, or—and this is why she stands so refreshingly outside momentary agenda—self-consciously clever. On the contrary—it's luxuriously austere theatrical art in relentless search of wellsprings, renewal, and nourishment.

The actors—all of them—are only terrific. Abkarian is locked into variety and presence in many roles, even as the Nurse in *The Libation Bearers*, as indeed are the flower-fragile Nirumama Nityanandan as Iphigenia, Cassandra, and Electra; Brontis Jodorowsky not-quite-hiding his sculptured bone structure in and out of the chorus and major roles; the remarkable Juliana Carneiro da Cunha as Clytemnestra and Athena, her lengthy perorations punctuated by a head, when it speaks, that could be a big-screen exclamation point; and above all, the sensual choral leader and Brechtian Erinye Catherine Schaub, who evidently can do anything, whether building costumes and accessories, or choreographing fourteen choral dancers who—forgive me—are more precise and certainly more breathtakingly primeval than the Rockettes ever dreamt.

Have I made myself clear? This is not your average drop-in, drop-dead theatrical experience. Be prepared for the discomfort of bleacher seats. Prepare yourself, also, to come early and watch the actors putting on makeup and costumes in their open cellular dressing rooms below the bleachers. Exchange a flirtatious glance, as I did, with the deliciously seductive Shahrokh Meshkin Ghalam, who will emerge from the frenzied chorus as a Rita Hayworth Apollo in a Burt Lancaster body, smiling at his own high-flying leaps and making you wonder why the Athenians couldn't find more comfort in carnal sex than carnal destiny. And don't flee quickly from the most noble and thrilling curtain calls in town.

I ask Mnouchkine if I might expect some redemption from *The Eumenides*. "No," she says, "it has to do more with peace, and peace is not justice.... What Athena says is—it has to stop, it has to stop.... The cry of the victims will not accomplish anything.... When peace is signed, the dead are forgotten. And it's not fair. Although Athena speaks of justice, she introduces something interesting, really. She introduces complexity."

A rare director, indeed. For a few autumn days in New York, for a passing moment during our national disaster when one criminal leader admits he'll do anything to win reelection, theatrical redemption is ours to cherish, a haunting reminder that what surrounds and suffocates us has to stop.

(September 1992)

Ibsen, Wilson, and the Play of Time

Gertrude Stein's "continuous present" is not far removed from Robert Wilson's theater, even less so, perhaps, when he is engaged in the reformation of a resistant text. Stein "found out a fundamental thing about plays...that the scene as depicted on the stage is more often than not one might say it is always in syncopated time in relation to the emotion of anybody in the audience." How characteristically delightful of Stein to see Wilson before he happens, and to see him, moreover, with wise qualifications sneaking into her sentences—"one might say" and "almost always." One might say, then, that with Stein following softly in the footsteps of her mentor, William James, who found the present "melted in our grasp...gone in the instant of becoming," that Wilson's theater is a natural blip in syncopated time, a logical step in what threatens to look like a peculiarly American fate.

The William Jamesian American is supposed to be a pragmatist, inventing his life according to practical reality. But who is this charming dreamer talking about? Surely not the banker, politician, broker, or lawyer busily allowing nothing to melt in his grasp except other people's money. Either James is wrong or we're all wrong about James. Another possibility: both James and Stein are the real realists, and so is Wilson. The practical reality summoned to war and the spiritual impoverishment of the zonked-out American viewer move into art as photographic realism; only those spending a lifetime voting against their own interests can fail to notice that such realism is merely a cunning rearrangement of the facts. An unmediated fact is that we divide our day into hours, minutes, and seconds while the mediated fact is that we divide and circumscribe our lives by the countless memories and aspirations that struggle ceaselessly with the orderly march of the clock. Momentary experience and the long stretch of perception are never the same, or at the least, they exist only in Stein's syncopated time.

Which leads me to the provisional conclusion that Robert Wilson's realism, like Stein's, is as close to the motion of the mind as our theater ever gets. Beckett's realism, for example, is finally closer to the unmediated clock, even as it freezes the experience of language into something like animated sculpture. Wilson's realism, unable on its own to cope with the mysterious, re-creative power of words, chooses by default a more aggressive diffusion of time as we think we know it. Hardly surprising, then, that like Stein before him, he's not much welcome in the theater, always the art most frazzled by its own disorderly possibilities. But unlike Stein, he has no gift for gab at all, meaning that as time begins to consume what he can do with architectural and dancerly images nourishing his theatrical imagination, he has to turn to other people's language after all.

Ibsen by Wilson? The next joke on all of us will be Shaw by Wilson. Meanwhile, this perfect Wagnerite, always needing to control everything —image, environment, actors, singers, and now the words he cannot consume himself—is reaching for his own quintessence through the medium of the first great poet of apparent theatrical realism. Fair enough that at A.R.T. in Cambridge last season he chose *When We Dead Awaken,* the last gasp if not the last word in the Ibsen revolution. What is surprising, however, is how this gloriously impossible text, with its need for Wagner as much as Wagner always needed a merciless Ibsenite eye, grinds Wilson down to a succession of display-window images (actors as pose, squeaks, and splats). Odd, too, how he alights upon some of the domestic crankiness while utterly failing to make sense or grandeur out of the avalanche. At ease only with his own insertions (Charles "Honi" Coles's down-home doggerel substituting for the tap-dance improvisations Coles can no longer do), he seems to be presenting the production as deliberate evasion, hoping to look as if he's been out-foxed rather than out-classed by Ibsen.

But Ibsen, I suspect, is not only in total command of split-level imagery, his characters' tongues always out of sync with their fleet-footed brains; he's also not in need of desperate humor or arbitrary shock. If anything, he's unfair to most contemporary directors if only because he's so fair to the best actors, none of them incapable of reality and transcendence in one focused suspiration. For the moment, then, Wilson has met his textual match. Taken as experiment, this production is precisely what should be done, a hint to Wilson perhaps, that great plays are not operas lacking compulsive music: they are pure unto themselves, and may not be seeking the coffee-table gloss of a modernist director agitated by his own wordless vocabulary.

Says Stein: "Anyway the play as I see it is exciting and it moves but it also stays and that is as I said in the beginning might be what a play should do."

(1991)

The Presence of Joe

Even over the most convivial uncorking of a decent vintage, Joseph Chaikin continues to be a genie of hard labor, committed at all hours to the transformation of thought into theatrical statement and image. His head crooked to one side, as if straight answers might emerge only from angular prisms, he allows a festive giggle to fill a parenthesis, only to return in the next breath to the primordial ooze that fuels all his best work as actor, director, and teacher. He's always been one of a kind, a guru to some, surely, but remarkably free of the postures that too often come with that self-appointed job. Unlike others similarly placed to demonstrate new strategies, his authority is as natural as breathing, never a demonstration of self, rather a communion with voices primed to reveal the actor as the clue essential to theatrical mystery.

I've heard it suggested only recently that this commitment to *the presence of the actor* (the title of his book) automatically marks him as an anachronism. Chaikin's actor—lithe, clarion voiced, wall-eyed, possessed—is a creation from another time, not working either the oedipal vein of tragedy or psychology, instead appearing onstage as emblematic modernist, transformative into animal, object, or idea yet never locked into story or character. If subsequent experiment has yielded still another image of the actor—something like the theater's version of postmodernism—I'm not sure I can identify it.

Instead, honorable as much of the work from Robert Wilson to Anne Bogart is, the presence of the expressive actor has given way to architectures and abstractions in holy obedience to the gods of millennial technology. Edward Gordon Craig's late-nineteenth-century vision of the actor as *über-marionette* merely had to wait out the century to come into its own. Leave your screen at home and you're likely to run into it in the theater, whether in the shape of everlasting family drama or the ubiquitous presence of T.V. monitors, body mikes, circus lighting, and ear-splitting surroundsound.

Allotted fifteen minutes of fame, it's just as well to be an anachronism. Chaikin himself, despite the aphasia he's been overcoming during the past decade, simply goes on. Last year (1995), he came to Ireland (and, at my invitation, to my own Exiles Theatre Ltd.) with Susan Yankowitz and former Open Theater Actors Shami Chaikin, Tina Shepard, and Paul Zimet for the first of what has become four reconsiderations of *Terminal,* Yankowitz's investigation into mortality first developed twenty-six years ago with Chaikin and the actors. Working with Irish students and American and West Indian faculty, Chaikin and Yankowitz were searching, in the company of mixed generations and traditions, for what Yankowitz sees as "a new layer of words and images which will intersect with the primary text." (Point of self-interest here: as co-director with Morton Lichter of Exiles Theatre, I was intent on demonstrating a part of our own history; we had both taken part in the Open Theater's work in the 1960s.)

That investigation continued in March 1996 with students at the University of California, San Diego, as part of a weekend conference honoring Chaikin. Then in April, and continuing in August, work began in preparation for an appearance of the latest *Terminal* in Belgrade's Autumn Festival—an act of faith, I suppose, in the idea that theater need not be reductive in addressing mortality to an audience that has known nothing but for the past five years.

The two Sams in Chaikin's life—Shepard and Beckett—are quite evident these days. While in residence at Exiles and San Diego, Chaikin performed *The War in Heaven,* written with Shepard in 1984 as a response to the loss of speech he suffered from the stroke that assaulted him during open-heart surgery. Defying expectations and the rules, he sits at a table in a hellish half-light, skin like transparent parchment, eyes caught in a space all their own, voice pitched to the stars, his vibrating frailty the very image of how strong theatrical simplicity can finally be. As an encore—an implicit tribute to the lieder recitalists he's always admired—he reads the poem Beckett wrote for him after hearing about his stroke. "Thought music" is the phrase Chaikin coined to describe his work with Shepard, and I can't imagine a more accurate distillation of Beckett's work, too. Since these readings are minimalism in maximum gear, I allow myself one disturbing question: If Chaikin can make so much by himself of theatrical possibility, why probe further with others and into his own theatrical past?

Suddenly I recall that, in those intoxicating sessions with the Open Theater in the sixties, Richard Gilman and I were there precisely to ask such questions, even if—as now—a defining answer would prove as elusive to the catch as a butterfly dipping and darting in the wind. We were encouraged, however, to keep trying. What I remember for a start is that, guided by Chaikin's sense of quest, we were for an instant on a mission to make theater as we were never taught it. The sixties get a bum rap today not only because of the usual code words—drugs and liberalism—but mostly because so many of us truly didn't give a damn about money. Or rather, the pursuit of it for its own sake. We couldn't go on, but we went on.

That loft in the West 20s where the Open Theater began its work was a sensible place to retreat from the spell cast over theatrical vocabulary by the witch-fathers of the Group Theatre and the Actors Studio. Surely, righteous indignation need not be the only guiding force in drama, mothers standing heroically by their stoves as Moses-like daddies hurled titanic threats at the dreaming heads of easily abused sons. There must be something in playmaking and acting that urges the imagination to look outside the home. Where was the theater that might dare to search for the theatrical equivalents of Mondrian's and Stravinsky's geometries? The wrong Russians had been colonizing our lives long enough: time to find new shapes for life on the stage, to declare freedom from acting as unlicensed therapy, to bring back the eloquent body, the unpredictable gesture, the resonant silence.

Not that anybody in the Open Theater actually talked with such missionary zeal or in brutal comparisons based on dangerous, clumsy analogies. The actors, as always, simply wanted to work. Once a week, however, they were encouraged by Joe to join a discussion usually led by Gilman or myself, or sometimes both of us together. Gilman talked frequently about painting, and I referred usually to the contrast I could see between the actors' work with their fantasy and the exercises I had witnessed for two years under Lee Strasberg's direction.

What a liberation—at least for me! If, as Harold Clurman would have it, Strasberg's primary gift was to look at the inside of an actor in much the same way as a Swiss watchmaker gazes at the timekeeper's moving parts, Chaikin's gift was to address Time itself. Strasberg collected classical recordings in such colossal numbers that he couldn't possibly listen to each more than once, if that. Yet he rarely mentioned to his actors what he was finding in Mozart, Dietrich Fischer-Dieskau, or Alban Berg. Chaikin, on the other hand, could barely contain his need to end sessions with music, more than once playing the astounding first act of *Die Walküre* under Bruno Walter with Lotte Lehmann and Lauritz Melchior caught in what must be the hottest sustained vocal embrace of all time. Somehow, Joe's actors were expected to make connections on their own, perhaps with a little help from me at the end of the week, but more likely putting the other arts into those free-floating containers of impulse and inspiration they were being urged insistently to trust while doing their work.

Years later I learned from Robert Pasolli's *A Book on the Open Theater* that Gilman and I had been viewed as "instructors in perspective," a dreadful codifying title that must have been invented to account for the strangeness of our presence. (With some relief this year, I heard Joe refer to me as his dramaturg, an acknowledgment that pleases me even as I have to say that others, such as Mira Rafalowicz, were truly dramaturgical over a much longer span.) Few of us at the time saw the group as an institution: like the actors, Gilman and I were to think, build, collaborate, contributing our five dollars a month toward the loft rental along with everybody else.

Years after the facts, I can't be certain that episodes such as *Walküre* happened as frequently as my memory would have it. What I recall, finally, is a time in which perspective was everything. I remember bringing friends such as Jean-Claude van Itallie and Gilman to observe this phenomenal grouping of actors; a few would-be directors (Peter Feldman, for one) were quietly as inventive as any in the gathering.

I recall, too, a gawky, loose-limbed eighteen-year-old playwright named Sam Shepard, who had allegedly written seventy-five plays by then. By 1966, when I finally accepted the charms of a regular income, joining Robert Brustein at Yale, there was also the haunting presence of still another boyish wonder named Robert Wilson, who made me feel old by declaring his doubts about Joe's work. The romance of good, hard, disinterested, intelligent, impolitic, engaged, sensual rehearsal seems to have come and gone so quickly.

All those exercises had been so much more suggestive and—yes— entertaining than anything being done in theater those days. (These days, too, for that matter.) I know, however, and said as much to Joe, that such a group could sustain itself only so long without an audience.

But as I said it, I wished I could take it back. Soon enough, there were Monday evenings in Sheridan Square, presenting a better version of Eliot's *Sweeney Agonistes* than the British ever did—or at least, so I thought at the time. Ahead without flinching were real producers—a world, in short, from whose bourne no traveler returns. So the Open Theater as we had known it was doomed to succeed: Megan Terry's *Viet Rock,* van Itallie's *The Serpent,* and all the rest were undoubtedly worth the loss of the original romance. Yet: *how* to live with loss? That is always the question.

Joe, I know now, was always decades ahead of us. The self-destruct mechanism was part of his plan anyway, and now it was ticking away more or less on schedule. Flash forward, as we must, and all the various destinies achieve a logic that could have been anticipated: after ten years, the Open Theater was no more, replaced in time by the Winter Project, even something called the Summer Project, and eventually a final entity called the Other Theater. Since some didn't want to leave when asked, they were often pushed—or is it purged? Others simply moved, as I did, in another rhythm to another place. Everybody, of course, got older.

Wheels always within wheels. Early on, Joe went to Minneapolis to act in Terrence McNally's *And Things That Go Bump in the Night.* His leading lady, the delicious, bitingly intelligent Leueen MacGrath, was herself close to Peter Brook and Natasha Parry; in time, Joe was in London working with Brook on his controversial anti-Vietnam collage, *US.* It was inevitable, too, that Joe and Jerzy Grotowski would meet, but whoever influenced whom, it's easy to notice that Joe's vocabulary and work are in the present tense, Grotowski's in the past.

From time to time, I make lists of those whose work had been touched by Chaikin at least as much as he's been touched by them—those already mentioned, of course, but also Joseph Campbell, Susan Sontag, Maria Irene Fornes, R.D.Laing, and Ellen Stewart. Unlike Strasberg, who in the end was training others and himself for the Hollywood camera, Joe was never a maker of stars. Yet I was amused to read that Michelle Pfeiffer's guru-teacher was the late Roy London, an Open Theater stalwart who might never have gone West without that push from the fold. The question of influence is always a mug's game. Joe had his teachers, too, though he rarely stayed with any long enough to become a fanatic for one acting method or another.

The least trivial wheel within wheels may be not the two Sams so much as the singular Brook. Certainly, neither Brook nor Chaikin has needed the other, but it must have been reassuring for both to know that, in far-flung corners, each was driven by similar demons: research before performance, thought before action, dedication before ambition. Alone with actors, they speak in almost the same hushed yet curiously sculpted phrases. Both tread softly through verbal thickets: twinned in their distrust of certainty, each nevertheless presents work after work marked by the precision of piston engines. They know how to wait for the crowning thought, the hard-earned image. To risk an image myself, I'd say that the theater's good fortune is that these two natural rabbis chose the more trustworthy house of worship.

In all this, I'm neglecting a major point of separation: Brook—nurtured by Shakespeare, celebrated once in the West End and on Broadway—has an almost automatic instinct for the marketplace, even when working in abstractions; Chaikin—nourished by philosophers, poets, and Beckett more than anyone—has never known the meaning of trade, commerce, or fashion. Brook has had empty spaces made over into theaters for him; Chaikin, totally itinerant, self-propelled, has had none. More power, of course, to Brook's evident sexiness for audiences, foundations, and producers, but let's never mistake it for the only way to be beautiful in bed.

Besides, it's beautiful anyway to see Joe airborne in more ways than one—traveling where the work is, floating into new rooms to cast his spell, as if he hasn't already done enough. *Terminal* has been taking energy from the young, as hoped and expected, but not always without tremors; even as many admit to confusion about an acting vocabulary by-passed in their training, Joe himself exerts his customary unforced persuasion. Too briefly, of course, he steps out of their theater history chapters to demonstrate an alternative: whatever happens next in their lives, it won't happen without a vivid memory of Joe's muted, yet demanding presence filling an empty space.

Meanwhile, the projects march on. This summer, he performed Beckett's *Texts for Nothing* at the Royal Court Theatre in London and at the Edinburgh Theatre Festival. And were it not for a conflict with his New York production of two Shepard plays at the Signature Theater Company— *When the World Was Green (A Chef's Fable),* another Chaikin-Shepard collaboration, which debuted at 7 Stages Theatre during Atlanta's Olympic Arts Festival, and Shepard's 1965 play *Chicago*—he would have been able to accept an Exiles invitation to perform the Beckett at this year's Dublin Theatre Festival.

Ahead lies a possible production of *Happy Days* in New York, and so far as I can make out, surprises well into the millennium. Shepard once called himself "an apprentice to Joe," and it would seem that all avenues are still open for successors.

Anachronism indeed. Suddenly I'm insulted by the implication. Chaikin is surely not obliged to meet the winner-loser lottery standards of the shopping mall, nor does his work require defense just because it has never shown ambition to be anything but itself. Reputation, as Shakespeare would have it, is just a bubble, transitory and likely to explode anyway. So why waste energy addressing its interlocuters?

Who elected the pundits presiding over every fifteen-minute hour? Who anointed the anointers who edit the magazines chattering to their own class? Whatever the medium or discipline, few artists can keep up with the managed celebrity of the market.

Consider the story and reputation of one painter, known almost exclusively to Beckett, and—if I can be allowed a flying leap—a figure not unlike our Joe. He's the late Bram van Velde, still awaiting anointment but once exiled in Paris from the Netherlands as Beckett was exiled from

Ireland. Confronted with the statistic that in his entire life he had produced fewer paintings than Picasso in his ninety-first year, he acknowledges the latter's "exceptional creative and inventive" work but adds that Picasso "was a stranger to doubt."

At last, a wheel within wheels that only connects: Beckett bought van Velde's 1937 painting *Without Title* and placed it on the wall opposite his desk; van Velde, in turn, reports that his gouaches are "born of the unknown—and not of habit, or know-how, or intention, or *of some recipe*" (my italics). But surely, I heard that first at Open Theater sessions when Joe assured the anxious gathering of actors and writers that his exercises were never intended to be recipes. Suddenly, we were on our own, abandoned to life.

Best tale of all, perhaps the only essential wheel, comes when van Velde wears a pair of glasses found in a dustbin for more than twenty years before visiting an optician. The specialist, insisting that van Velde can't possibly be seeing anything with those spectacles, asks him, "What sort of job do you do anyway?" To which van Velde replies, "I paint my interior life." Not a convincing formula for every endeavor or conventional success, it nevertheless will serve to describe what Joe Chaikin has been offering the theater all his life. He paints our inner lives, finding in them a palpable source for the animated spirit, the talking body, the enacted event, returning theater to something not often celebrated by the performing arts: a precious moment or two of articulate, intimate communion.

(November 1996)

Playwriting

Transfer at Elysian Fields

So the last scene wasn't the natural inevitable death he had always feared, but only a household accident. Ironic melodramatist to the end, Tennessee Williams didn't die from the unwashed grape Blanche DuBois thought might finish her, but from an inhaled bottle cap. Not quite the exotic, hothouse ending he might have written, but close enough to bring the wry smile that he could always solicit amid the languid sighs and cracked hearts that keep colliding in his plays.

To be a playwright in America, as Williams knew better than anyone, is to depend on the kindness of strangers, few of them really dependable. He was lucky to have found success on Broadway when he did, but it was almost the death of him even before last week. Broadway and Hollywood were generous for a time, but they are never patient with aggressive delicacy or an intelligence tirelessly searching for repose. They are especially suspicious of an artist who peaks too soon. Williams's instincts and temperament were more like those of American actors than American writers. Like Orson Welles, Marlon Brando, and all our great young actors from John Barrymore and Tallulah Bankhead to Geraldine Page and Kim Stanley, he was not given much room to grow at all, let alone grow old gracefully. He was doomed by the right success in the wrong place.

But it was only a public doom. One can die in the marketplace while staying quite alive at home. Current obituaries notwithstanding, it is too soon and too easy to bury his last twenty years just because *The Glass Menagerie* and *A Streetcar Named Desire* hypnotized the world into early submission. Always a better scenewriter than playwriter, he was less an architect than a pointillist painter of shimmering portraits. *Streetcar* drove itself hard, like an organized drama, but it was really a terrific succession of high moments, eleven astounding scenes that didn't need to search for a play. Illusion—as Blanche would have it—was everything. There is one scene in 1979's *Vieux Carré,* however, with more tension and tenderness than anything in *Streetcar.* His fitful rhythms and blotchy style kept getting messier as confidence waned, but his fall from favor was also the price that had to be paid for eccentricity, tenacity, and the refusal to be a good little messenger from established domains in literature, politics, and morality.

Literature wanted him to be southern like Faulkner, but despite the accent he was really American like Poe. Politics thought he was less committed than Miller (or Bellow or Mailer); instead, he was committed to the forgotten–gallant survivors who knew instinctively that ideologies are even more ephemeral than plays. Williams's characters were "the fugitive kind" because he had discovered in battle that running is the best revenge. It followed, then, that his moral sensibility couldn't really find its public; like Oscar Wilde, he was gay before his time but never comfortably and predictably gay in his work. He was simply dissenting from all establishments, writing undisguised real women better than anyone else in our theater, presenting macho men who spent their frantic energy trying to disguise the women in their souls. His biggest crime against traditional expectations may have been that his women were always brighter than his men.

Does it really matter now if the rush to judgment rules him better or worse than O'Neill? Neither of them, after all, was up to the best in Beckett and Brecht. Surely the important reminder is that he was better than the marketplace deserved: play after play with curving, voluptuous phrases unmatched by anyone in English in the past forty years; dramatic situations that are breathless in their intensity; roles as actable and mythic as almost any in the tragic-comic tradition; an epic imagination that might have carried him to worlds uncharted if *Camino Real* hadn't been so stupidly rejected on Broadway; and not least, a wondrous gift for titles that were the clues to everything–smoky rooms, chanting, haunted voices, butterfly people floating through theatrical space as if time, the enemy, could never crush them.

At New York cocktail parties, Williams once wrote, he used to consume martinis almost as quickly as he could "snatch them from the tray." It was that "febrile thing" hanging in the air. "Horror of insincerity, of *not meaning,* overhangs these affairs like the cloud of cigarette smoke and the hectic chatter." The horror, for him, was about the only thing left unsaid at such parties. And so he said it in his plays. "About their lives," he went

on to say, "people ought to remember that when they are finished, everything in them will be contained in a marvelous state of repose which is the
same as that which they unconsciously admired in drama." I hope
Williams remembered at the finish, and was finally content with the pride
and repose in his drama that will remain his singular triumph over time.

(March 1983)

While one doesn't have to die to inspire a biography, it certainly helps.
When Tennessee Williams swallowed that bottle cap in 1983, agents and
publishers must have been signaling each other like lions in heat. Tennessee
had always been good copy not only for the columns but also for the classrooms and scolding reviewers. Like Dylan Thomas, Brendan Behan, and
even Eugene O'Neill, he led a reliably tormented life, appealing to those
who love to feel above their betters. Making it easier for them by being
brazenly homosexual and visibly miserable, he also satisfied a craving—so
common to Americans—to lavish crocodile tears on artists who seem to be
failing at their work. His last decades were mostly awful: nothing he did,
whether writing plays every morning fueled by vodka and red wine or acting in *Small Craft Warnings* Off Broadway in 1972, brought him the satisfaction needed to warm his divided soul. He had never required much evidence to confirm doubts about himself. Always ahead of the scolds and
Calvinists, he was his own worst critic, much more efficient at misplacing
his gifts or accounting for disaster than his neglected or traitorous friends.

Until now. Two new books on Williams could scarcely be more
opposed in spirit and execution. In the end, however, neither goes far
enough in rescuing Williams from the loathing he heaped upon himself,
and both go too far in confirming different myths that keep colliding
with the artist who actually worked every day at his craft. In *The Kindness
of Strangers*, Donald Spoto compiles soiled laundry lists; in *Tennessee: Cry
of the Heart*, Dotson Rader natters about a pal with Falstaffian sexual
appetites who also just happened to be famous. Rader is decidedly better
at anecdote than Spoto, offering in one story after another more sense of
character than Spoto conveys in more than four hundred labored pages,
but even Rader can't seem to grasp what it was inside Williams that gave
him the will to work.

What is worse, both Spoto and Rader are enthralled by the same critical premise that Williams accepted too easily himself, all those rules and restrictions about playwriting that had so little to do with Williams's amazing gift for spreading gargantuan human images across a stage. The great miracle of his career (as opposed to his work) is that he succeeded so well and so long on Broadway without ever presenting an entirely conventional idea of a play. He was always agreeing easily to thwart his own instinct for building extraordinary structures out of fugitive, scenic fragments. Available to manipulation and distortion, he was probably a natural candidate for the conventional biography (Spoto) and the narcissistic memoir (Rader).

Williams deserves more stimulating, sensitive recorders. Even at their sloppiest and unfocused worst, his plays were never caught in the downward draft of prose like Spoto's—a windy drone, boring enough to stun an ox. Neither were they flip and cool, like the more readable phrases of Rader. Williams may have failed to develop as both artist and commodity, but he never wrote a line without shape, color, or emotional density. Reading Rader and Spoto, one might think that Williams was mainly a consumer of sex, drugs, and booze rather than a writer with a voice all his own.

Perhaps he invited such an emphasis by living in so much obvious distress, swept away by tidal waves of paranoia, unable to rely on anything more than a performing self. Spoto in particular is critical of all the work after *The Night of the Iguana,* but even then he never seems aware that his reporting and analysis could just as well be describing a Bowery bum as a major artist. Overloaded with the testimony of friends and colleagues, many of whom had contributed to Williams's problems, he reports facts that are rarely allowed to yield mystery or surprise. His book reads more like an accountant's ledger than a life as it is led: choosing the forward motion of foursquare chronology, he neglects the inward, meditative motion of experience.

It's possible that Williams would have laughingly preferred it this way. According to Rader, who claims to have recorded Williams's life after 1960 either on tape or in "notes, letters and journals" written soon after events, Williams once said that he traveled so much "because it's hard to hit a moving target." That he slips less easily out of Rader's grasp than

Spoto's is simply a function of Rader's prescient opportunism. Playing Boswell to a raunchy Dr. Johnson comes easily to Rader, if not quite so elegantly: rummaging through memory, he saves his book from celebrations of his own sexual prowess and big-baby-bear devotion by quoting Williams at length on almost every other page. Where Spoto finds only routine despair, Rader presents conversations and scenes that might have slipped routinely and entertainingly into a play. Against the model of Spoto's sober gloom, Rader's version of the life can be counted a partial success, if only because he remembers "good times, laughter, pranks, outrageous camping," reminders that Williams in much of his work was a master of ironic, startling wit.

Spoto's interviews and schoolmasterish research seem only to leave him in a trance dominated by one mundane, familiar and questionable idea—that Williams's main characters were repeated versions of himself. (Biographers often identify their own occupational therapy with everybody else's.) Sometimes this leads him toward speculative detours that trail disturbingly into the interpretive void that marks most of his book. Suddenly, for instance, he notices that three of Williams's women have the same initials—Amanda Wingfield, Alma Winemiller, and, as if she too were in a play, his agent Audrey Wood. He is intrigued to discover that Tennessee worked once with a Stanley Kowalski and that he knew a Harold Mitchell, but so what? Shakespeare, after all, had a son named Hamnet, news that would probably derail Spoto forever. A virtuoso with dangling particles of truth, Spoto is continually in meandering pursuit of countless dead ends.

Better such idle chat, however, than his occasional remarks about dramatic technique or theater. Spoto's authorities are marketplace sages like Brooks Atkinson and Walter Kerr, both friendly witnesses whenever the plays were not too steamily sexual or apparently shapeless as an unmade bed. Spoto calls *Ten Blocks on the Camino Real* "formless and experimental," missing—as Williams finally allowed himself to miss—the signals through the flames that might have led him more authoritatively into a developed epic technique. Spoto's acquaintance with drama has barely crept past the well-made play, so it's not surprising that he should use "experimental" as a dirty word, or that he would be disturbed by Chance Wayne's final address to the audience in *Sweet Bird of Youth,* calling it an "intrusion of authorial voice...permissible in a Mozart opera, but difficult to sustain in a modern-dress play." Isn't it just possible that the wicked, exploitative, sexual Williams, leaping over towns, countries, and beds in the company of beautiful, exploitative, unquestioning boys, was merely running away from stuffy Spotos telling him incessantly how *not* to write a play?

Maybe that is where Rader comes in, claiming now to have been a friend, but unmentioned by Spoto. (Whom should we believe?) What Rader does best, even if it wasn't his intention, is remind us that Williams was probably escaping into himself whenever he descended to his own lower depths. Spoto looks for clues about characters and their models in life. Rader looks for fun and sentiment. Neither, however, finds what Williams discovered down there, probably because biographers often mistake behavior for the man. Flawed as he was, Williams had the native courage of a displaced Jacobean, locating, in some of the best plays ever written, the crushed yet magisterial importance of sex in all our lives.

(July–August 1985)

Vienna Woulds

This century's late discovery of Arthur Schnitzler's plays, densely packed, like Mahler's symphonies, with sinewy passages of longing and chaos that burst almost discreetly into occasional screams, has not been a discovery shared fully in New York. About lost time and a time lost to us forever, the plays are also about life lived among others. Only a theater equipped to spread that life lavishly upon the stage – with hordes of actors and explosions of Klimtian glamour – can hope to meet Schnitzler's terms while honoring his moral weight. That New York lacks such a theater is not exactly a secret.

Das Weite Land, called *Undiscovered Country* in Tom Stoppard's version, was produced by the National Theatre several years ago, more recently in Hartford and Washington, D.C., and is currently in repertory at the Mark Taper Forum, Los Angeles. An astonishing work, it places twenty-three characters in a crowd of twenty more hotel guests, waiters, bellboys, and elevator operators. While only ten characters are central to the story, the presence of the others gives Schnitzler the space and time he needs to delay action so that the major figures need not be rushed into contrived decision or mechanized fate.

Slowly, then, they curl around each other to make their choices. The play is haunted from the start by the apparent suicide of a young pianist, Korsakov, who fell in love with Genia Hofreiter (Blythe Danner), the wife of a wealthy philanderer, Friedrich Hofreiter (James Naughton). He, in turn, is just bounding back from an affair with Mrs. Adele Natter (Teri Garr), an affair completely understood, if not accepted, by Genia. The Hofreiters live in a villa outside Vienna where friends, including a doctor (Peter Riegert), keep congregating to gossip and play tennis while plotting vacations and assignations. Everybody is polite, if only moderately, and it is only a matter of time before new alliances are formed—Friedrich with Erna Wahl (Laila Robins), who is being wooed chastely by the doctor, and Genia with a young naval officer, Otto von Aigner (Dylan Baker), whose mother (Carrie Nye) is an aging actress stupendously weary of men and all their faithlessness. The play ends with an offstage duel between Friedrich and Otto that is more shattering and worldbreaking than the duel between Solyony and Tusenbach in *The Three Sisters*.

Schnitzler has, in fact, refined the usages of offstage action: only at the end is it possibly to believe that Korsakov might not have killed himself; that Friedrich might have murdered him emerges—and is deliberately never resolved—in the play's final moments. Similarly, major characters, such as the entire von Eigner family, are never seen together onstage. Images of their lives, indeed all the lives, steal upon us, permitting the play to resound as powerfully after the end as it does throughout its intricate actions. Schnitzler is not so much leisurely as he is expansive and detailed. Reality, for him, is the absence of predictable shape, but on the other hand, the almost certain presence of the price that will be paid when private impulse is confused with public honor.

Stoppard's version and Nikos Psacharopoulos's production share a commitment to Schnitzler's leisure while driving the play forward with compulsive energy that sometimes undercuts the gravity of Schnitzler's subliminal story. Stoppard can't resist an occasional self-conscious flirtation with English euphony: "between the drizzle and the drivel" or "frantically, romantically." Once, he overreaches into an unacknowledged Marxist phrase that can't be Schnitzler–Friedrich taking "from each according to his needs." Stoppard is sometimes like a boy sent to do a man's job.

Psacharopoulos is, of course, the wizard of Williamstown, daring to organize the impossible so that it looks like the probable. Even he can't quite get his actors to equal his actresses. When Peter Riegert's doctor tells Erna that he "could show you another world where the air is purer," he might just as well be guiding her to a meal at Windows on the World. James Naughton offers only the clenched bluster of Friedrich, never his complexity or ironic humor. As usual, however, Blythe Danner saves everything: in a production richly dressed by Jennifer von Mayrhauser and spectacularly endowed by David Jenkins with a real elevator for the Dolomite hotel, she provides the most consistent lift to all the action. A true match for Schnitzler's mysterious fusion of worldliness and eagerness, playing with a strand of hair as she retreats from her own seriousness, she is Mahler's earth song, suspended in time, heartbreakingly real.

(July 1985)

Harmed Play

Santouche, in Mac Wellman's seventy-minute epic fantasy, *Harm's Way,* is male America on a rampage. In eleven brief scenes with music, he manages to kill five people: first a mother who has just murdered her stubborn child because the kid refused to eat American cheese and baloney on Wonder bread; then the leader of a gang; next a man calling himself William McKinley who has been trying to get a dead Grover Cleveland to bury him alive; then a con artist named Crowsfoot (also revealed as a carnival beast named Guyanousa) who has stolen Santouche's girl; and finally the girl herself. As the lights dim to the steady musical beat that has underlined every moment in George Ferencz's *Horror Comics* production, a chorus of three little kids in tuxedos and bowlers chants, over and over again, "Who you gonna kill next, Mister?" Santouche, exhausted at last, seems to fade out with the lights.

Which may be the only wishful thinking indulged by this mercilessly imagined, densely packed, weirdly articulate political play. Wellman's targets are bigger and more elusive than Santouche's. Clearly aware that national life and theater have developed the most refined techniques for burying the truth about our lives, not least through a barrage of images that make each experience look just as unimportant as the last and the next one, Wellman barrels ahead with a plotless odyssey that piles image on image as if he alone might escape the fate of the nation.

If he doesn't quite do so, it's partly because he's caught in the inescapable clutches of today's production techniques, the director illustrating everything with darkly lit pictures that never let imagination or the play alone. Politically at least, the nightmarish journey of Santouche from one death to the next is gotten off the hook because it doesn't look enough like the everyday world. Seen by Ferencz as a literal dreamscape, its theatrical seductiveness carries it too far from the hard interiors of Wellman's political conscience.

(A confession about my perspective might help here. Having missed the first three scenes because I was unaware of the 7:30 curtain, I was rescued later by a copy of the play and an article by Wellman in *Performing Arts Journal* 24 called "The Theater of Good Intentions." With these in hand—a practice, by the way, common in Europe—I was able to match the percentage of Ferencz's production that I saw with Wellman's full intention. Clearly, however, I had to fight my way into the lures of Ferencz's work, if only because I was trying for ten minutes to locate and recover what I had missed.)

Wellman is not, like the production, hell-bent on borrowing pop music and art for the sake of effect and impression. America, after all, is not a rock show. But you would never quite know it in Ferencz's version. Where Wellman is meditating on obsessive evil, not something boxed into traditional American corners, where powerful men (the McKinleys and Clevelands) are merely victims, Ferencz falls into the trap of a physically satisfying Good Show, all those rhythmic bodies surrounded by sound and light that keep masking Wellman's marvelously rapturous words. Wellman isn't trying to be subtle, but he *is* trying to be clear. In his only scene with a genuine Pop figure, the words need to be heard, especially the repeated use of "my way," which immediately casts the image back to Sinatra, our true psychic president. Ferencz goes for the entertainment—loud, text smudged, as hypnotic to watch and just as unrevealing as a Sinatra (or anybody else's) close-up.

In his *PAJ* essay, Wellman suffers a lot about naturalistic theater and the insidious ways in which method acting has led us into a world of unreal, "rounded" characters, always explicable, sympathetic, and reductive. For him, rightly, the great characters—Hamlet, Lear, Woyzeck—couldn't fit neatly and completely into modern American drama. Santouche may not be Woyzeck, or even Little Caesar, but he wants to be liberated in production into the fullness of the social disaster surrounding him. It doesn't matter that it may also be within him. For Wellman, what counts is the familiar landscape, the revelation that entertainment, and the news as entertainment, keep standing in the way of what has always been there to see. And to see what theater is all about.

Ferencz and his company are alive, energetic, and always inviting to the senses. Yet they might just as well be doing Sam Shepard or Len Jenkin or even a Lee Breuer animation. Wellman deserves his own individuality: in a better (production) world, he wouldn't have to wait five years, as he did here, for his play to be produced. (Hence the ironic, faded linkage, through Guyanousa, to the mass suicide in Guyana.) Nor would he have to be merged with anybody but his own distinguished self.

(December 1985)

Coup de Lace

Getting away with murder is what all good comedies try to do. *Arsenic and Old Lace*'s enduring charm is that it doesn't pretend to be doing anything else. Compared to the carnage seen on an average evening of flipped channels, *Arsenic*'s two dozen corpses, three attempted murders, and imminent homicide at the curtain represent a triumph of discretion, modesty, and healthy humor. What's more, the murders are offstage. *Arsenic* floats on subliminal clouds in which the horrors of the real world are always being mocked by the simpler lunacies of an imaginative realm.

That realm doesn't fuss about Great Themes, but it does recognize a chastening logic all its own. Reduced to a philosophy, this logic would be terrifyingly dangerous; presented nakedly as a contrast between good and bad killers, it stands as a challenge to conventional pieties. The Brewster sisters poison lonely old men in order to release them from perceived misery, but their horror-movie nephew, Jonathan, transformed by plastic surgery into the image of Boris Karloff, kills for the love of it.

In every respect but their dotty hobby, the aunts are community paragons. Of course they poison people, but they wouldn't "stoop to a fib." Like all good citizens, they respect religion, distrust foreigners, and hate "scary pictures." Jonathan's motiveless malignity is unbearable to them. By the end, however, he is the fool who discovers that their quiet, homebody methods were far more efficient and far less strenuous than his worldwide rampage. Jonathan's punishable crime may be murder, but his aesthetic crime is the fear he inspires. His aunts' crime may also be murder, but they are beyond earthly punishment because of their evident harmlessness. Their victims would surely not agree, but they could scarcely deny that what really killed them was trust in appearances.

So much for community standards. Joseph Kesselring's peculiar achievement, helped apparently by the play-doctoring of his original producers, Howard Lindsay and Russel Crouse, is that doubts and equivocations never invade his airtight storytelling. *Arsenic* is a leisurely farce, refusing to be pushed too quickly into inconvenient corners. Much of the comedy springs from situation rather than wisecracks. Even better, the funniest moments are visual—the last-minute rescue of a potential victim; the stage lit only by matches as bodies are moved from one hiding place to another; the unpredictable, insouciant escape of Dr. Einstein, Jonathan's creepy accomplice.

When the wisecracks come, they are almost always about drama critics and the law, a perfectly witty, natural combination. Evidently, Lindsay and Crouse were responsible for these broader satirical thrusts. Mortimer, the aunts' good-guy nephew, is a newspaper reviewer who used to write about real estate, which—as Aunt Abby says—"he knew something about." Finding this vein irresistible, Lindsay and Crouse mine it for all its suggestive possibilities, even letting Mortimer provide his own criticism of the play he's in—a dazzling, presumptuous observation that the Brewster household is Strindberg crossed with *Hellzapoppin'*. Mortimer may be as unconscious and unobservant as most drama critics, but it's marvelous that he's caught in humor so willing to stand outside itself. One of the visiting cops turns out to be a secret playwright, relentlessly neglecting his duty while trapping the hapless Mortimer into listening to his endless plot. The Kesselring-Lindsay-Crouse team knew that even death might be better than a rotten play.

They also knew how to write playable roles. In Brian Murray's graceful, confident production, most of the characters come alive with all the fullness and self-contained logic of the play itself. The original Abby and Jonathan were played by Josephine Hull and Boris Karloff: with her quizzically crossed eyes and miniature dumpiness, Hull looked like an innocent fugitive from a Charles Addams cartoon; Karloff, of course, was Karloff, adding still another dimension to *Arsenic's* flirtation with Pirandellian send-up. While Jean Stapleton and Abe Vigoda are inevitably part of a less eccentric tradition, they bring honest, endearing humors of their own. Stapleton's Abby seems to know everything and nothing, all birdsong and homemade jam happily living in a time-warped fairy tale. Vigoda looks like Karloff, but doesn't aim for Karloff's quiescent, slurred menace. Instead, he glowers and lurches like a bratty kid too big for his clothes.

Mortimer was a role that came close to defeating the brassy charms of Cary Grant in Frank Capra's frantically sentimental movie version, and Tony Roberts doesn't do any better. It isn't easy to build a stage life on a prolonged series of gargantuan triple takes, but Roberts's frenzied shouts can't be the best route. That it is possible to exaggerate without limit while constantly coming up with surprise is proved by William Hickey's wonderfully smarmy Einstein. Borrowing shamelessly from the stretched vowels and monstrous frailty of his *Prizzi's Honor* role, Hickey is a sonic and visual knockout. His reluctant enslavement to Jonathan is as palpable as his mini-tantrums when arms and legs look like they might swing out of their sockets, breaking lamps and windows. His last exit is breathtaking—a dip and turn that would do honor to Makarova.

Murray's direction is particularly good at releasing those mercurial, vivid moments. When Polly Holliday's Aunt Martha heads for the dry sink to get poisoned elderberry wine for their latest victim, she can't resist a lovely hopping skip. Marjorie Bradley Kellogg's traditional set has especially keen details—colored, diamond windowpanes, a splendidly high-beamed ceiling, all those doors and levels that suggest a zany, never-never-land spooked house, a Brooklyn that never was; as one character puts it, "the virtues of another day all in this house."

Which is why the play retains so much acceptable simplicity while effortlessly going about its topsy-turvy business. Neither great nor gag-ridden, *Arsenic* emerges faithfully from its own dark time (1941) like a sentinel reminder that good plays are never as violent or immoral as our lives.

(July 1986)

Not Fear Itself

Franz Xaver Kroetz is merciless about most people's little acceptances. Taking jobs or joblessness as natural conditions, Kroetz's characters inhabit a landscape in which each sees the other as an ectoplasmic bundle of displaced energy and numbed accommodation. The joke—and the mercilessness—is that none of them see themselves. Living on the edge, yet rarely tipping over, they are finally protected by their own hysterical gestures or accidental insights. Kroetz knows what his characters acknowledge only in passing: that while action and talk can mean momentary rescue, resolution is a lie.

The Kroetz landscape, therefore, comes into focus only though accumulation. *Help Wanted,* as presented by Mabou Mines, is a resetting in America of six brief plays, roughly ten minutes each, in which a man and a woman (not necessarily married or even familiar with one another) are seen in the ongoing middle of their histories. In *Steps,* an unemployed husband, greeting the day with a cry of "good morning, misery...shit and despair," eats a breakfast served by his giddily complacent wife, who can't understand why he can "only see the bad things." *Conversation* offers two people on a park bench, the man claiming to be a cop protecting a boy whose grandfather was killed by terrorists, the woman a silent, apprehensive mother understandably moving from doubt to terror. *Poor Poet* presents a writer in bed with a woman, simultaneously helping her with a crossword puzzle, flipping T.V. channels, and telling someone on the phone that he refuses to sign a petition or demonstrate. In *Homecoming,* a husband gorges himself on fried chicken while his wife stares disbelievingly into space: he is arguing deliriously that her loss of work is just as well because, home alone all day, she can appreciate his company all the more at night. *Last Judgement* shows a raggedly dressed old couple, evidently just good friends, busily mixing brown paint, which they plan to splatter over newsstand copies of the *New York Times,* each trying to convince the other that they're not alone in "the idea of resistance." And finally, *Time Out* catches a couple at the highest pitch of misery and despair, punching the air rather than each other, frantically mourning an abundance that has failed to release them from terror on earth and in their dreams.

JoAnne Akalaitis's version of these plays has to be the best late-night cabaret entertainment in town (performances begin at 10:30 P.M.), even if that is not precisely Kroetz's intention. Akalaitis is superb at mapping the territory that captures her cool, dispassionate imagination. Diamond-hard, her production keeps releasing those fleeting moments when bland, matter-of-fact activities suddenly assume heroically ironic proportions. All rhythm without the blues, seeing the world in exquisite flashes, Akalaitis dashes through these plays without looking behind, leaving the actors and the rest of us to pick up and discard the pieces. She is a strict constructionist of elegant machinery, ideal for Kroetz's icy, distancing images but less adaptive to his darker consciousness. In the original text of *Poor Poet,* for example, the couple is not playfully in bed and the woman is not doing a puzzle; rather she is listening attentively to the man's political arguments. Amusing to watch while remaining humorless, Akalaitis's accumulations are in love with theatrical immediacy, but they are finally too far removed from Kroetz's immediate realities.

One reality, in fact, is that Kroetz wrote not six but fifteen short plays under the title *Fear and Hope in the Federal Republic of Germany* (the echo of Brecht unashamed and deliberate). Evidently, the accumulated effect of the original three-hour German production in 1983 was of a very specific Germany in which the big, corrosive theme of the day was unemployment. The war as experienced by Germans, and their Nazi past, continued to haunt Kroetz's original characters, even those born after 1945 — not a vision that can be shifted accurately and comfortably to Akalaitis's bland, featureless America.

All unhappy societies are not alike. But even if they were, and even if translation from local vernacular is always elusive, one important dividend of translating contemporary drama (done so fluidly here by Gitta Honegger) is that one's own local world can be seen in such vivid relief— but only when the playwright's own world is respected. On their own, these swift reductions are smart and welcome, but what they might accomplish can't be done in an hour. At best, *Help Wanted* feels like a rehearsal for *Fear and Hope*.

Akalaitis is directing disappearing acts rather than illuminations. Her actors have oddly arresting moments—Ellen McElduff's dizzy stares into middle distance, Ruth Maleczech's perpetual motion as she pours her paints—but most have just as many moments of fuss and muddle, sometimes falling into stridency, where Kroetz is probably more contained or plainly factual. Coloratura interludes dividing each play seem decorative, loud, and arbitrary. Driven by demons that have little to do with Kroetz, Akalaitis shows here the courage of small convictions. Why Kroetz, anyway, if she isn't willing to see him whole, German, and unevasively political? Sometimes, sadly, less is truly less.

(February 1986)

What is so splendid about Ruth Maleczech's performance as Annette in Franz Xaver Kroetz's *Through the Leaves* is its bounce, the extravagant pleasure she takes in rising above circumstances that could so easily batter both actor and character into withdrawn silence. Not that Kroetz's chatter, more like postsynchronized dubbing than dialogue, would allow Maleczech to digress into despair: for him, language is what is used instead of communication, conversation viewed without mask or evasion.

Annette keeps a diary that punctuates her scenes as working butcher and late-life lover of Victor (Frederick Neumann), and in it she even voices the punctuation itself—"parenthesis...dot dot dot...exclamation point...period"—but she can disclose only what her buried consciousness allows her to say. She boasts about her imagination and even recognizes that Victor is dumb, but nothing she can dredge from experience gives her the assurance of an active intelligence. She enjoys her work more than the brutal, perfunctory sex she shares with Victor, but she still goes for the sex. Always fussing, she doesn't think: for her, busyness—and business—are next to sexiness.

Maleczech is uncanny in isolating her performing intelligence from Annette's seducing drone. When Peter Stein directed the German premiere of Edward Bond's *Saved* in 1967—an acknowledged influence on Kroetz, Rainer Maria Fassbinder, and other German playwrights—he wanted "to create an equivocal impression in the spectator which would not always allow him to distinguish between the personality of the actor and his artistry," precisely what happens when Maleczech pops her eyes into question marks while suddenly slipping into a joyous riff of her hips. She's Winnie in Beckett's *Happy Days* momentarily liberated from her mound, unaware that butchering and Victor are even more paralyzing than primordial ooze. On she goes, the giddy actor neither commenting nor behaving, simply being carried away by performing instinct into a world that Annette will never know. It's a marvelous double image—actor not only ignoring character but also making a joke of drama's rule-book solutions. Against Maleczech's freedoms, fate doesn't stand a chance.

This may have little or nothing to do with Kroetz's programmed intentions, which after recent events look more and more like received Marxist intuitions draped over rational nausea. What can be worse than being alive in such disgusting times except not being alive? Kroetz's pitiless observation of Annette and Victor's stupid exchanges never begs for analysis any more than it seeks sentiment. Drama is the patient etherized on the table, Dr. Kroetz not particularly caring whether he or she lives or dies.

That it lives here is not only Maleczech's achievement but also Neumann's, who looks like an animated version of the beef slabs and innards sliced and pounded by Annette's sharp knives. He's as blunt, gross, and uninflected as the pigs' heads in Annette's display case, so it's not a surprise when she says her "Victor is really a pig sometimes." Roger Downey's cunning translation is unabashed by such echoes; he's quick to jump on just the word in English that can stab a heart with irony: Annette says, "You've got to hold on to the good things you come up *against* [my italics] in life, then you've got something to look back on." Writer and translator may be above or beyond their characters, but if they're cruel, it's only to be kind.

And accurate. Which is too often more than JoAnne Akalaitis wishes to be. For all her trust in actors and her dazzling command of imagery and rhythm, she continues to place equal faith in textual shifts and weird, displacing smears that keep getting in the way of Kroetz's severe, undecorated, presentational simplicity. As in *Request Concert* in 1981, she moves the action from Bavaria to America, this time to a Queens that is supposed to harbor specialty butcher shops where meat is cut and sold for domestic pets. This leads not so logically to the trivial revision of Kroetz's Martha and Otto into Annette and Victor, as if Germany and partly German names were so exotic we'd all miss the political and dramatic points. When Victor asks Annette for "a hum job" (Downey's inspired euphemism for a blow job), she claims she's never done it, but Akalaitis has already directed her to try one earlier, making both of them look dumber than they really are. Then, too, there are the interpolated songs between scenes, none more needless and sententious than the one declaring, "This is not a love song."

Perhaps Akalaitis's is an exhausted nod in the direction of postmodern vocabulary, behind it the premise that we're awakened by the abrasive mix of the literal and the abstract. So be it, then, especially because Akalaitis can't disguise her fundamental mastery of theater as an actor's event in which clarity is finally what is seen rather than embellished.

(October 1989)

Les Liaisons Abstruse

Heiner Müller may not be everybody's idea of a humorist, but for Robert Wilson, Müller's *Quartet* "is funny because it's about role playing." Unlike his source, Choderlos de Laclos's *Les Liaisons dangereuses,* Müller's version places the marquise de Merteuil and Valmont—those horrific ritual seducers—into one masquerade after another. Wilson calls their antics "parlor games," a clue to his continuing hesitancy to judge or interpret. He is hard on French directors who have made *Quartet* "too romantic," and he's equally dismissive of German directors who "make it too tragic." Like Müller himself, who finds all his plays "relatively funny," Wilson's take on this text, while characteristically detached, is relatively light, swift (only two hours), and eager to be fun.

Which is not the same thing as being funny. Müller doesn't make obvious gestures to humor or, for that matter, to anything like narrative coherence. His text is a series of monologues separated by fleeting exchanges: Valmont and Merteuil speak an incandescent rhetoric more to empty space than to each other. Actors in their own self-perpetuating drama, they shift almost invisibly from one tense to another, treating time as infinitely malleable. Their seductions never take place before our eyes. This deliberate deprivation is Müller's way of exploding theatrical expectations; he's relinquishing the usual playwright's prescience, relying instead on the sheer intensity of his words.

And so there it stands—a text that can be humorous or sensual only by insinuation, a page full of signs, yet nonetheless a blank expanse waiting for response. Wilson's response to Müller's *Hamletmachine,* a more blasted artifact than *Quartet,* was to fix contrapuntal images over the words, so that what was spoken had nothing directly to do with what was seen. This time around, however, the basic Wilsonian scenario—Merteuil in a chaise on one side of a scrim that diagonally bisects the stage, with Valmont more often than not on the other side—threatens to approximate the context and direction of the words.

Not that Wilson is ever more than glancingly literal. Establishing his presentational credentials with a fifteen-minute prologue in which Merteuil and Valmont are joined by three added characters—an Old Man, a Young Woman, and a Young Man—Wilson sets up an essentially silent series of painstaking, slow encounters over a table backed by a gigantic, florid, act curtain based on Albani's *Diana and Acteon.* The painting is the opposite of a Wilson frieze: his groupings are usually angular, tensile, almost stunned into sharp-edged silence; Albani's picture is of nine voluptuous nude women surprised into openly fearful retreat. The argument between painting and table is Wilson at his purest: two texts without words, each describing a different way of coping with sexual threat.

Merteuil—bare-shouldered, one arm gloved, wearing a purple top over a long black skirt—is caught in vivid light, moving in sudden starts and stops. The others enter, one by one, in equally distinctive getups— the Old Man formal with a monocle, the Young Woman in a green slip and high heels, the Young Man all in white with a double-breasted jacket draped over his bare chest, and Valmont in deep maroon and cadaverous face. For a moment, the prologue could be mistaken for a dance version of some Transylvanian fable, disrupted finally by the Old Man's sneeze, the Young Man's hand holding his crotch, as Merteuil moves to sit, Merteuil placing her arm over Valmont's hunched shoulder, his head weirdly out of sight as if he might suddenly be headless, and the Old Man's shooting of the Young Man just after the women pivot in their chairs. Whether by accident or design, the episode recalls Wilson's *I Was Sitting on My Patio . . .*, with its silvery, straight-backed chairs reflecting some kind of dispassionate observation that the formal dining table is a disguised bombsite where people ignore or destroy each other. As the Young Man crawls toward the wings with Merteuil sitting on his back and the Young Woman sputtering and laughing, the soundtrack offers a baroque harpsichord accompanied by shattering glass.

Müller's play begins when the Albani painting disappears. Not surprisingly, the gorgeous framing of the action—five luridly red side curtains, looking like entrances for *Sleeping Beauty*—calls attention to itself as insistent statement, possibly more important than the words. That this isn't quite the case is a tribute to Wilson's dependable pacing. As with *Hamletmachine,* the text can be experienced apart from the installation images. But it is text as dreamscape: the beautiful dumbshow goes on while the ear picks up Valmont's low animal growls or the proliferating visceral images that, in Carl Weber's pungent translation, sound like a view of life's tensions as so many body parts. Blood, orifices, umbilical cord, veins, the wicked body, the slimy bottom ("Of your soul!"), the tongue protruding—these are the coinage of Müller's vision, almost always sounded against Wilson's shining choreography.

The prologue's perfection sets a standard unmatched by the play itself, despite its isolated beauties. The words never exalt in the same kind of textured, measured distinction given to the movement, lighting, and set. Lucinda Childs's Merteuil is the perfect emblem for the production's divisions: sleek, emphatic, totally in command of wrist and elbow, she's strikingly deficient in vowels, consonants, and phrasing. Even Bill Moor—unlike Childs, an actor first rather than a dancer—seems confused by the perceived need to speak quickly while moving slowly.

The most effective performances are by Jeremy Geidt as the Old Man, Jennifer Rohn as the Young Girl, and Scott Rabinowitz as the Young

Man—who all belong more to Wilson's drama than to Müller's. Their precision, concentration, and expansive sense of freedom within Wilson's dancerly restraints are quite dazzling, and—yes—fun to watch. That none of this finally feels like comedy or even like a wholly realized theatrical experience matters less than the suggestions throughout that Wilson's recent drift toward text may yet flower in extraordinary visions we can scarcely imagine—Racine or Corneille, for example, finally released into an English that, like Wilson, aspires to the condition of music.

(March 1988)

Comedy of Mannerisms

When an actor enters with his hands tightly woven behind his lower back, you know that you're in for one of life's encounters with the Prince Philip School of Acting. That mysteriously prestigious genre, the comedy of manners, may not be responsible for all the crimes of the twentieth century, but surely it accounts for some of the coldness and indifference found every day wherever people congregate to make each other miserable. Plays like Somerset Maugham's *The Circle* (1923) and S. N. Behrman's *The Second Man* (1927) are frigid models of the not-so-comic way in which "civilized" people wreck each other's lives.

The genre is meant to be harmless, no more than a passing glimpse of those sympathetically unhappy people, the rich. Maugham's characters gather for a country-house weekend, familiar from plays if not from life, in which major changes will occur in relationships without any real acknowledgment that some of the people are getting hurt. Arnold Champion-Cheney's mother, Lady Kitty (Geraldine Page), who had run away thirty years before with Lord Porteous, returns for a visit just when Arnold's father, Clive, is also a guest. The first-act crisis is about how Arnold can maneuver his wife, Elizabeth, into keeping his parents apart. Arnold doesn't know yet that Elizabeth's romantic fascination with Lady Kitty's escape from marriage is a clue that Elizabeth wants to do the same with young Teddy Luton, whose lower back and hands, by the way, are noticeably different from Arnold's. The only surprising event would be a shock of recognition, some sense that there is more to living than idle chat and restless bodies.

Maugham seems more bored than his characters. Moving them on- and offstage must have been, for him, like moving elephants up moun- tains; sometimes the transparent effort is almost endearing: "There's only one course open to me now," says Lady Kitty when she realizes that her seduction of her former husband isn't working, and that is "to dress for dinner." Earlier, Maugham brings on a houseguest called Mrs. Shenstone, who, with good reason, doesn't seem to know why she is there; all she had to do was to read the program to discover that she's Lady Kitty's understudy. Hoping, perhaps, that we might not notice, the playwright simply keeps her offstage for the next two acts. Edmund Wilson nailed Maugham's "bogus motivation" years ago; his language, says Wilson, "is always banal," and does not even have "an interesting rhythm."

That cannot be said of S. N. Behrman, though he allowed himself to be trapped by the same unyielding manners. *The Second Man,* however, is deliberately self-conscious about the genre. Behrman's antihero is Clark Storey (Daniel Gerroll), a young writer who knows he'll never be mar- velous. Unlike Maugham, Behrman keeps to essentials: four characters shuttling in and out of Storey's West Side studio in three acts and eight- een hours, Storey wishing audaciously to marry the glamorously doting Mrs. Frayne for her money while a dizzily naive Monica wants to nab Storey instead of Austin Lowe, the brilliant, rich, and boring scientist helplessly in love with her. Behrman is always on the screaming edge of being real. Storey's attempts to get his money are constantly thwarted until the end by the others' refusal to perform his scenarios. Storey advises Austin to "cultivate superficiality" if he really wants the gift of Storey's gab, but Austin is agitatedly lost in Bertrand Russell's rarefied mathematics, where it is possible—in the best line of the play—"to escape from the dreary exile of the actual world."

If the best line comes from Russell, the twists and upsets come from Behrman pushing headlong into fulfilling the threats that Storey deserves. When Austin in his anguish proves to be a lousy shot, the moment is almost as farcically sensible as Uncle Vanya's failure to shoot the professor. That it doesn't reverberate with similar tremors is the fault of Behrman's refusal to murder the genre: he is more committed to neat conclusions than shattering realities. Luckily, he can't quite hide behind Storey all the time, so that when Storey declares that he had to give up "real emotion and real feelings" because "that's civilization," it's possible to hear the writer's shame.

Comedies of manners are not quick to recognize shame or any other emotions. How difficult, therefore, must they be for actors unwilling to surrender to what one acting manual describes as the "studied nonchalance" required for the genre. With Wilde or Coward, verbal dexterity fills in the empty spaces, and actors can enjoy the relaxed pleasures of acting from the neck up. Verbally, Maugham *is* the elephant, assigning words like "ripping" to Teddy, or cruelly finishing off Lady Kitty and Lord Porteous by having him condemn them as "trivial people."

Trivial they may be, but don't try to persuade Geraldine Page that she's anything but a passionately confounded woman continually alive to the next hilarious possibility. If the text offers only bumbling foolishness, Page offers an alert, eccentric woman constantly in the ecstasy of thought. Her hand might wander to her ex-husband's knee, or she can be caught weighing with her hands the tall tales she is about to spin, or finally she might grab a cookie to staunch her frustration at the news that Clive loves "old wine, old books, and young women." In an instant, the cookie becomes Clive's tongue, Page biting into it with a charged gusto that otherwise eludes her somnolent playwright.

Daniel Gerroll is almost too incisive for Behrman's Storey. In a role once played by Alfred Lunt in New York and Noel Coward in London, Gerroll seems to be caught in a less nonchalant world: his words may be flippant, but his collar has to be sticky and gray. It's an honestly frantic performance submerged by a play pulling away from its own honest hysteria. Ivar Brogger's Austin, all teeth, hollowed chest, and splayed legs, is a miraculously compelling bore, so wet, earnest, and wounded that he keeps suggesting the play Behrman didn't write. If the comedy of manners would only blow its cool more often, it might be able to contain these actors' wit, strength, and unmannerly inventiveness. As it is, Maugham and Behrman—Maugham especially—reveal that the most "trivial people" on those stages are the detached, trivializing writers.

(March 1986)

Posing for Playboy

When the "glory be to God" hypocrites rioted over Synge's *The Playboy of the Western World* in 1907, they were said to be ranting about a supposed insult to women in Synge's use of the word "shift." Yet surely some darker insight was at work, some intuitive shock that Synge was not one of them. Without judgment or disdain, he was plainly showing men at their worst and women as their resourceful, sex-starved victims. That early audience couldn't be pacified by the play's poetry, those extravagant phrases uttered on one arched breath as if words and their sounds were more important than life itself. Yeats wrote of Synge's "great art" with its "coldness or its strangeness," deriving its authority from something that might seem "capricious...as though it had fed on locusts and wild honey." Synge's audience was just hiding under women's shifts. What really disturbed them, like all moralizing fakers, was that Synge—as Yeats added—"had no life outside his imagination."

Playboy tells of an autumn evening and day in which a small country parish makes a hero out of Christy Mahon, a self-confessed murderer of his father, terrified of hanging, in love with his image, irrepressibly charmed by the discovery that he's charming to others, particularly the unravished ladies. But it's about more than the town or Christy: Pegeen Mike is Synge's finest creation, a proud, overworked woman in charge of her drunken father's pub and the center of everybody else's life; Synge catches her in flight between a fixed marriage and those breathless hours in which body and soul are being touched by desire for the first time. Amazingly, she misses her moment, preferring to share the violent righteousness of her community. What's worse for her, however, is that she knows she's missed it. There are few more wrenching moments in modern plays than *Playboy*'s last, when Pegeen admits her loss.

Synge's characters survive through their language, lifted only in part from what he heard on the Aran Islands: what worked for him was less his documentary ear than his instinct for intoxicating rhythm and the blunt utterances that, by now, the Irish borrow more from him than from themselves. "Is my visage astray?" asks Christy's brutal father while showing his wounds. Christy finds himself handsome in Pegeen's mirror, remarking that his father's "would twist a squint off an angel's brow," one of those casual asides that can't fail to Synge its way into memory. Over and over, he stuffs the characters with the lyricism of gods, making bleak events look like storms pierced by rainbows. The men in his play might be posing and strutting all the time, but Synge is telling what he wishes they could hear.

The danger in producing *Playboy* is that it will be nothing but sound swimming away from sense, the stark tale caught in an everlastingly picturesque undertow. The Druid Theatre of Galway is clearly trying to work against the tide. Pegeen is found onstage as the audience files in, brooding by the fireplace. When the lights rise, she begins her chores—cleaning food from dishes, washing her hands, disappearing beneath the bar to get an inkwell and paper, bringing the paper up as if she were balancing gold nuggets, and finally mumbling the words of the order she is writing to her father's distiller. With admirable reticence, the play's director, Garry Hynes, is not allowing the play to show anything but a subdued woman at work. As it turns out, unfortunately, this statement is the beginning and end of her capacity for reality and understatement.

As soon as Pegeen has to talk out loud, the play takes on rearrangements of reality. The set, for example, is loaded with props that look substantial and used but are part of a teal-blue backdrop encasing a cutout cottage that could just as easily serve Hänsel and Gretel's mother and father. Pegeen butters the edge of a loaf of bread for Christy, then slices it precariously against her breast, but once this fine, local detail is out of the way, the two of them talk at each other in that noisy, self-absorbed manner assumed by actors who know only how to act rather than behave. Hair strands fall artfully over every woman's brow.

Synge's masterful third act almost rescues the company from its travelogue routines, though it's difficult not to stray into thoughts that they're really rehearsing the Agnes de Mille production of the Rodgers and Hammerstein musical that—glory be to God—was never written. When Synge turns Pegeen and Christy momentarily into Jessica and Lorenzo, a pair of Shakespearean exiles caught in the intoxicating drift of moonlit prose, Hynes turns the lights down. Olwen Fouere and Maelosia Stafford are fearlessly exultant, bright stars in Synge's gorgeously satin sky, but they aren't helped by Hynes's transparent artifice. There they are—

Christy sensually bare to the waist, Pegeen just beginning to touch him and be held—yet never do they give themselves to tentative play, to the discovery of each other's curves and flesh. Yeats was struck by the "sting and tang" of Synge's reality. The Druid goes for pretty pictures and sometimes the wildness, but in the end, they've done nothing with the locusts or the honey.

(August 1986)

Samish

No point in waiting for the perfect *Godot*. If nothing else, Mike Nichols's new production passes the time, which—as Gogo says—"would have passed in any case." That one wants the play to pass into other realms, stopping time perhaps, is the unreasonable expectation set up by Beckett's severe perfection—his ingenious purloining of tradition for new purposes, his insistence on the stage as a pitiless, enclosed universe, his refusal to solve anything. Theater, however, rarely shows pity to playwrights: Beckett's theatrical universe today is as hard a nut for us to crack as *Lear* used to be until Jan Kott and Peter Brook gave it a Beckettian turn. No longer the obscure dramatist who puzzled his earliest incredulous critics, Beckett is by now the maker of an absolutely clear set of theatrical rules, a voice like no one else, the writer trapped like his characters in a demanding, overly familiar style that can't be escaped.

Better than any psychiatrist, he has told us what we're suffering and that the grave is the only way out. What's surprising, however, is that this play with no obvious closure now seems to be delivering a message almost as banal as the news in conventional plays that love conquers everything. Just as Didi and Gogo are stuck where they are, so too is the play locked in its own definitions. Beckett made the way for new possibility, but in so doing, he couldn't stop time from demanding something else.

The perfect *Godot,* if there is ever to be one, will have to come from a more Brookian director than Nichols. Brook's *Lear* deliberately denied the play's apparent romance. Goneril and Regan shed their Grimm visages in favor of more brutal, exhausted cruelties, the play itself catching up with the dispassionate dispersal of evil in this century. Similarly, the director of *Godot* for the next century will have to account for theater's need to be the most open form of all. It's not sufficient to cast the play, as Nichols has done, with the best clowns imaginable: before anything else, the director must release himself into a vision—and an energy—of its own.

Not a concept. What *Godot* needs now is another way of seeing. Nichols's visual gloss on the play is Georgia O'Keeffe's landscapes—pockmarked sand, bones, and, for updating, the hubcap, truck tire, and wheel rim that have been added to her desert by our death-defying technology. These elements are his tremulous additions to Beckett's simple indication of a country road and a tree. The tree is there, of course, but surrounded now by what also looks suspiciously like the great American Western-movie landscape. Nichols may be seeking myth more than vision, which might work if he could make anything more than the bloodless gestures attempted in this neutral production.

He starts well: Steve Martin's wry, offhand Didi, sniffing his armpits, picking at hairs in his stomach, and lighting a match to dispel the stench, is a mercilessly amusing portrait of unaccommodated man, never to be outdone by Robin Williams's equally raw assumption of Gogo's sweaty humanity. Their early encounters move swiftly from music-hall turns to the edge of embitterment. Having missed the spectacle of his own pissing, Martin's "Will night ever come?" emerges from a truly enraged heart. Williams's ecstatic consumption of the carrot he'll never forget, its green stalk waving hysterically before his face, is one of many moments he embodies with his flashing, staccato attack. For a time, it looks as if the two comedians won't let Beckett stand in the way of their limitless capacity for breathless, comic survival.

Nichols binds them, however, to a show-biz vocabulary that neither sends them into their own delirious stratospheres nor illuminates the experience of the play. Like Mozart approaching the cadenzas of his piano concertos, Williams could easily bolt off into his own riffs and curlicues, though his right to do so would surely remain open to question. Yet Williams contained is Williams outside of himself, the best of him not truly satisfied by dips into English and southern accents, or a wickedly apt imitation of John Wayne. Williams is instinctively no less musically alert than Beckett; to make the best of him, nothing can be sacred.

But this is a production frightened by Beckett and haunted by its own limited experience. These movie quotations are just about all Nichols can call upon. F. Murray Abraham offers a dashing, juicy Pozzo, filled with the miseries and glories of performance, but it takes only a moment in the first act to realize that he's allowing himself to be shadowed by William Hickey's hoarse godfather in *Prizzi's Honor*. Williams turns the beaked jawbone of an animal on Bill Irwin's starkly envisioned Lucky, bleached white hair encasing his parched personality, but in what seems like momentary desperation, the jawbone is made to serve as a movie clapper, with Williams adding a new line, "That's a take."

And so it goes. What matters, though, are not the passing reductions or even the speed with which Beckett's famous pauses and silences are traversed; Nichols is fielding a spirited cast, pound for pound more alert and intelligent than any seen before, yet he can't bring himself to embrace Beckett's ooze, that screaming quietude, that haunted rage. What's more peculiar is the lid he's placed on Williams's and Martin's humor, as if to prove how much funnier—and moving—they can be with less complex material.

Could it be otherwise in our theater, so much in a hurry to go nowhere? To be fair to Nichols, it may be that Beckett's notoriously tight-fisted control over productions of his plays has stifled him or that *Godot's* awesome, monochromatic presentation of one man's horrified glimpse into the abyss is no longer the only possible story. Something's radically wrong when Didi's and Gogo's adventures can pass by almost as if they never happened. In this version, at least, the play has pacified the terror.

(November 1988)

Feat first. Frederick Neumann unwavering gaping. What words for what then? What words so many learn so. Go on must go on. Act with words with nohow words somehow. The say? The said. Words alone on page there. Not meant for stage there somehow no how no way.

Dim light source known. Jennifer Tipton. Dim black sees the seen. Clear shade again. In the dim voiceful void. Light sees more than dim words. From good to better. Never better duet with light dim words.

Begin again. Ghostly light. Nothing seen sound echo. The voice.

Shovel flash in dim void. Lift and flash. Neumann voice from sunken head. Ask not where it can go. Neumann head hands in void. Shovel drop in dark deep never better. Sound on. All not still gone.

Not Ophelia's grave. Neumann not the digger. Bones and skull on steep rake nowhere but up. Dim light on head and hands. Black in back. Say on.

Say first the body. No. First the place. The place not Shakespeare's. No wit no way.

It stands. What? Small body back in dim ghastly light. No move. Words say picture tells. Know minimum. Know meremost minimum. No choice but see. Neumann up and stand. Bit by bit go on from there. That or groan. The groan so long on its way. No groan. Simply pain he say. No more but less.

A time when Beckett played with play. No more. Play with words. Dim words. A time when try see. Try say. Half light flow. No more say. Why play?

No future in this. Alas yes.

Bit by bit up and on. Thenceless there. Old man and child in dark light now. The child hand hold the old holding hand. Backs turned both bowed with equal plod they don't go.

Waiting for the game end. Slowly with rarely a pause plod on and rarely recede. Worst in—

Pause a thought? New thought remake the thought past thought. Plod on fast from pause. Make word move fast in faster thought. Sing phrase but pause. In the dim voice words move fast then slow. Bit by bit old man and child part from hold. Many others would do as ill.

Try again. Fail better. The unworsenable. New word arrives. Secrets. From bad to worsen. All at once in that word new thought. Beckett moveless. Moves. The better best is yet to come. Not to come. No knowing what it is secrets the words. Neumann knowing enough still to joy knowing Neumann. Not enough for others. So enough still.

Words for what then?

Blanks. Neumann plod on. Better some words than others. The ooze. Some words from soft of mind they ooze. The skull the bones and snare of words. True. True! And yet say first the better word lest last become the first to know. That said plod on. Blanks for nohow on. Time gone. Worse. Less.

Leastword on. Dim less dim. Light on black in back. Old man and child kneel. Old man and child fade. Fadeless more than kneel. Dimmed to dimmer still. Tipton best of best. Thought worse than most. To dimmost dim. Utmost dim. Leastmost in utmost dim. Dim go. Ooze on back not to unsay dim. So far dim still. Somehow worse. Dim dim. Dim some.

What words for what then? Deny. The stage deny some. Faintly preying. Heard as praying. Faintly longing still. Faintly vainly longing still. For faintest stage life. Still.

Back to worsenable void. Dim go. Light on point. Rise Tipton better best. Ooze back toward end in sight. Sightless end in backless void. One hour all there is. All enough. Gnawing. Gnawing to be gone. Gone for good would do as ill. All gnaw on.

Neumann say. Enough. Say enough. Flick, hand. Hand, flick. And glance. And without blood. Ooze there is when blood not whatsoever there. Act without words better still. But when? For what then?

Where on from here? Nowhere but down go. Beckett say last gasp then. Nothing but voice ooze and words snared. Stare at snare then. The whole narrow void. Two black holes gaping unwavering. Stare clamped to bore. All at once waiting game for end. Happy days not here again. Not I to love what stares at snare.

Begin again.

(September 1986)

All-Consuming and Condescending

"Trust me, trust me, Armand, trust me," says Marguerite in Pam Gems's extravagantly awful *Camille,* a revision of Alexandre Dumas fils's *La Dame aux camélias* evidently meant to rescue Marguerite from male romantic clutches. What fate could be worse, however, than Gems's miserable prose? It was easy to lose count of the "trust me"s during the play's waning moments; when Gems can find nothing to say, she says it again. Poor Marguerite, less in need of pseudofeminist twists than she is of a distinctive eloquence that might truly liberate her. Gems roughs up Dumas's story a bit, giving Marguerite a beloved little son and a timidly etched lesbian friendship, but in the end she's just a closet romantic in occasional naturalistic drag.

And what a drag. Nothing timid about Ron Daniels's Long Wharf production, with Ming Cho Lee's gorgeously parqueted floor leading spaciously to upstage corridors and alcoves separated by sliding paneled doors and windows; Jess Goldstein's swirling gowns, wedding-cake hats, and splendidly slimming jackets and trousers add to the production's camp pleasures—eighteen actors sweeping on and off as if in search of the nearest sound stage. Daniels offers the Technicolor denied to Garbo, properly interpreting Gems's stylistic ambivalence to mean that if Gems can't be clear about the real world, the unreal one might as well look luscious. Placing a huge Steinway before the panels while asking the pianist to underscore much of the storm and meringue with Liszt, Chopin, and Debussy is Daniels's way of rescuing Dumas from Gems.

What does Gems want, anyway? Like Dumas's Marguerite, hers is dying not from oppression but from consumption. Gems gets real stage blood from Marguerite's coughs, but that's the extent of her "realistic" revisionism. Claiming to write "from a sense of outrage," yet also admitting that she has "no plan...the activity is only semiconscious," Gems has consciously written about feuding women who are opportunistic, bitter, angry with one another, or just plain stupid. God save feminists from Gems's missionary semiconsciousness: when she isn't throwing women into catfights, she's condescending to them in one way or another.

The worst is dippy Clémence, the eternal dumb blonde, nabbing a Swedish count, the most available bore in town. They've "seen every country in Europe, except Japan." She saw Venice, yes, "but it was flooded." How did she find Italy? "It took a week or two," she replies, true only to Gems's meretricious hold on character knocking. Not much better is Marguerite's older, supposedly wiser friend Prudence, milliner to courtesans and arranger of alliances. Sasha von Scherler brings a diamond-hard sparkling dryness to the role but can't make a resonant sense out of lines like "There is nothing so vacated as a woman my age." Who could? Gems doesn't seem to know that there is nothing so vacated as a text without the right words at the right time. To Marguerite's lover, Armand, she is "lion, tiger, leopard," as if all big cats were the same: Gems is master of the blurred image.

With plenty to wear and little to say, Kathleen Turner's Marguerite strides through the actions with sturdy energy that almost builds a case for the modern character eluding Gems. In movies, Turner is warm bubble bath, crème brûlée, a Brahms intermezzo, an alert welcomer of a world that ought to have the good sense to embrace her as she is. The plot—in, say, *Prizzi's Honor*—may wipe her out, but she leaves behind the memory of survival power, as if nothing could kill a spirit so in love with wonder and adventure. More substantial, more soiled than Garbo, she nonetheless treats the camera in the same way—a friendly eavesdropper on her floating consciousness. Unlike Meryl Streep, that scholar of emotions, burrowing in the archives for card-indexed feeling, Turner lets anything happen. She's large, but never so proud that she can't be intimate.

Onstage, she is less secure. Not only because Gems hasn't made guiding decisions but also because of this production's need to pitch her out of the intimacy she embraces so casually onscreen. No reason why Daniels's direction couldn't be adapted instantly into a Peter Brookian *Traviata*. Without textual lyricism, however, all the effort shows. Too often, Turner strains her lungs just to be heard in an unaccommodating space; it's not so much that she shouts but that she can't spare more than a moment for quiet repose. The play is even more fragmented than the average screenplay, but here Turner never seems to trust in her power to make the fragments look like a whole. It's as if she has let the stage cut her down to ordinary size. Too busy projecting rather than being, she suddenly notices that a long reminiscence to Armand might also involve her discovery of his hair or brow. A natural feminist statement in movies, she's reduced onstage to directorial subservience.

Damn Gems with her spurious claims on a politics she only insinuates into her play's arrangements. Pandering to our need for romance, she unloads pounds of nostalgia for a world never known while denying her actors the words and actions that might jolt them into the true modernism they know how to do. "The writing," she says, "comes off the end of my pen." The blunt end, that is, the end that doesn't begin to address the magic of her protagonist or the agony in the romance.

(December 1986)

Bound and Gagged

Neil Simon isn't kidding: after the longest, most remunerative apprenticeship in playwriting history, he still wants to be a Jewish Chekhov or Tennessee Williams. *Broadway Bound* is the obligatory first play he never wrote, the one in which the dramatist celebrates his presumed talent by showing us his roots.

Driven, perhaps, by similar demons, Chekhov wisely avoided his own history, choosing in *The Seagull* to group family and friends as a metaphor for the distance between the will to create and the gift. Chekhov is hard on everybody: for him, nothing will rescue the mediocre from their pretenses and shabbiness.

Closer to home, Williams in *The Glass Menagerie* stands almost in the wings, giving center stage to his gorgon mother, a woman who finally looms as a writer-manqué—inventing and destroying imaginative lives as she goes along. Williams's genius at the time was that he knew how to let a character invade his play and make it her fictional own.

Simon, on the other hand, knows mainly how to invade his plots—and now his autobiography—with jokes. *Broadway Bound* moves on three generational tracks at once: Eugene and Stanley Jerome, two young writers who want to do radio comedy, are laboring in their Brighton Beach household against the ebb tide of their parents' marriage and the discouraging noises made by their cranky Trotskyite grandfather. Surrounded by so much lovelessness, the boys keep up what is probably meant to be a brave front of humor in adversity. More often, however, it's heartlessness in perversity. Simon's insistence that dread and misery always can be overcome by a confessional moment—Grandfather's "I am not an affectionate man"—or a self-deflating gag.

Sadly, Simon is not an affectionate joker. He may think he is, lathering the action with so many "I love you"s from one character to another, but most of his humor betrays a fundamental lack of interest in character. Just as he's setting up the boys' aunt Blanche as a generous, intelligent woman seeking reason and love from her father, he has her tell Eugene of a new grandson called Myron Isaac Eisenberg. Not because her marriages or daughters or grandchildren will figure in the plot but to prepare us for

Eugene's wise-guy observation that the poor kid will have a rough time trying "to date a girl from Mt. Holyoke."

Simon's jokes have a way of making his seriousness suspect: if the humor keeps spinning dizzily away from the truth, how can the depths be believed? With one exception, each character is no more than a characteristic. Grandfather, for example, can't remember anything, yet after Eugene tells a joke about two people kissing each other in the cold and sticking together, Grandpa later tells his daughter to ask Eugene to tell her "about the people who got stuck together." Is Simon saying that Grandpa always fakes, or is this just a convenient mistake on Simon's part? He doesn't let his characters escape into complexity: like Reagan's photo opportunities, his humor is meant to cover up what he doesn't want us to see.

Thanks to Linda Lavin and Gene Saks, however, we do see Kate, Eugene and Stanley's house-whipped mother. Simon's methods don't make it easy for a real character to emerge: Kate pads around the household and the play like a peripheral figure much of the time; too often, she is sidetracked, as if Simon really thinks that the brothers' writing blocks and lousy ambitions are as compelling as their mother's anguish. His near-refusal to show her whole—she says that she has friends, but they're never seen; her lunch date with Blanche can't take place in a play that is as homebound as she is—threatens to sink his jokes without a trace. Two scenes save the day: Kate confronts her husband in the first act with her fear of abandonment, and in the second, she retells the story of her teenage encounter at a dance hall with George Raft. Confrontation and monologue are masterfully written, entirely free of Simon's usual subversions. For once, the joke is that he doesn't tell jokes.

Lavin's performance is one of those textbook lessons in great acting that in Paul Muni's, Lee J. Cobb's, Alfred Lunt's, Laurette Taylor's, and Kim Stanley's days used to astound Broadway with pleasing and alarming regularity. Her mouth is in perpetual silent motion, lips and tongue constantly tasting or chewing unseen debris, as if she might stop breathing should she ever let her teeth alone. No object is free from her polishing hand or cloth; after talking to her mother on the phone, she drifts automatically into dusting the receiver. Gathering wool into a ball while listening to her sons' CBS broadcast, she moves silently from attentive pride into suspicious hurt, always on the precarious edge of exploding into her real life, yet always—always—restrained. In her reminiscence, she shifts with mercurial swiftness from herself when young to her friend Alice, bug-eyed with awe, to George Raft himself, the very image of elegant sin which she long ago gave up as a model for her own life. Then, within seconds, her body crushes itself into the awful present. Only by the end is it clear that Lavin has turned Simon's pencil sketch into an oil, providing Kate's missing history. With the power available only to an actor at the height of her own command of detail, she tells the story of a life otherwise barely told. Simon can't resist giving her a joke or two, but Lavin rescues Kate from her playwright.

Saks is equally good with the essential actions. Kate folds a tablecloth with methodical concentration while fighting for her life; Eugene folds his blanket the same way when momentarily discovering his own vulnerability. It's a pity, however, that the production is finally like the play itself, cosmetic to a fault—clean snow and empty Brighton streets, standing lifelessly there as emblems of the reality Simon doesn't wish to confront. "A hard life can knock the sentiment out of you," says Eugene of his mother at the end. For Simon, however, a soft mind can't keep the sloppiness at bay.

(December 1986)

A House Is Not a Poem

Heresy to say so, but Federico García Lorca's *The House of Bernarda Alba* is an opera without music and therefore not a good play. Drama, the cruelest art, was no kinder to Lorca than it was to other modern poets. Better ones—Yeats and Eliot—tried either divine afflatus or parched authority. Yet nothing worked: the dramatic center could not hold. Meanwhile, lesser poets such as Maxwell Anderson and Christopher Fry, huffing and puffing toward the condition of music, ran out of breath before even reaching the condition of drama—in which characters are in the grip of ideas and passions that defy resolution.

Lorca's brother Francisco argued forty-six years ago in his preface to the three tragedies *Blood Wedding, Yerma,* and *Bernarda Alba* that "standards of criticism applicable to a realistic and psychological drama" should not be applied "to a drama that is poetic in conception and symbolical in its essence." Yet just as goodwill and prestige can't fill an empty stomach, poetry and symbolism can't automatically satisfy our need to be engaged by dramatic necessity, or to stay awake. Francisco was troubled by Federico's "tendency of purging lyric elements from his drama." Evidently, he couldn't acknowledge his brother's plausible self-awareness. For Federico, "musical essences" were precisely the source of the plays' power; much as he admired the relative austerity of *Bernarda Alba,* he was attracted even more to the play's traditional—and Spanish—heaviness.

Sopranos can make a meal of doom, but actors need other voices, even other dooms. *Bernarda Alba* is relentlessly in the service of one force alone—the sixty-year-old mother (Bernarda) compelling her five daughters to live without sex. The only relief from Bernarda's awesomely monotonous pressure is Poncia, her maid and contemporary, trying against the odds to keep the house in tenderly felt order. Making two will-o'-the-wisp appearances is Maria Josefa, Bernarda's eighty-year-old mother, a crone Ophelia, exiled to her room and fantasies by Bernarda. Offstage and never seen is Pepe, the hot-blooded fiancé of Bernarda's oldest daughter, Angustias, and late-night wooer of her youngest, Adela.

In one corner, then, obstinate domestic fascism (Bernarda); in another, desperate frustration (Angustias); in a third, uncontrollable, wet sexuality (Adela); and in a fourth, an invisible macho brute who sounds like he's rehearsing a nightclub act in a flamenco bar. Throughout and at the end Bernarda shouts "Silence," thus signaling that this is a play about chattering women struck dumb (finally) by a vicious oppressor who is no more complicated than a hydrogen bomb. While sentiments are never in question—who can't be upset by Adela's totally predictable suicide?—nothing more is left to ponder than the monolithic intensity of coercive, unforgiving experience. Lorca is telling not only what is known, but what can be seen and felt the moment he sets his ever-so-Spanish epiphanies in motion.

Oh, that Spanish soul. Francisco Lorca sees it everywhere in his brother's work, and I'm certain he's right. But how can it possibly move into a language and realm where the soul could be scarcely more remote?

Nuria Espert's production in London, framed by Ezio Frigerio's majestic, white-walled courtyard with its splendid gray-blue slate floor—real!—is the best argument imaginable for the play. Joan Plowright's Poncia is one of those confident statements about character that elude most actors: overflowing with contained wisdom, she lives onstage as if—like the play —she's never left those walls. Talking with moderate cynicism about the impossible Bernarda, she spits suddenly on Bernarda's chair, only to turn back for a moment to wipe it off—everlastingly the peasant rebel with the bourgeois spine.

Plowright isn't alone—the daughters tear into their furious deprivations like a pride of hungry lions—but she isn't enough to rescue the play from its deprived music. Glenda Jackson's Bernarda is inexplicable—more rigid than the pope and not even relieved by fake charm, headmistress of a depraved St. Trinian's. If she's true to Lorca, so much the worse for the play and its inflated reputation. Spanish soul is no excuse for dramatic stasis. Lorca was not only murdered by Franco, he was crippled by his incapacity to free his drama from its primordial, outmoded, melodramatic instincts.

(February 1987)

All My Plots

All My Sons shouldn't work, not even for an instant: Arthur Miller crammed so many transparent story lines into the single 1946 day and night spent in Joe and Kate Keller's backyard that the play feels constantly as if it might drop dead from exhaustive coincidence. That it lives at all is a tribute to Miller's reliable advances into what Ibsen used to call "the great scene." Neither in plotting nor in scenemaking is Miller equal to Ibsen's best—he's too soppy and schematic for that—but despite the sweat, he finally finds those end-of-the-tether moments when characters are released from plots into experience.

Still, what a mess of old, sorry plots. Not content with bringing the whole weight of Joe's criminal past down on him in one day (he had knowingly sent defective cylinder heads to the army air corps, which were responsible for twenty-one deaths and the suicide of his eldest son, Larry), Miller adds interfering neighbors, a marriage proposal soon threatened by the play's circumstances, a symbolic fallen tree, a reference to a gun (they always go off, don't they?), and a strategically delivered letter read separately by three concerned characters. The play is like a festival of false starts, every one a story in itself, constantly diverting energy from the play proper, in which Joe merely has to be exposed as the all-American "innocent" liar he really is.

Miller offers leaks rather than facts, as if terrified to reach the end. Meanwhile, he fills in the blank spaces with genial chat and folksy goodwill. After an act of this, however, it's easy to recognize that each relaxed moment is just a setup for the next angry bash. Miller's technique is about lulls before storms: he's determined to turn a small idea into an opera.

The idea, fortunately, is good. With prophetic power, Miller unearthed the American nightmare—the continual urge in public discourse to lie, cheat, and forget, while forgiving the victimizer rather than the victim. Joe Keller is that common American leader and rare protagonist—a real shit. Toward the end, Miller flirts with the sentimental notion that Joe has learned something—they're all his sons, Joe says—but he doesn't linger on it, letting Joe go the way of Donald Manes, in this case with the obligatory gun. Maybe it would have been truer to let him fail his suicide like Robert McFarlane or get shipped into a hospital like William Casey. Characters in well-made plays never seem to learn the melodramatic lessons easily drawn from real life.

If there's any irony, it's that Joe's death is the only way to end all those shouting confrontations. Without it, we would still be there, patiently waiting for the characters onstage to learn what the audience already knows. Miller keeps arranging late climaxes: Kate reveals inadvertently that Joe let his partner take the rap; the partner is Ann's father (Ann had been in love with Larry and now wants to marry his surviving brother, Chris); Ann has held on to Larry's suicide letter just so that she can pull it out for a third-act confirmation and those three explosions; Kate is pulled from her protective fantasy that Larry is still alive; and Chris discovers that if Joe may be "no worse than most men," he isn't any better.

Tiring as all those manipulations may be, they give way finally to Miller's gift for sustained outburst. Father, of course, will have to face son: that we always knew. Less successful because it's more diversionary is one neighbor's attack on Ann. The arrival and accusation of Ann's brother, George, are too convenient by half: suddenly, on this day of all days, he has chosen to believe his own father's story after avoiding him for three years. By then, however, it's clear that Miller has been pacing himself for the big moments when Joe can't escape anymore and Kate has to give way to Ann and Chris.

In Arvin Brown's respectful, detailed production, those episodes rise naturally out of the crowded mass like Bruckner's horns bursting away from the orchestra's murk and delays. Hugh Landwehr's gray clapboard house doesn't look rich enough for the outside of an industrialist's home, but it fits neatly into the text's peculiar evasion of class issues. Another evasion: would people scream at each other so uninterruptedly in the backyard at two in the morning? Miller's rhetoric lacks color and heft, but its crescendos give actors an opportunity to let their bodies swing into signals and actions before their mouths find the words. Jamey Sheridan's Chris and Jayne Atkinson's Ann are particularly adept at releasing their energies in clear physical stops and starts. Joyce Ebert takes Kate into unashamed operatic realms—true to the script, she lets her husky booming alto tell part of her anxious story. And Richard Kiley leaves customary good-guy sweetness behind: his Joe is shifty, gritty, and totally revolting. Standing safely outside the fuss of Miller's playmaking, he's the plain image of what Miller does best when he's willing to do it—the honest presentation of a dishonest life.

(May 1987)

Serving Two Masters

Strange how two comic unearthings, so distant from each other—Luca Ronconi's painstaking four-hour traversal of Carlo Goldoni's *La serva amorosa* (The loving servant-girl) and Jerry Zaks's butterfly remaking of Cole Porter's *Anything Goes*—should choose to emerge in their first moments from twilit darkness and tentative hush. Ronconi begins almost as if unlocking a vault: his diaphanous act-curtain has barely swept mysteriously across the proscenium when a voice is heard from one of two figures in silhouette, "In this room we can speak privately." Here, surprisingly, is anything but formula commedia dell'arte; in an instant, Ronconi has banished the clowns.

Zaks, playing a different game, starts with an old Victrola recording of Porter singing, "In olden days a glimpse of stocking was looked on as something shocking," the scratching sound soon overwhelmed by the band, on an upper level, hidden behind one of those luxury drop curtains that instantly hollers show biz. This is at once homage and aggression. Fifty years ago is just as far away for Zaks as two hundred is for Ronconi, but the American pulls himself quickly from tintype into polished brash where the Italian pushes deeper into darkness and the previously unknown.

Not that it should be otherwise. For Porter, God knows, anything goes but nostalgia. Surely the toughest of our lyrical wits, he wouldn't take kindly to hero-worshiping pretense, to any notion that behind formula lurks a glamorous hidden agenda. Give him, as Zaks does, a shiny uncomplicated setting for the clown jewels he sprinkles all over the place —those jack-in-the-box inner rhymes springing from cushioned tunes— and that's all he needs. *Anything Goes* in its Lincoln Center incarnation is proof enough that Porter's ease is a hard act for book-writers to follow: Porter did the double-whammy act of music and lyrics alone, but here it takes six writers (Guy Bolton, P. G. Wodehouse, Howard Lindsay, and Russel Crouse for the original book and Crouse's son Timothy with John Weidman for today's revisions) to fill in the spaces before welcome song cues. For some reason American musical comedy buffs care as much about the book as the songs. Why not admit that in Porter's work the book scarcely matters? I fly so high with a guy like Porter because it's my idea of something to do.

That the book musical used to have so much more trouble with the book than the music is puzzling when you consider—as in Goldoni's 116 comedies—how much hangs on situations and characters that are already known. Basic elements are remarkably consistent: thwarted love, generational conflict, class differences, the need to scheme, and the pressure to survive. Perhaps part of the problem lies in the American refusal to move money into the more serious corners of the plot. Goldoni, on the other hand, is never far from the bitter truths that drive families apart and servants into breathless manipulations. His poor, his young, and especially his women are smarter than the rich, the old, and the men. Porter's writers, however, need only supply uncritical diversions and jokes sour enough to make Porter's more supple inventions show up more clearly as the graceful punctuations they already are. Playing phrases like "Indoor China" against "Outdoor China" is the perfect way of throwing into relief Porter's incomparable "tinpantithesis of melody."

Wanting only to be giddy, America's formula comedies may never need a Ronconi to pump them into a new generational life. It's probable too that Goldoni wouldn't recognize himself in Ronconi's shadowed mirror. Even so, this *Serva amorosa* (not to be found yet in English translation!) is a remarkable resurrection. The elements may read business-as-usual—Corallina, old Ottavio's servant, must maneuver between Ottavio's new young wife anxious to cheat Ottavio's son of his inheritance and old Pantalone's daughter not so anxious to marry the son unless he's rich—but Ronconi infuses them with a deliberately lugubrious, unrelieved passion. Think of Mozart's *Figaro* caught in Wotan's supremely troubled undertow. A matter of tempo, perhaps, but also a question of every other detail—the persistently amber lighting hovering over a stage littered with armoires, beds, tables, the odd chair or two, and giant mirrors, all of them shifting from one scene to another, sometimes bisected by a Brechtian white curtain or, in one scene, joined by three Beckettian trash bins. Call it perverse if you like, and you'd be right, especially since there's scarcely a risible moment all evening. Yet the story keeps submitting to its own reversals, like a glossy photo returned to its negative.

And what acting—deep, quiet, unafraid of filling the lofty theatrical space with the power of exhausted pause, frantic yet rarely hysterical, possessed always by thought, disturbance, tremors of doubt. Ronconi gives the actors freedom, or instructs them, to inhabit the stage as they might their homes, backing into a room rather than assaulting everything frontally, or disappearing behind a curtain or offstage for a moment while the scene continues, gazing intently not on a partner but in one of the mirrors. Self-absorbed, they are nonetheless performing all the time and always for each other, devoid of psychology but endlessly behavioral. Furniture represents obstacle more than decoration. By the time Annamaria Guarnieri's harsh, angular, hunched-over Corallina declares that "love is a passion, but hunger is a stronger passion," the play's buried veracity has been completely validated: gestures have been established as the play's meaning; these are actors shielded by scrim and candlelight (Franco Quadri, Ronconi's Boswell, calls this production Ronconi's *Barry Lyndon*), yet unprotected by the usual trappings of illusion. Reluctantly, they offer text as naked, inexorable structure.

We're a long way, then, not only from Italian formula but from American comedy. How current Goldoni feels, how charmingly antique the Porter. *Anything Goes* was new in 1934, five years after the Crash, and ought now to have a subliminal connection to us, only days after our latest drubbing. Jokes about the stock market notwithstanding—rich man to money-grubbing widow, "If it's any consolation, I was just coming out of the stock exchange when he [her husband] took off from that ledge: he jumped like a Yale man"—the production understandably wants only to be delightful and de-lovely. With songs neatly lifted from other Porter shows, and one song new to me—"Buddy, Beware"—deliciously sung by Linda Hart with the clear diction and spontaneous presence missing from Patti LuPone's energetically hostile star turn, the revival efficiently dodges comparisons with the past—Ethel Merman, Victor Moore, Ginger Rogers—while confirming once again that Porter's the top.

But there's something bottomless about the American theater's need to pacify and please. New York's "official" theater celebrates retreat and escape; the region of Umbria and the hill town of Gubbio, where Ronconi's production originated, subsidized archaeological research and a glorious, too often ignored, page of dramatic literature. Asked by the Lincoln Center management not to review my first visit to *Anything Goes* because LuPone had been replaced by her understudy, I returned to see what I had been assured I missed. No question that LuPone knows her formulas better than the half-prepared substitute, who was forced to play Reno Sweeney without LuPone's costumes, but on balance do they want me to come out humming those costumes rather than those stretched, contoured tunes? Much as I enjoyed repeating the Porter concert, I get my kick from Goldoni's vintage champagne.

(November 1987)

Half-Caste

Poor Phaedra, usually played by stunning gorgons draped decorously in tunics and operatic passions. Hard to imagine a scholar like Jan Kott writing *Racine Our Contemporary;* even for the French, the idiom remains distant and lofty, treasurable for its resistance to our compulsions, its steady gaze backward to ancient models. Neglected by her warrior husband, Theseus, Phaedra has all the time she needs to fall silently for Hippolytus, her stepson; when she thinks Theseus dead, she reveals all, first to Oenone, her nurse, and finally to Hippolytus. Not dead yet, Theseus returns, only to banish Hippolytus when Oenone denounces him as the sexual aggressor bringing shame to the royal house. With Hippolytus gone, his drowning reported by his faithful servant, Phaedra poisons herself just before admitting her guilt to Theseus.

At the Comédie-Française in the 1950s, the audience used to fuss restlessly between Marie Bell's arias, evidently preferring her breath control to the play. Not that they were wrong: grasping the curtain with an upraised arm, she would start slowly, letting Racine's rhythm steal across her immobility until body and soul were joined in an ecstatic dream. This was never acting as we usually know it. Bell's realism was in the back of her eyes, the gleam in her throat, crescendo and climax the sum total of an art always closer to music than drama.

It's daring, then, for Tony Harrison to confront this tradition not with a direct translation but with a verse drama borrowing Racine's contours, charting essentially the same story reset in the British Raj several years before the Indian Mutiny of the 1850s. Phaedra is Memsahib, the governor's wife, hopelessly in love with Thomas, her stepson. Inevitably, Harrison's thematic variations lead to undertows of race and imperialism: Thomas/Hippolytus was born out of Governor/Theseus's philandering with an Indian, and Thomas himself is now in love with Lilamani, the surviving daughter of a noble Indian family murdered by the governor. I suspect, however, that Harrison is less engaged by the politics than by the opportunity to release Phaedra from classical restraint. Her arias are still there but no longer freighted with ancestral resonance. Harrison is good at conjuring India's relentless sun and isolation as demonic forces driving Memsahib to her disaster, but he can't move events far enough from prim, domestic roots: this is less *Phaedra Britannica* than *Phaedra, White Lady from Kensington*.

Not that Carey Perloff's carefully wrought production encourages any drop in cosmic temperature. With the help of Donald Eastman's imposing design—three grand, white-pillared arches looking out on slatted shades against the sun, topped by a red strip with grating over every arch—Perloff makes the tiny Classic Stage Company stage seem like a temple built by the gods. When Thomas's tutor Burleigh tells the story of Thomas's hideous death, a lamp placed on a bench casts his looming shadow against the pillars. The arias, too, are frank about their intentions: underneath them are Elizabeth Swados's impressionistic sounds—a timpani beat behind the Governor's bewilderment, a cello making an extended sound on a single string, a flute accompanying Memsahib's early confession to Ayah, her servant. Stateliness, for Perloff, is next to godliness, and she finds vibrant, questioning life in both.

Seen at an early preview, many in her cast were only beginning to find similar command. The oddest contrast may be Caroline Lagerfelt's Memsahib with Bob Gunton's Governor: where Lagerfelt's lamentations seem to be reaching for unaccustomed size, Gunton's exhausted fury is always titanic, an embodiment that easily signals his readiness to take on the real Racine, Euripides, or Seneca. His entrance in the second act comes as a great wash of authentic splendor after the miniseries tactics of the first. Rajika Puri's impeccably pointed, beautifully voiced Ayah matches him in presence and thought, but it's the wrong match. Lagerfelt keeps leaning forward from her waist, as if her dress or the task is pulling her down. She's best when lashing out at Ayah with sudden flashes of pitiless humor, seeing through herself better than anyone else. Yet even as she suffers, she looks and sounds like that competent governess in *The King and I,* not likely to make such a fool of herself over a mere boy.

Even so, *Phaedra Britannica* is more than just a worthy try. When Lagerfelt settles in, stands up straight, and stops acting so strenuously—when she allows Memsahib to breathe—she'll find a play and production that, for the most part, can support the austere yet lush Racinian design that survives so eloquently in Harrison's text. If I'm still not persuaded that Racine in English has to be Racine in England, I'm delighted with the risks taken. Harrison's rhyming couplets and steady beat work well as correlatives, even as they verge occasionally into nursery babble ("The little Princess is it? Lost your heart? / I'm going to find my father, and must start"). How often these days do we get a glimpse into the singular glories of the pure, spoken theatrical act, the insistent grandeur of the poet who loves the theater for what it is?

When Robert Lowell offered his verse translation in 1961, he was, if anything, more humble than Harrison, nevertheless finding cadences and inner heartbeats close to Racinian awe. "His poetry," said Lowell, "is great because of the justness of its rhythm and logic, and the glory of its hard, electric rage." With Gunton supplying the voltage, Perloff the heat, Harrison's solutions come close to the same justness sought and found by Lowell. Racine may never—mercifully—be our contemporary, but this production suggests, at last, that he's nearer than we thought.

(December 1988)

Still in the Woods

It's an ominous moment when a serious play begins with a joke. Certainly, Lee Blessing's *A Walk in the Woods* finds a surprising quantity of laughter in the sour subject of U.S.-Soviet arms negotiations. The long-winded opening joke, however, is a hint that, like diplomatic strategy, the humor is a ploy to seduce an audience not likely to find the issues gripping enough on their own. Who would have thought that the tedious manipulations of governments and the terrifying realities of nuclear bargaining could yield the most charming play of the season?

This isn't Graham Greene "entertainment," one of those cunning narratives thinly disguising its darker purposes under the cover of chase scenes or sexy diversions. Blessing is more austere: taking his cue from a walk in Geneva's woods by the U.S.'s Paul H. Nitze and the Russian's Yuli A. Kvitsinsky in 1982, when the two negotiators actually returned with a simple agreement later rejected by Washington and Moscow, Blessing presents four walks in the woods, taken by John Honeyman (Sam Waterston) and Andrey Botvinnik (Robert Prosky), each walk occurring in a different season. In a formal sense, Blessing is setting up what can only be a play of ideas, since his characters exist entirely within the decorously arranged framework of their walks; mercifully, they never refer to wives, kids, or any other life outside their discussions.

Neither, however, do they refer much to the actual content of their negotiations. Blessing gives each character a moment of personal reflection when all the buzz-words are trotted out, not merely to give the play authenticity but to remind us that this isn't only about two simple men enjoying and disappointing each other. Not unlike Hugh Whitemore's *Breaking the Code*'s acrobatic avoidance of the Enigma code itself, *A Walk in the Woods* manages to keep all the "boring" details at bay. Or rather, they're shoved into conveniently forgettable lists—SDI, SALT, human rights, megadeaths, Afghanistan, etc.

In their place is the charm, most of it given to Botvinnik in the play's only flirtation with dangerous politics. A delightful character, quite capable, as he says, of contradicting himself because he'd "go to any length to keep a friend," Botvinnik keeps the play humming with the appearance of maverick ideas. Whether suggesting that they should both be embarrassed to be Russian and American—"the world's fools"—or blaming Switzerland for their troubles, since they ought to be doing business "at the bottom of a missile silo," Botvinnik is in almost complete charge of the best arguments and the play's vitality. For him, Americans and Russians are too alike for comfort, with the Russians just as likely to have murdered the Indians as we were. Where we believe we're idealists, and they believe they're realists, he knows that both are illusionists, better at hiding truth from themselves than from others. All Honeyman can muster against this is the feeble charge that Botvinnik is a cynic.

Now that we've had the Gorbachevs in our living rooms holding hands while swaying through a singalong, Blessing's Botvinnik assumes a kind of bizarre believability, not least when he's crooning—briefly—"Blue Eyes Crying in the Rain." But it's never clear if Blessing is trying to humanize the Russians or merely saying that sentimentality can redeem us. Both characters are sentimental in their own ways, Honeyman insisting on "hope" as a negotiating tactic, Botvinnik relying on "friendship."

The Russian, in fact, gets one of his gentler laughs when reflecting on their rejected proposal, which he liked: "I will miss it," he says, almost as if he wasn't referring to an event that could blow up the world.

While a few of the more devastating facts creep into the text—such as the news that thirteen treaties have left us with fifty thousand warheads rather than the original three or four hundred—Blessing's play is finally more about wishful thinking than anything else. If only Russian negotiators could be such fun, if only the more priggish Americans could nonetheless be sincere good guys, if only the whole damned thing could be left for walks in the woods, if only the idea of history as geography—America's oceans meant conquest without opposition, Russia's vast frontier meant conquest against the odds—could be understood by the public, if only everybody was aware of how many weapons systems have been unveiled *after* treaties, if only Americans realized that Russians have hawks and doves, too...

For all his good intentions and sprightly dialogue, Blessing is not Shaw, not only because he doesn't turn ideas on their spinning heads but also because he reveals so few driving convictions of his own. Sure, he's likely to write happier endings than the one here, in which Botvinnik predicts that "talks will go on for hundreds of years—if we're lucky." Where, however, is the imaginative lift that would admit that the real negotiators can only be shits?

Paul Nitze was distrusted by Carter and used by Reagan. How in heaven's name could he ever be a good guy? Why trust the evidence of a dramatist willing to confuse the issues by jamming these walks into a single year while pretending that the progression from Brezhnev to Gorbachev actually takes place within the play's timespan? Would these negotiators go on and on without ever naming their bosses by name? What kind of credibility or suspense can there be when we all know that Honeyman wouldn't stand a chance in the company of Reagan's real favorites—North, Casey, and Max Kampelman?

Blessing's fantasy is in good company, if one can include it in the same breath, say, as Beethoven's *Fidelio,* where trumpets announce the last-minute rescue of the prisoners. But let's not kid ourselves that this is history—with or without geography. Blessing is not only lucky to be as fluent and sweet as he is, but also to have found such an affectionate production team, led by Des McAnuff. This is elegant work throughout: Bill Clarke's woods, framed by white walls with the black one displaying a photograph of still another forest, are arresting and properly claustrophobic, as if commenting on the play's essential unreality; the movement from one season to the next, with an especially voluptuous drop of autumn leaves between the first two scenes, provides the occasion with sensual respites much needed after so much talk; and Michael S. Roth's musical underscorings at those crucial sentimental moments are honest in the context, if not so welcome. Waterston's Honeyman could have stepped out of *Mr. Smith Goes to Geneva,* the Frank Capra type of film this might yet become. Slim, folksy, as irrepressibly honest as Jimmy Stewart ever was, he's the perfect comforting image of the American abroad we haven't seen in these sleazy years. Best of all is Robert Prosky's Botvinnik, a beautifully composed portrait: listening with intensity, talking with a rare sense of commanding intelligence, never missing a heart-tugging twist, a deeply felt truth, or a good passing joke – part of the problem, surely, but not his fault. This is a play that has buried its politics and thought in the treacherous precincts of the well-meaning human heart.

(March 1988)

Party Games

Four years after writing *The Birthday Party* in 1958, Harold Pinter gave a talk describing the pleasure he finds in using words. Like a character in his plays, he suddenly jumped into reverse: "At the same time I have another strong feeling about words which amounts to nothing less than nausea... words written by me and others, the bulk of it stale, dead terminology, ideas endlessly repeated and permutated, become platitudinous, trite, meaningless." That hemorrhaged condition, a sense of permanent dislocation, words failing to protect us from going over the edge, haunts every moment of *The Birthday Party,* perhaps more consistently than in his later plays with their more confident hold on a cool, distanced style. Early Pinter, like early Hitchcock, makes paranoia look almost normal. Even a box of cornflakes or its absence can be – as in *The Birthday Party* – a throwaway source of menace.

Amazing now that Pinter could ever have looked obscure. *The Birthday Party* is quite plainly a whacking good story about Stanley, a man hiding from the world in a seacoast boarding house, finally found out by Goldberg and McCann, clearly a team of hired killers prepared to break him down and whisk him away to a fate unknown. But is it unknown? Pinter may omit as much as he includes, but when Goldberg casually refers to the "right" size of his car's boot, there can be little doubt that Pinter is planting an image of murdered Stanley stashed there before whatever form of disappearance Goldberg and McCann will arrange. Stanley himself had earlier taunted his adoring landlady, Meg, with a similar image when he suggested that the two new guests she's expecting might cart her away in a wheelbarrow. Pinter may be spare, but he's never careless: the few facts he includes are usually all we need to know.

He's always reminding his audience that plays, like life, rarely explain anything. Or rather, playwriting is unlike life whenever it assumes utter prescience, pretending to have all the answers. A marvelously piquant version of this is Meg's remark in the third act that Stanley and his pursuers must be old friends. As much in the dark as any member of the audience, fatuous old Meg is quick with mundane explanations as far from the profoundly horrible experience of the play as she can possibly make it. The threat to Stanley is not his domestic history, it's his hopeless desire to escape the consequence of being alive.

Peter Hall's justly acclaimed productions of *The Caretaker, The Homecoming,* and *Old Times* not only set a standard but placed a stranglehold on ways of doing Pinter that might stray from expressionistic suggestion—the precariously exaggerated pitch of a staircase, for example—and hushed, anguished pauses. Hall arranged Pinter's characters like a curator setting sculptures at their best angles, the distance between them telling as much of their story as the light catching them in profile. With the best English actors—Donald Pleasance, Alan Bates, Paul Rogers, and Vivien Merchant—this aesthetic approach highlighted their own emotional austerities, much of the narrative suspense emerging from the expectation that at least once during the evening their dams would burst. Hall left nothing to chance.

Carey Perloff's direction of *The Birthday Party* acknowledges, first, that the play is more grounded than its successors, not a likely candidate for Hall's tiptoe styling or withdrawn breathlessness. If there are any sequiturs here, only a music-hall comedian would recognize them. Pinter fights his nausea by playing with words, even allowing his Jewish idiom a turn or two:

Goldberg: We'll make a man of you.
McCann: And a woman...
Goldberg: You'll be a mensch.
McCann: You'll be a success.

Perloff rushes at these exchanges as if she's worried that, without her headlong energy, they may fade into the sickly chintziness of Loy Arcenas's straightforwardly realistic design. Unlike Hall, she's in a hurry and she's having unashamed fun.

If anything, she plays the fun cards too soon. The first scenes start abruptly, with Georgine Hall acting up a self-conscious storm as Meg, pointing every line and moment with rubbery smiles, thick grimaces, knowing thrusts of head and arms. Surely Stanley would find her more excruciating and threatening than the world he's running from. It's not surprising that David Strathairn as Stanley should look so suppressed before he's had a chance to feel Goldberg's and McCann's menace. Elbows clinging to his cardigan, one arm frequently wrapped around his waist, Strathairn offers a Stanley more shy than put-upon.

Fortunately, he begins to come into his own for Stanley's crucial second act, catching some of Perloff's playful spirit for his scenes with Peter Riegert's lubricious Goldberg and Richard Riehle's submissively aggressive McCann. Even if they're not as haughtily in command as the Sydney Greenstreet–Peter Lorre team Pinter surely had in his thriller-obsessed mind, they possess a similar kind of performing impulse, which releases them breezily into the calms and tempests that keep succeeding one another in this melodramatic comedy. In the self-effacing role of Meg's bewildered husband, Petey, Robert Gerringer is solid and plain, a reminder that a Pinter character can have a totally unresonant existence. Wendy Makkens, as Lulu, the young neighbor brought in to spice up Meg's macabre party for Stanley, has both sauce and bite—and is wonderfully overdressed (as is Meg) by Gabriel Berry. She's particularly effective at letting the story happen to her rather than infusing it with some kind of "acting" knowingness.

Seen in a preview, Perloff's work was already more than a sketch for the colorful, anti-atmospheric Pinter production it wants to become. All it needs is less from Georgine Hall, more from Strathairn, and a restraining hand on moments now rushed. Pinter needs this kind of refresher course, but he also adores his mystery.

(April 1988)

The Seductions of Cynicism

Three audiences converge on David Mamet's perversely funny morality play, *Speed the Plow*—Madonna-watchers, committed cynics, and those (like me) who know that, whatever else he does, Mamet will make language sound like spoken jazz. Madonna's crowd has to wait for her entrance, and then they may not recognize her: in the drab role of an office temp, she's sleekly handsome rather than shockingly gorgeous, too subdued a presence to hold her own as the good-guy half of the argument but, admirably, not trying to do more than she yet knows how. If she's unequal, it's partly a response to the wimpy inequality built into the role. Mamet can't let a wise woman into his universe.

Plow works more as energy than idea. This play—three acts racing by in an hour and fifteen minutes—doesn't have time for true debate. Instead, Mamet gives the good lines and the charm to his scoundrels, Bobby Gould (Joe Mantegna) and Charlie Fox (Ron Silver), two Hollywood nogoodniks about to join in producing what Karen the temp calls a movie of "degradation . . . rage, sex, violence." Nothing new about such a setup, except that it skips lightly over the familiar types whom F. Scott Fitzgerald, Budd Schulberg, and Nathanael West used to look at with loathing and awe.

Mamet's not pretending to write characters according to the rules. Forget complexity, roundness, or even twentieth-century notions of sympathy. Like a latter-day Ben Jonson, he's getting his charge from his own verbal reconstruction of the way masculine evil talks to itself. Real Charlies and Bobbys may drop a Mamet-like phrase here or there, but for the most part, their days are not spent in moral doubt or in delight with vocabulary. Mamet's guys are trumpets and drums, fabulous riff-makers skimming breathlessly over extended justifications of their uniquely stupid, valueless pseudo-philosophies. "Don't fuck people," says Bobby to Charlie, "because people's what it's all about, there's lots of fuckin' people."

The plot couldn't be more schematic. Bobby can "greenlight" any movie he wants to under ten million dollars. Beyond that, he has to go to Ross, the studio head, for approval. When Charlie brings him the hot news that a big star is willing to do his "prison" movie, he dumps the package with his old pal Bobby so that together they can get Ross's approval the next morning. Enter Karen the temp: Charlie and Bobby bet five hundred dollars on Bobby getting her to his house that night and into bed. Bobby asks her to do a "courtesy" read of a book he knows won't "get the asses into the seats," a book about the effects of radiation on our lives. Karen persuades him that the book should be filmed because it's about the fear we all fear. By the third act, Bobby is ready to drop Charlie's "prison" movie in favor of Karen's "radiation" mission. Since nobody could possibly believe anymore that sex, like one-night-stand pregnancy, can create a complete reversal of motive and character, it follows that Charlie will find the way back for Bobby, and Karen will find her way out.

Plow's internal logic wouldn't have it otherwise. Charlie can easily rescue Bobby from his momentary lapse because Karen's book and her motives are pushovers. Mamet makes the idealist sound like another form of asshole: "All radiation," quotes Karen from the book, "has been sent by God to change us." Karen is a sex-object born again as . . . a sex-object with a public conscience. That it won't wash is a foregone conclusion. Bobby wouldn't be the likely recipient of a delegation from Sane/Freeze anyway, so where else can the plot go?

Mamet boxes himself into a narrative corner where villainy triumphs. Not surprising, then, that Charlie's victory brings cheers from the cynics— not necessarily what Mamet the hemi-semi-moralist might have preferred. "If you ever show up on the lot again," Charlie says to Karen after Bobby surrenders, "I'm going to have you killed." The audience loves it—and him. Ron Silver's Charlie, waving his cigar like a rifle, is an astounding talking machine, ingratiating as Jonson's Mosca and Volpone never were: he's thrust, sweat, and parry, a bearded wonder with a mouth like a sewer, so completely in charge of his third-act passion to bring Bobby back from the morality brink that he begins to transform rottenness into the purest of ideals. Joe Mantegna's slippery Bobby is no less seductive, creamy as his pastel clothes, looking every inch the king-clown poised to thank his mother at the next Oscar ceremony. Mantegna fits so seamlessly into Mamet's horrid universe that he almost makes the threatened reversal look real: without him, *Plow* wouldn't have any suspense at all.

Mamet's success as a natural theatrical force is weird and scary. Charlie's cigar is like Mamet's pen—both instruments operating outside civilized constraints. I'm not sure what he's actually hearing in Hollywood or New York, but I can tell you what he's hearing inside himself: American men as King Kongs who fling Fay Wray from the Empire State Building before getting away with murder. Even if they have the same killer instincts as their prototypes, the same vulgar tics, the same foul mouths, they wear them with a Mamet difference, poets in spite of themselves. Mamet forgets—or wants us to forget—that he has never made it clear why Charlie needs Bobby so badly to sell his surefire prison movie to Ross. Charlie has to be Karen's adversary, and that's that. If Mamet were to let his plot meet complication, he might have to make his characters meet life as it's lived.

His way is simpler. He's lucky to have actors who know how to pick up his tumbling cues, making them sound like the most exhilarating conversation ever invented; he's fortunate, too, in Greg Mosher's musically respectful direction, letting Michael Merritt design a simple, yet grand, utilitarian set framed by tomato-peach drapes. No phony realism here—only a theatrical world where words divorced from thought can display American power as it is. Too bad Mamet doesn't yet know how to make discussion and passion as real for himself as words and worldly despair. His short-winded plays keep playing into the hands of the monsters he's putting down. Catching them in their disgusting facts, he's joining them, maybe reluctantly, in their winnings. God knows there's a play in that sorry story.

(May 1988)

Ahead of Himself

If rage could guarantee a good play and doors a funny farce, then Larry Kramer might easily go to the head of the class. As a proud, card-carrying conspiracy theorist, I'm ready to go anywhere he wishes to take me in suggesting that the most successful hideout for big-time criminals is government itself. And though I can't quite believe that a play is likely to be an effective weapon in any of our dolorous battles, I'm delighted to applaud Kramer's lonely frontline commitment not only to politics but to theater as a political instrument. Brave beyond the call and undoubtedly crazed, like many of us, by Americans' taste for snake oil, his new play, *Just Say No,* risks everything by turning rage to farce—and back again.

Or rather: unable to contain his demons, Kramer drifts continually from wholesale paranoia to hit-or-miss oneliners, and finally from giddiness to melodrama. That the play never takes off satisfyingly in any direction is hardly surprising. Farce may be precisely the form Kramer doesn't need to tell his ghastly, outraged tale. If anything, his plot and its inevitable echoes are too stark: building the antics on thinly disguised versions of the Reagan family, their sleazy friends, and Ed Koch, Kramer is not merely exposing betrayals of public trust, he's also alluding to decades of murder in high places.

While the play proper skips nimbly through the entrances and exits of several visitors to Foppy Schwartz's Georgetown townhouse brothel in what is supposed to be the country of New Columbia, the play central is obsessed with those *guignol* allusions. Scarcely a moment goes by without reference to the disappearance of people in New Columbia who knew too much. Foppy (David Margulies) plays host to Trudi Tunick (Julie White), who's carrying a hot tape of orgies that ought finally to blow the administration apart. As confidante to Mrs. Potentate (also known as "Proud Mommy"), Foppy initially wants to cover up the tape. With the arrival of young Junior Potentate (Richard Topol), out of the closet and wanting to be a dancer, Foppy begins to acquire a conscience and a mission—to blow his own cover by blackmailing the administration into fighting AIDS. Other arrivals, including the mayor's young lover Gilbert Perch (Keith Reddin), who falls in love and in bed with Junior, lead Kramer to his own orgy of slamming doors, an apparent death in the middle of coitus, the momentary disappearance of the tape, and, by the end of the first act, the arrival of Madame Deus herself, Mommy Potentate (Kathleen Chalfant).

From this point on, Kramer's farcical spirit fizzles while his anger burns. Part of the problem is that the wicked tape and the possible exposure are never as frontally urgent as Kramer's often potent search for the monologue he might more sensibly have written. Loud, pretentiously sub-Noel Coward, Margulies could easily take the stage alone. Kramer might have had him Tell All to Bill Moyers up in heaven. Who wouldn't believe his shocking account of murdered witnesses, sexual hypocrisy, ruthless suppression of the facts? As it is, *Just Say No* finally suppresses Foppy's humor and its own by digressing into horror: Mommy has Junior's lover incarcerated for the murder she has ordered, thus proving— as if that's what we need to know—that Kramer has no hope anyway.

Not that I doubt him or disagree. Kramer is eerily right to let the Potentates' daughter Eustacia say that she loves "Mommy and Daddy as long as they don't tell me about the dark." But his farce hasn't earned the right to be so categorically sage. David Esbjornson's production is, if anything, more formally ambivalent than Kramer, never getting a grip on the mounting rhythms demanded by the genre. The best of the actors seem to be going it alone: Topol's Junior finds the high-flying dumb sweetness in his role, Reddin the blithering, vein-popping dottiness in his, and Chalfant the sinister glaze of Nancy that we're never allowed to see in the text.

No wonder even they're bewildered. Kramer pins lines on them as if he were putting tails on donkeys. Alluding to Mommy's insatiable taste for cock, he has Foppy use the same pun twice—"she will perform any act to get ahead"—the second time only because he can't resist another pun—"now she's gone down on history." His profligate, forgivable anger brings him down on his play, and no amount of goodwill and good politics can save it.

(November 1989)

Triumph of the Words

Now that Michael Holroyd's biography is reminding us that it wasn't easy for loveless Sonny Shaw to turn himself into devilish G.B.S., we may be compelled to view his plays with more of an eye to their reluctant melancholies. Yet there was never any doubt that, putting all his genius into work rather than life, Shaw also rescued drama from its easy slippage into comforting solutions. Dick Dudgeon's apparent sacrifice in *The Devil's Disciple*—letting himself be hanged to save Judith Anderson's husband, Anthony—is anything but a conventional move. Judith (and the audience) may wish to cling to love as his motive, but Dick insists on his right to shock: life means nothing to him unless he can act on instinct.

Luckily, Shaw's dramatic instinct always jumps out of thought infused by feeling. Try as he might, he can't be cold in his intelligence. Dick's romantic trappings—handsome face and irrepressible charm—expose the nonsense in everybody else's head. His granitic mother, Mrs. Dudgeon, covers up her highly developed capacity for hate with standard pieties; in his turn, Dick invents pity for the devil, still another twist of the Shavian knife. Wearing badness on his sleeve, Dick's pity is for outcasts. Shaw, as usual, sees mischief as the only way to wake slumbering hypocrites from their deluding dreams. He's positively hot with passion to disrupt.

Wonderful to see how well the mischief still works in the theater. Accustomed as I've been to slumbers induced by earlier Stephen Porter productions, I was delighted to find myself caught here in Shaw's whirlwind energies, every moment charged with those dizzying leaps into stratospheres where words are sovereign, ideas are loved. It can't be easy to negotiate Shaw's frontal rhetoric on the Circle in the Square's awkward stage, where actors must constantly angle themselves to reach at least two-thirds of the audience most of the time. Porter's solution, helped immeasurably by Zack Brown's cleverly disguised proscenium design—an upstage revolve that makes the four scene changes move as swiftly as the play—is to strike a neat balance between intimate discussion and direct address.

If anything, Porter's splendid cast simply takes the antagonistic stage as one more reason to match Shaw's quicksilver intelligence with equally active feet. These performances are entirely faithful to Shaw's wish that they "represent conduct as producing swiftly and certainly on the individual the results which in actual life it only produces on the race in the course of many centuries." Nothing less will do than champagne exhilaration, the actors' only subtext their thrilling discovery that Shaw is carrying them on his ample wings, the headiest reality their minds at work.

What's particularly pleasing is the way Philip Bosco's hilariously haughty General Burgoyne doesn't arrive in the last scene as comic relief after the earlier Dickensian melodrama in which Mrs. Dudgeon curses Dick when she's written out of her husband's will. Dick allows himself to be mistaken for Anderson, Judith faints from his kiss, and Anderson evidently runs for his life. Funny as he is—every vowel merging into a question mark—Bosco doesn't have to save Shaw's reputation as a humorist, since the other performers have already been flying on currents of wit and irony.

Rosemary Murphy begins the play with a Mrs. Dudgeon who is no mere prune-whipped curmudgeon: bitter as she may be, she practically trembles with joy whenever she can safely retreat into merciless denunciation. Of her husband's will, she observes, "He will be punished for it in both worlds," as if the pleasure of that thought can make up for her losses. Remak Ramsay's Anderson, his acid tenor continually betraying his insincerity, is a ramrod-straight scoundrel whose reversal at the end is all the more convincing—and comic—because he's been so seriously awful before. Roxanne Hart's Judith, her bewildered hands threatening to drop from her wrists, is caught in the breathlessness of her unfamiliar urges, an easy mark for Dick's unpremeditated seductiveness.

As it must be, however, Victor Garber's Dick drives all before him. Going from strength to double-strength these days, Garber is a perfect Shavian actor, at ease with the long, legato phrase and those sudden stops and starts. Wearing his glamour like an old shoe, the last to notice what he's got, he's living almost entirely in the byways of his mind. Yet he's also the master of Shaw's occasional, heart-stopping pauses. A collector's item, this performance, not to be missed.

As might be said of Shaw's masterful transformation of melodrama into high comedy. He was moderately worried that when the "novelty of… the advanced thought of the day" wore off, *The Devil's Disciple* would be "exposed as the threadbare popular melodrama it technically is." One can't help adoring that *technically*. Shaw had to know that his ideas could influence a few even as his comedy would entertain many, but the novelty, as such, would never quite take. Despite the melodrama, the play still lives, inevitably reminding us how far we haven't come. "The contrast," says Shaw in the preface to his collected prefaces, "between the wisdom of our literature and the folly of our rulers and voters is a melancholy proof that people get nothing out of books except what they bring to them." Shaw's play wins the battle, even if the rest of us are losing the war.

(November 1988)

The Fugitive Play

That London's West End is the home of what must be the best Tennessee Williams production in thirty years is only part of America's mounting national and theatrical disgrace. Let Rocco Landesman and Lincoln Center snipe at one another, the bloody awful truth remains that Broadway is now what Carol Cutrere, in *Orpheus Descending,* would call "the local bone orchard," unable to fulfill anything but its own prophecies that the public will buy only high-tech trivia or spin-offs from soppy tube dramas. Peter Hall's lucid, passionate production of *Orpheus* is at the Haymarket, one of London's oldest and coziest comfort stations for the exhausted middle class; since Jerome Minskoff is one of his coproducers, it's plausible to expect a Broadway move, yet so far, despite the London success, there's no sign of a crossing. Evidently, Broadway prefers death to the honor of going down fighting on behalf of a great American play acted with harrowing accuracy by a splendid cast.

A great play? Certainly, when presented with tact and sensibility, as if it belongs—and it does—in a line stretching from Webster to Strindberg. Apart from the equally underrated *Camino Real,* Williams never tried to put so much of the world into one play. It took him seventeen years to get it right: the earliest version, *Battle of Angels,* was trashed in Boston in 1941. Master of self-doubt, Williams scratched at the text until he was able to orchestrate its multiple narratives into one grand symphonic design, an image of America devouring innocence: on its outer edge, menace; inside, possibility destroyed.

In Hall's production, the menace is unrelenting. Lady and Jabe Torrance's dry-goods store, in a small southern town not far from Memphis, opens at the back to a raised street and high brick wall. Williams offers a frank exposition in which two characters speak directly to the audience about the terrible Klan burning ("the Mystic Crew") of the vineyard joyfully owned by Lady's father ("A Wop from the old country"), so Hall boldly underscores the action with headlight beams, barking dogs, tropical storms, and dark musical rumbles. Yet even as he fills the stage with detail, he's making a statement about the way theater can concentrate its energy on violence's invasion of intimacy. The great mountain-climbing staircase reaching up to Lady's and Jabe's separate bedrooms is just one sign among many that this is a play and a production unashamed of grandeur and symbol.

Williams's control is astonishing. Moving with uncommon stealth between hushed and explosive encounters, this is drama in quasi-sonata form: a portentous introduction followed by allegro statements and development, slow movement, scherzo, and grand finale. Lady's extended scenes with Val Xavier, the young drifter who leads her from the hate she feels for everybody into an ecstatic rapport with him and with herself, are alternately languid and breathless; surrounding them are the fugitive appearances of white-faced Carol, like Lear's Fool, the repository of the play's fearful, oppressed ironies. Finally, the big public confrontations end with Lady's discovery that Jabe led the Mystic Crew to burn her father's vineyard, Jabe's emergence from his deathbed to murder Lady, and the town's execution of Val with a flaming blowtorch.

Pressure and release, the refusal to be submerged by the personal or consumed by the drift of one idea alone: these are among the play's virtues, its amazing insistence on the truth of an outsider's vision. *Orpheus* reminds me that this particular way of seeing the world—the antiphonal scene- and phrasemaking, the thick impasto of the characterizations, the desperate adoration of life despite the evidence—didn't exist until Williams created a theatrical language all his own. How casually he's been dismissed, partly because he wore his insecurities on his open heart but not least because major Williams productions continue to be so few and far between.

Word is out that, with their usual hindsight and spineless lack of imag-

ination, several of our regional theaters are now planning *Orpheus* productions next season. Evidently, we still need London to give us signals.
Yet it would be a small disaster if Hall's production is not allowed to set
the standard in New York, especially since Vanessa Redgrave's Lady is a
transcendental definition of theatrical acting. From her gray, sullen opening scenes to the final moments when she bursts like a gawky sunflower
into the surrounding meanness, she moves mercurially from one texture
to another, letting events catch her with a child's surprise. Her voice is
only one of her instruments—a deep rasp shading into burbling, momentary soprano. British critics have been questioning her ripe Italian accent,
not noticing that it makes her the ultimate outsider Williams clearly
intended; more than that, it marks her as her "Wop" father's daughter.
To quarrel with Redgrave's authority is like arguing with Niagara. It's
wonderful to watch her tall figure hovering over and finally embracing
the relatively small Jean-Marc Barr as Val. Barr gives a lovely, sweet performance of a youth who doesn't know why he's wanted yet wants only
what Lady has to give. The two together are like a great birch touched
softly by a willow. When Jabe fires on Lady, she dies with a shocking
shrug of the shoulder—the tree felled, yet still questioning.

Is New York afraid to welcome one of the few great actresses alive,
forgetting that her political commitments are part of her amazing emotional power? In London, there's no other play or performance to match.
Worse, a new play that's also about innocence destroyed, David Hare's
The Secret Rapture, is almost a clinical demonstration of how not to bring
politics into a play: Williams trembles with inevitability, Hare manipu-
lates with contempt. And wouldn't you know it? *The Secret Rapture* will
be coming to the Public Theater.

(January 1989)

She's still a magnificent birch reaching heroically for her place in the
Pleiades, but Vanessa Redgrave's Lady Torrance is no longer being nudged
by a quietly windswept willow. For reasons that elude me, Peter Hall has
turned his London production of *Orpheus Descending*—its grandeur sinister
and stealthily appalled—into a less startled, more emphatic, noisy cartoon.
What was once weighted and balanced to present tarnished innocence

colliding with amiable brutality now leans heavily on the brutal side: sound levels are up on Stephen Edwards's electronic score, some of the women's costumes are in more garish colors, and Val Xavier has been transformed from willow to oak, not noticeably different in spirit or voice from the redneck monsters pursuing his skin.

Some of this looks like carelessness. With Tammy Grimes's Vee Talbot stumbling early into the Torrance dry-goods store wearing a printed red dress, the bursting image of Lady suddenly in red for the triumph she is planning at the end can only seem unexceptional, perversely underscoring Grimes's misplaced effort to bring the same kind of liberated energy to her role that Redgrave gives to Lady. Similarly, it may have seemed plausible to replace Jean-Marc Barr's short, balding, softly voiced Val with Kevin Anderson's lanky, long-haired, histrionically contentious version, yet it doesn't read as anything more than a whim to match the uncommonly tall Redgrave inch for sporting inch. Unlike Barr, Anderson can't stop acting in italics, illustrating shifts of temperament with lunges, leaps, and jabs at the walls, caught in a perpetual audition for his high school football team. Barr's quietude was like a slate on which women could dream of warmth and protection while men wrote a history of violence and envy. Anderson looks and sounds like one of the boys.

In revising for New York, Hall may have been seduced by American voices that could easily seem idiomatic to a British ear, though they're often uttering sounds heard only in theaters. Grimes couldn't be farther from her London predecessor, Miriam Margolyes: by now she can lead only from that famous plum stuck helplessly in her throat, as if simple, human sounds might frighten her into actually thinking about what she or anybody else is saying. Vee is still another version of Williams's fugitive kind, plain, vulnerable, desperately tender; Grimes is a version of her musical-comedy self, mannered and untouchable, Eve Arden slumming as Zazu Pitts. It's easier to understand how Hall might have expected from Anne Twomey the intensity and diamond clarity of Julie Covington's Carol Cutrere. Williams asks her to be both chorus and character, compelled to shift public and private gears in an instant: Twomey is giddy as both, caught in the downdraft of her monotonous, pleading voice. She's all attack and no finish.

Fortunately, these rude comparisons are only half the story. Almost all the others are more vivid than their London counterparts, especially Sloane Shelton's Beulah and Marcia Lewis's Nurse Porter. Saddled with one of the boldest expository loads in dramatic literature—Beulah shadowing the past and foreshadowing the future in between what Dolly calls her "evil laugh"—Shelton is a *Macbeth* witch blowsy with sardonic, hideous wisdom; she alights on her first word to the audience—*fire*—like the moralistic flamethrower Beulah might like to be. Shelton lets her words bite and sting, drawing blood from them as she embodies the image of a world devouring the living to feed the dead. Nurse Porter is, if anything, more cunningly stupid, and Marcia Lewis makes the most of her brash refusal to know anything but what she already knows. In *Orpheus,* Williams is positively Jacobean in his portraiture, slashing at the canvas with quick strokes that ask of the actor equally sharp colorings and shadings: Lewis crackles with similar authority, finding the arid joy that leaks from an evil heart ready to accuse the wounded Lady of having no shame.

This production's extravagant joy, preserved and enriched beyond measure, is Vanessa Redgrave's quicksilver Lady, illuminating every flashing moment with passionate intelligence. Her vowels and consonants emerge now from hectares of Sicilian dust, eager to release unexpected laughter, embracing sudden furies as quickly as they melt into possibility and hope. Like all the great Williams roles, Lady is a mix of appetite and deprivation: Redgrave is enormous in her incarnation of both. She reads Val's reference letter in a syllable-slapping mockery of formal English, but when she can't resist Italian it bubbles from her effortlessly as overwhelming testimony to ancestral loyalties. If arms could be wings or eyes burn enemies, Redgrave's would do so; as it is, they are components of an acting instrument that confounds limits. Shot down in midflight, her insides seem shattered, her arms jerked from their sockets like a brutalized dying swan. For Williams, Lady's death means irretrievable loss. For the stage, Redgrave's death scene and all that precedes it are reminders that the union of shameless visionary writing with generous high-wire acting is an art without compare, ready against the odds to defy even Williams's sense of tragic destiny.

(October 1989)

Lost Soul

Albert Innaurato's *Coming of Age in Soho* can't resist the confessional mode. The leading character, an ambisexual writer named Bartholomew Dante, admits at the beginning that he is looking for a plot. Since it is reasonable to deduce that he is very much the author's voice, it is clear that Innaurato will keep revealing doubts about himself; indeed, that he won't be able to hide either the absence or contrivance of plot. The play fails, but honorably: Innaurato can't make dramatic or even comic sense out of his writer's turbulence; neither can he disguise his elemental honesty. There is something endearing about plays that know they aren't working.

His honesty, however, is only about writers, not people. Bartholomew, known affectionately as Beatrice, is suffering not so much from writer's block as writer's avalanche. "Guide my fingers to the words," he says toward the end, but where—given his situation—would he ever find time for any kind of guidance, let alone fewer and better words than Innaurato is able to give him? Trying to live alone in a barely finished Soho loft, Beatrice is scarcely past the obligatory exposition scene with Patricia, his wife of fourteen years whom he hopes to shed, when he comes under assault from the rest of the cast: Dy, a runaway fifteen-year-old WASP boy in search of freedom from WASP-hood; Patricia's hoodlum brother Pasquale, acting as deputy for Patricia's offstage (god)father; a working-class handyman friend of Patricia's named Danny who is there to be handy for the elusive plot; Beatrice's teenage German son searching for his hitherto unknown father because his German mother is an imprisoned terrorist; and finally, the WASP's loathed elder brother on his break from Harvard searching for the runaway. In short, your average convocation of unlikely characters, who, in real life, would be smart enough to elude the succession of flimsy motivations and ditsy coincidences that bring them to Beatrice's loft.

People named Dante, Odysseus, and Trajan McDowell (the WASP brothers) and Puer (the German son—given the Latin name for Boy as we are repeatedly reminded) are not exactly people who meet in lofts or anywhere else. I doubt that they would be found even at a Modern Language Association convention. Innaurato probably wants to establish zany credentials for the comedy he doesn't really have the will to write.

Beatrice's anguish, which doesn't quite rescue the play's integrity, is nonetheless a visible, audible, terrible thing. But even more terrible is that it is so remorselessly sabotaged by the playwright's temptation to be wise and cute at the same time.

The wisdom, in any case, is airlifted from Great Books and Great Music. Innaurato's assembled implausibles are always quoting someone–Unamuno a few times, Valéry, Suzanne Langer, and, just to jazz up the occasion, Alfred Kinsey. The music is a soprano singing a *verismo* aria as the lights rise on the first act, and Elisabeth Schwarzkopf opening the second with Mahler. When the young brother and Beatrice discover that they can embrace without sexual threat, the music by half-light is Mahler again. Some, but certainly not all, of these rubbings might add convincing substance to livelier characters, but who can really believe that emotional crisis can lead so many inept people on schedule to the apt quote? Can found music make up for lost drama?

Not that real issues are ignored. If anything, Innaurato's problem is that he can't relinquish a digression or a joke. Any one of Beatrice's concerns could have made a play: whether to be above or beyond labeled sexuality, whether to reach for intimacy or race to convention, whether to see women and boys as people or objects, whether to write or not to write. (And then, too, there's Catholic misery shadowing Beatrice's every choice.) By the time the play is over, the theme of fathers and children looms more visibly than the others, if only because Dy's father weeps over the phone when Dy calls to announce his homecoming, and Beatrice discovers that in his own son, Puer, he has found joy. This isn't a play, it's a conference call.

At one point, Beatrice calls his agent, announcing that he's "caught in a trap," which the agent recognizes as a quote from Blanche DuBois. Innaurato's charm and misery are in continual collision. Luckily, he can't help revealing his own traps. Unluckily, they are not very compelling, and they don't lead into an interior life that might nourish his characters. Language keeps defeating credibility: working-class Danny is Pasquale's dictionary, supplying him with words such as "sexist" and "euphemism." Then there are irresistible puns blocking the action while mocking emerging feelings. (Dostoevsky had a foot fetish, which is "why there's so much soul in his work"—to say nothing of its "narrative arch.") Begging his questions, Innaurato is also begging for an editor.

Which is why he shouldn't have been his own director. Under the circumstances, he has done well with most of his actors, particularly the teenagers. Ward Saxton as the Einsteinian monster from Germany, wizard of computers and fountain of therapeutic wisdom, brings an eager, playful energy to his encounters, despite the patronizing way in which the character is viewed by Innaurato and almost everyone else. (Puer is an offspring of that wickedly intelligent German child in Lillian Hellman's *Watch on the Rhine:* someone might cop a doctorate with a study of American playwrights' fascination with youthful German precocity—better still, their fascination with each other.) Scott DeFreitas's Dy is direct, unsentimental, and sparkish. Indeed, both boys have a supple, easygoing gift for slipping away from the awkward, demi-operatic snares set by their author, suggesting that their director trusts kids at least as much as he distrusts his material, a fortuitous reversal for them.

Even so, what the play needs is a director who can tell the playwright when to stop, when to listen, and when to start the whole thing over again. Puer tells Beatrice that "simply to write is not to fail." Director Innaurato should have told Playwright Innaurato that simply to write is not enough.

Whatever track he may be on during the amiable humors of *Gus and Al,* Albert Innaurato returns repeatedly to his apprehensions—and loathing—of critics. Perhaps he's taking out a small insurance policy on his writing life. And who can blame such a charming, decent playwright for inventing a fabulous scene in which his alter ego, Al—who has miraculously escaped from 1989 to fin-de-siècle Vienna—meets his own grandfather and asks him to change his name to Mamet when he emigrates? Luckily, Grandfather Innaurato doesn't know what Al is talking about; unluckily, grandson Innaurato is either too modest or too self-loathing to give Grandfather any reassuring lines about Al's talent. A critic, however despised, is free to report that the world is big enough for both Mamet and Innaurato.

If Innaurato is right—and he may well be—the world isn't equally free to accept a *Village Voice* review. When Al meets Gustav Mahler in 1901, the composer and playwright move quickly into a comparison of their bad notices, Gus suffering from a Vienna critic's judgment that his Fourth Symphony is "alien noise," Al smarting from New York's rejection of *Coming of Age in Soho*. "You have the temerity," says Gus, "to read me a notice from a village newspaper?"

Innaurato's temerity goes further: teaming Al with Gus, while everybody in Gus's household makes cruel allusions to Al's excessive weight ("a fat genie," says Mahler's sister), Innaurato is dangerously on the edge, simultaneously applauding and knocking himself in a pose only critical judgment could rescue. But he rarely tips over that edge, a sign that he's ready now to transform doubt and anger into unself-conscious art. Mahler's achievement is daunting, but much as Al envies it, he also discovers that the cost for him would be too great. While churning ice cream in the room he shares with Mahler, he has to admit that sweets are "better than death, music, women, and fame." Mahler, not so happy to hear that Richard Strauss's music has survived to 1989, is only partly comforted by the news that he is worshiped. *Gus and Al* plays like a declaration of independence, Innaurato not so much eaten by envy as making a hearty meal of it himself.

His fantasy and jokes are irresistible. Al lives with an ape called Kafka, who has invented the time machine that Al used—against Kafka's warnings—to escape the lousy reviews he's anticipating for his latest play. Kafka's judgments were cooler than Al's: "Nothing wrong with failing," he says, "it's persevering after failure that's dumb." On the Ringstrasse and in the country with Mahler, Al meets Natalie Bauer Lechner, busily noting down Mahler's every word in her journal. Like a Schnitzler character strayed into a Chekhov comedy, she has been trying to get a proposal from Mahler for fifteen years, only to be thwarted by young Alma Schindler's arrival. Her formality and stuffiness couldn't be more endearing: she's fond of taking "refuge in solecism," and when she thinks about Mahler's other worshipers, she insists quietly that "it is pleasant to love a violinist, but not original."

When Gus and Al argue about art, the stakes quickly mount, Gus unwilling to be infected by Al's despair. He can't believe Al's hair-raising descriptions – and demonstrations – of T.V., break-dancing, and minimalist music: "art must matter," he says. But Al, in turn, tells him furiously that 1989's museums are missile silos, that people dying from a plague are insulted by southern senators, that there's no censor where he comes from because "no one cares about theater." "How strange," says Mahler, "theater is so powerful here."

Gus and Al's mixture of drollery, satire, and anguish is commandingly balanced by Innaurato. Just as he leads you to think he's about to weigh the play down with a consultation scene between Mahler and his neighbor, Freud, he slips delicately into the meeting between Al and his young grandfather, with its dangerously suggestive moment when Al – not yet aware of who the handsome gardener is – clumsily makes a pass. Apart from the shrill aggressions he gives to Alma, Innaurato is eminently fair to everybody, leaving a trail of spiky tenderness behind each relaxed scene. In this play, at last, he's no longer locked in family nightmares.

Like Jim Youmans's beautifully painted Vienna Werkstätte designs, opening the play to a wondrously funny world, Innaurato may be opening his formidably antic imagination to more engaged, yet less frantically obsessive, possibilities. David Warren's production is, for the most part, gentle and unforced. Wearing a fat suit under his shirt and trousers, Mark Blum makes a gallant, sweetly reticent Al, just as Sam Tsoutsouvas presents a surprisingly unanguished Mahler, his dignity often mocked by his foolish, serenely dumb goodwill. Best of all is Cara Duff-MacCormick's earnest, bewildered Natalie, all hands and flutter, "smudged and splattered as my life is" – one of those Innaurato creations saved from self-pity by last-minute, breath-catching humor.

Even if he's still too hard on his surrogate at the end, letting Mahler orate about *himself* as "the greatly gifted" and Al and the others as "the merely hopeful," he wins a victory by having Kafka rescue Al from 1901 with the news that the reviews were only mixed. Maybe this time, too, he'll find out that what matters most is that good work is even better than sweets – and good reviews.

(March 1989)

Three-Inch Pickings

Charles Ludlam used to say that "the shortest distance between two points is playwriting," a deconstruction of mathematical wisdom he didn't always observe. In his own work, two points are never bridged the easy way. Midway in the studious mess that spills over the stage in Ludlam's first play, 1967's *Big Hotel,* the bellhop races in to voice what Ludlam wisely suspected most of us would be feeling: "Somewhere along the line, I've lost the thread of the narrative." This could have been his way of thumbing his nose at narrative anyway, a quick escape clause from the happy chaos he knew he was causing. That it comes too late and is ignored thereafter only proves the lunatic point he was scoring all over his playwriting map; what he does best, finally, are the detours taken from one dramatic point to another.

The big joke in *Big Hotel* is that there was never any narrative thread to lose. It takes only a moment into the play to realize that the prologue preceding it was Ludlam's way of setting up antinarrative expectations. God in a teased blonde wig, wearing earrings like giant biscuits, confronts the Devil, but only to put him down with an inspired allusion Milton never thought of—"Get away from here, you three-inch fool." Ludlam's innocently raunchy high school pillow party sets its terms quickly: the playwright's attic is being ransacked for recycling—and remaking—old clothes, old jokes, and old ideas of dramatic license, with new spins on bad taste the name of his free-falling game.

Unfortunately, *Big Hotel* also demonstrates that Ludlam was still more apprentice than sorcerer. Useful as it is to be reminded of Ludlam's beginning, it's not much fun going to the theater as an archaeologist. A swift glance over the cast list turns out to be more reliably entertaining than many of the scenes themselves: assembled under Big Hotel's roof are Norma Desmond, Lupe Velez, Trilby and Svengali, Mata Hari, somebody called Chocha Caliente, a Hollywood agent named Chamberpot, and a suicidal ballerina, Birdshitskaya, who might have astonished Diaghilev. If anything unites them, it may be the arbitrary way in which they are fighting either for survival or self-destruction. I have a feeling, however, that nothing was ever meant to unite them, least of all their destinies in and around Big Hotel's marvelously unlikely lobby.

Or it may be that they are united by Ludlam's urge to throw everybody into suggestive bodily contact, as if they were all magnetic fields expelling electric charges from any part of them that moves. Never have so many bumps shifted imperceptibly into so many grinds. Darting tongues are even more splendidly filthy than dildos and false tits. Meanwhile, Everett Quinton's eyes, particularly when mimicking Gloria Swanson's Norma Desmond, seem to erupt from his head like marble medicine balls. Hands and faces can't resist whatever might be hidden between legs; whether the ample, melonesque contours of Christine Weiss are on blindingly white-dressed display, or young men are stripped to bare their washboard tummies, the comedy finally comes down to whatever flesh is heir to—sexy, yes, but strangely and sweetly demure.

Ludlam's verbal wit is never as free or well developed as his physical comedy. When Norma is forced to look at her face in the mirror, she shatters it with one glance, that joke repeated later when the mirror is broken by Trilby's screeching soprano. But Norma is also there to elicit one of the show's few attempted puns, torturously arrived at by the route comparing Desmond to Bellini's *Norma:* "When I think of 'Casta Diva,' I want to cast a diva into the river." Even the mirror gag is topped by Svengali's writhings—H. M. Koutoukas looking spookily like Ludlam—as he begins literally to climb the wall.

A narrative thread might have helped. As it is, Susan Young's costumes are wittier than the play, and nothing is funnier than the *ding* everybody utters when ringing for the elevator. Quinton directs the company with fierce energy, but he can't disguise the hard labor. Given the long wait between jokes that work, it's only too easy to find the mind wandering past the bellhop's lament into the unwelcome thought that, unlike Ludlam's later plays, *Big Hotel* might not even offend Jesse Helms.

(October 1989)

Anniversary Schmaltz

In a year when banality kept reaching for new definitions, the most emblematic nonevent occurred in late September when the *New York Times* mourned our apparent neglect of Maxwell Anderson. It seems that, like Eugene O'Neill, he was born in 1888, yet only his widow, son,

Helen Hayes, and Professor Alfred S. Shivers, his biographer, were truly celebrating. I had been successfully dodging O'Neill's centenary—no arguments so far with partisans of *Dynamo* and *Marco Millions*—so I could scarcely feel sanguine about an Anderson centenary, with battles looming over *High Tor* and *The Wingless Victory*. Yet Mervyn Rothstein of the *Times* suggested nothing less: "What is it," he asked with an innocence that always invades the arts pages whenever the editors decide to guard our cultural health, "that has made one playwright endure and the other fall from favor? Is it simply talent or is there something else involved?"

Anxious to find out if still another conspiracy had been uncovered, I pushed on. Rothstein complains that *The Reader's Encyclopedia of World Drama* gives "page after page about O'Neill, and only a handful of paragraphs about Anderson." He doesn't tell us that, after noting Anderson's "serious subjects" in more than thirty plays, the encyclopedia offers one devastatingly simple reason: "a tendency to reduce issues to a simple struggle between good and evil left too little room for the complexity and richness that distinguish the greatest drama." Rothstein instead seeks the answer elsewhere: in Shivers's comment that "poetic works are not in vogue," or Arvin Brown's reductive statement that it's "all a matter of fashion," or Hayes's "language is out of style." Anderson, despite what Joseph Papp calls his "strong belief in democracy," was evidently too fragile for this world, clearly not a match for the mighty O'Neill.

But what about his talent? Shivers gets no argument from me when he claims that, compared to Anderson's dialogue, O'Neill's "is quite clumsy," yet he is drawing a distinction between a hippo and an elephant. In *Winterset*, Mio is confronting his nemesis, Gaunt:

> *Go home and die in bed, get it under*
> *cover,*
> *your lux-et-lex putrefaction of the*
> *right thing,*
> *you man that walks like a God!*

At an equally high point in her emotional life, Anderson's Queen Elizabeth (played by Hayes when language was presumably in style) tells Bacon that she is a queen:

> *Where I walk*
> *In a hall of torture, where the curious*
> *gods bring all*
> *Their racks and gyves, and stretch*
> *me there*
> *to write.*

If it was clever of Rothstein to avoid direct quotation from the plays themselves, it was equally wise to ignore those critics in the thirties and forties who were less enchanted than the *Times's* own Brooks Atkinson. In a review by Stark Young, he would have found a twenty-three-line quotation from *The Wingless Victory* (1936) meant to show Anderson's "tired rhythmic patterns, superfluous images and lyric clichés." From George Jean Nathan's description ten years later of *Joan of Lorraine,* he would read about "porpoise verse," and a belief that Anderson "enjoys all the attributes of a profound thinker save profundity." True, some of us might say the same of O'Neill, but Nathan, O'Neill's fiercest champion, goes on to nail Anderson as the presumptuous mimic O'Neill rarely was: "Shakespeare has outpoetized him...Schiller outfelt him...Twain out-witted him...Shaw outthought him."

Rothstein, similarly, has been outfoxed by his impossible assignment. Caught in the airhead game of answering a question – "Where's Maxwell Anderson?" – nobody else has bothered to pose, he could only assemble his own set of not-quite-lyric clichés. Though Anderson was not always as wretched as I've drawn him, he was never a true contender. The *Times* is always nagging us to respect popular entertainers like Anderson, Oscar Hammerstein II, and Ronald Reagan as more than what they are. For-give me, but the only conspiracy I could find was the *Times* up to its old tricks – preparing the way for a reconditioned, retooled, reimagined George Bush. Had Rothstein dug deeper, he might have found the Rea-gan doctrine buried forty years ago in a little volume called *Five Broadway Plays,* in which two Detroit High School teachers tell their students that the hero of *High Tor* faces the problem of "how to keep the things they love as they want them, in other words, how to stop things from under-going change." Anderson's problem is that he surfaced too soon.

Luckily, Rothstein's trial balloon never got off the ground. But if

Reagan's final days in office can coincide with the threat of an Anderson revival, what dismal theatrical prospects will the *Times* unearth during the next four years? With Maxwell Anderson on the edge of resurrection, can Archibald MacLeish be far behind?

(January 1989)

Trip to Fanciful

God bless our bushed middle class, devoted to family, amazed by nature's wonders, crazy about babies, delighted by memories of a happy child-hood, yet—and on such a "yet" Tina Howe builds still another of her exercises in privileged melancholy—desperately uneasy about morality. In *Approaching Zanzibar's* universe, as hermetically sealed from real anguish as any 21-inch T.V. screen, the major issue of the day is how fast life's going. No matter that Wallace and Charlotte Blossom and their preteen son and daughter, Turner and Pony, travel southwest for two thousand miles, failing to uncover anything more disturbing than a thunderstorm, as if distressed farmers or nuclear installations might not have given momentary pause to their squeaky-clean encounters with mountains, streams, sunsets, and lakes. This is a world in which, with a little nudge from the ever-so-poetical Howe, even cancer can be joyous.

The Blossoms are on their way to pay their last respects to Charlotte's dying aunt, Olivia Childs, an eighty-one-year-old artistic mischief maker whose fuzzily described creations sound like *Redbook's* idea of what Georgia O'Keeffe would have been up to had she wanted to be modishly avant-garde. Anxious as Charlotte is to reach Olivia before the end, she's not treating the case as an emergency. Sure, they could easily fly to Taos, but Charlotte's fear of thunder is matched only by her fear of flying. Consequently, we see the Blossoms first in their car, spending seven of the play's nine scenes contemplating the magical reminders they experi-ence about birth and death and the little discomforts in between. The kids make noise in the back seat, their parents holler at each other, Dad takes Turner fly-fishing in Asheville, Mom pours champagne over herself in her brother's boat on Lake Thunderbird in Oklahoma City, and—in the most excruciatingly impossible scene of all—they change places in the car so that the kids can imitate their folks' squabbling behavior. Earlier, Charlotte declared in that gosh-oh-gee American manner, "Daddy and I have some rights," but she had to know she'd long ago surrendered them, if only in homage to her awe about the splendors of birth.

In the Blue Ridge Mountains, they meet an equally awestruck Dad cuddling his three-week-old baby, followed by a grandmother and her deaf, psychic grandson, who scares the hell out of everybody for a moment when he "signs" Baby Williams's future as a brave, great thing who turns into a scary bad thing. Meanwhile, Dad tells Turner his reassuring news that our souls return to the waters, so the trout they're trying to catch are really after-life humans; later, however, Pony seems to believe that we begin as fish. Either way, *Approaching Zanzibar* keeps approaching ga-ga.

For some reason, Charlotte is always hot wherever she is, even on the Oklahoma lake—hence the champagne shower. This, I take it, is Playwriting's shortcut to menopause, just as the family's earlier encounter with a crazed old man who merely cries out that he's "lost her" is their first overt confrontation with death. No wonder that precocious, noisy brat Pony is always blurting out terrible truths, such as "He's deaf," or "She's dying." Pony has yet to learn the kind of restrained decorum that, presumably, a steady diet of Wonder bread has brought her elders.

Howe doesn't write scenes so much as prepare the route to punchlines that unmistakably make The Point! The lake trip gives Charlotte and her brother, Scotty, the opportunity not only to drink and waste champagne but to remember the story of a lion in a zoo who once pissed on them. Whatever else happens in the scene, such as the Blossoms' meeting with Scotty's pregnant girlfriend—Hoy Ballad!—is nothing compared with Charlotte's last line. "We had a great childhood." Along the way, Charlotte's weird detachment looms large as she screams ecstatically how much she loves little boys named Turner, who is at the other end of the boat, as far from her alleged warmth as he could possibly be.

That peculiar distance may be Carole Rothman's directorial choice, though it looks throughout as if she doesn't know how to react to Howe's phony lyricism. And she may be right: the trouble with the play is that it's genuinely, sincerely phony; it doesn't want to do anything else but scrape the pain back to the blahs. When the Blossoms finally reach

Olivia, they're faced with what looks like a supremely terminal case: Olivia doesn't recognize them in her waking stupor, mistaking poor Turner for Scotty's daughter, Amy. Appearances are misleading, however, since Olivia is evidently putting on an act. No doubt she's really dying, but after the play presents her various helpers (one of them, Sybil, a one-legged doctor who's not complaining since she's had "a great life...but there's so much more she wanted to do"), Olivia asks to be alone with Pony. Lo and behold—proving that chemotherapists have nothing on playwrights—she goes into remission, though it's possible she's been there all along. After telling Pony about her love for a man she met on the way to Zanzibar, the two of them jump on the bed, now miraculously looking and acting like a trampoline, shouting "Paradise": all very well for the privileged nine-year-old, but perhaps not so comforting to the menopausal and the dying.

Even so, the white curtain sweeps closed over this wondrous copout, no less frightening to those of us less bewitched by the official discovery of family than the not-so-dissimilar image of Heidi rocking her adopted white baby in Wendy Wasserstein's equally unreal, vapid accommodation in The Heidi Chronicles. Susan Hilferty's costumes look as if they were pulled from the Gap's windows—pastel greens, blues, and beiges spread over two thousand miles of an America vaguely worried about sic transit not-so gloria mundi. The kids, as usual in Howe's monomania dramas, talk like no other kids you've ever heard, or would want to hear, though their spontaneous raucousness is moderately more "connected" than their elders' folksy—and fussy—earnest sincerity.

Heidi Landesman's ingenious deployment of parachute silks that serve alternately as car, tent, and sails makes Howe's odyssey look like a rehearsal in search of a movie, pointing the way to wasteland American theater out of touch not only with the desperate emergencies on our front pages but with the unmanipulative journeys and hard poetry that drama used to be privileged to present.

(May 1989)

Angels in America, Devils in the Wings

As one who lives a life rather than a "lifestyle," I'm not sure what a gay play, let alone a gay fantasia, might be. But there they fly, those miniprovocations and tiny half-thoughts, now glued permanently to whatever may be dredged from the experience of seeing George C. Wolfe's musical-comedy version of Tony Kushner's *Angels in America: Millennium Approaches,* subtitled "A Gay Fantasia on National Themes." Well, if not exactly a musical comedy, a play now underscored with so much musical blather instructing us what to feel or think that it might just as well go all the way. A few years ago at the Public Theater, Wolfe made a lovely, sensual Caribbean mess out of Brecht's *The Caucasian Chalk Circle,* a scattershot entertainment that never enlightened but was intoxicating fun to watch until the awful Azdak came on, proceeding to be weighty and witless. At the time, it looked like Wolfe's bad luck with a not-so-good actor. With *Angels* in mind, however, it looks like Wolfe's revenge on complication and intelligence.

Poor T.K., caught now in the national theme he's too astute to suffer gladly: the success that dislodges good work from its resolute rage so that a huge public might see it as a user-friendly temper tantrum. It's tiring to repeat Steven Marcus's captivating phrase from years ago—"In America, nothing fails like success"—but from one era to another, it's likely to rear itself again as the most succinct, if not the best, explanation. *Angels* is inescapably the newest case in point, moving from the usual fifteen minutes of famous workshops and readings where, if history is witness, it might have quickly reached the usual oblivion, to a groundswell of attention that followed hard upon Declan Donnellan's production last year at Britain's National Theatre. Suddenly it became flavor-of-the-year, just in time to attract the attention of all those producers—Off Broadway, regional, and Broadway—who had let it slip away while mounting their clone-seasons: *Oleanna-Glen-Seagull Meets the Baltimore Waltzing at Lughnasa.* At last, went the newly coined, quickly conventional wisdom, a serious play both funny and—oh those words tripping off the press release again—relevant, meaningful, haunting, about something, desperately moving, movingly filled with meaning about the most desperate tragedy of our time, short of Bosnia and Somalia, of course.

Not to be outdone by flacks, the dutiful army of reviewers has checked in by now with their own hyperbolic yelps, led by Warwick the Kingmaker, Frank Rich of the *New York Times,* forsaking his available dash and gift for the fluent, colorful line in favor of hard sell—"the most thrilling American play in years." And what a relief that must be for the thirteen Broadway producers, already high on what one of them, shouting to the rehearsing company, referred to as "our Pulitzer Prize." (The exact quote: "We did it! We won the Pulitzer!") Maybe Kushner feels a flashing moment of pain at his evident loss of ownership, but why should any American playwright begrudge his own hard-won fifteen minutes on the yellow-brick road to movie contracts and half-ownership of Chemical Bank? Somebody has to be one of the Chosen, every few years at least, though it can't be easy to recall the last twenty years of Tennessee Williams, banished from Broadway and hounded as a failure, the curse of Marcus striking again.

The worst of it for Kushner is that he surely doesn't need Warwick to tell him he's good, though with the system what it is, he's not likely to be king without an official crowner. So once Rich's review was dispatched from London, the rest fell into place like all those dominoes that used to strike terror into the American imperium, still another reminder that in late-century America battles are often won while wars are always lost. To be fair, Kushner's options were not enviable, however well he might reason from the evidence of his own play, in which similar tensions between heroism and sellout loom over every decisive encounter. As James Joyce once put it, surely not imagining American theater's distorting mirror yet nonetheless aware of any artist's essential loneliness, "The artist, like the God of creation, remains within or behind or beyond or above his handiwork, invisible, refined out of existence, indifferent, paring his fingernails."

Gnawing is more like it for the American playwright, likely to lose something along the way, whether remaining semivisible or dubiously indifferent. In New York, at least, he has to know that Broadway has no recent record of playing host to delicately poised new work, having long ago arranged matters so that two thousand years of dramatic literature would intrude only on those rare occasions when subsidized imports (the Royal Shakespeare Company's *All's Well That Ends Well*) or a movie star's periodic need to confirm his out-of-practice pedigree (Dustin Hoffman's Shylock) would act as what merchants used to call "loss-leaders": profitless merchandise meant to lure customers back for more conventional goods. Otherwise, only partisans lifting themselves on billowing clouds of denial can have missed the plainly visible signs: producers now are faceless conglomerates, leveraging the various sellouts over which they preside in order to meet their not-so-original perception that the public can be seduced for an instant from the tube only by offering what the tube does all the time, usually more efficiently. And what an irony lies there for collectors, the moguls battering the public into submission by claiming they know what is wanted while viewers sink deeper into sofas, meekly letting the laugh track inform them that they're happy.

Enter George C. Wolfe, Warwick's truly Chosen One, hired by the New York Shakespeare Festival to direct that *Chalk Circle* extravaganza, ready in the wings, as it finally turned out, to replace JoAnne Akalaitis at the NYSF after Warwick's ceaseless shrieks for her head, just as he was miraculously in place when all previous directors of *Angels*—Donnellan, David Esbjornson, and Oskar Eustis—were out of the picture for one reason or another. Now, let's try fairness again and concede that some of those reasons could be sound, especially for Kushner. Unlike me, he might not have been mightily impressed by Donnellan's London production, clearly conceived for the small, black-box Cottlesloe Theatre, furniture rolled on and off by actors to the bare stage backed by the largest American flag ever seen, through which the Angel crashed in *Millennium*'s final moment. (Still another one for irony collectors: the Broadway flying machine, no doubt a technological improvement over the Peter Pan machines that used to work well enough, was evidently so far ahead of the mere mortals charged to run it that the opening had to be delayed for a week.) Esbjornson, who had directed a San Francisco workshop production, was never really a New York contender, and despite John Lahr's insistence in the *New Yorker* that Eustis, in Los Angeles, had directed a better production than Donnellan's, the pressure was already on for Kushner to scrap both designer and director for the Broadway sweepstakes, thus inadvertently declaring that New York can have only one Warwick and it ain't going to be Lahr, no matter how hard the new *New Yorker* tries to move to the head of the chattering class.

Oh dear, what a thickening of plots, enough to nourish entire armies of conspiracy theorists. But wouldn't it be better to try fairness again? Somebody may have reminded Kushner of how Frank Rich hollered "Hallelujah" when Caryl Churchill's *Serious Money* played in London and opened later at the Public, leading Joseph Papp to move it to Broadway in the reasonable expectation that Warwick would come through again. Unaccountably, it was not to be: turnabout in reviewing is never fair play, but the *Times* enjoys immunity, so if Warwick entertains a second thought, who can ask for anything more? You win some, you lose some, thus runs the world away, as the man said while not killing the Kingmaking King in Elsinore.

So what's a playwright to do?

Let's track this rueful morality play more carefully, at last. In April 1993 Kushner permitted his friend Michael Mayer to direct third-year students from the Graduate Acting Program of New York University in *Perestroika,* part 2 of *Angels.* In "A Letter from the Playwright," published in the program, he tells us that he had hoped originally to use the NYU production "to try out rewrites" for the projected Broadway production in October. Before playing in the November 1992 Mark Taper Forum production, *Perestroika* had been a five-act play, "twice its current length." With admirable candor, however, Kushner reports that rewriting time eluded him as the Broadway production of *Millennium* became more consuming than he could have guessed. "I've been crazed with anxiety and distracted to the point of madness," he writes, "and so we've decided to go with the L.A. version intact, warts and all."

No need to search for subtext here: Kushner lost months of rewriting time not only by submitting to interviews coast to coast, but by giving himself over to the full play of hysteria common to all Broadway productions, thirteen instant experts fussily protecting their investors' cash flow while still another director—Wolfe—plots new blocking for many of the same actors who had evidently negotiated their roles with some effectiveness for Eustis in November. Meanwhile, Robin Wagner was rigging swiveling panels, automated platforms sliding on with set-piece furnishings, sometimes decorated with pastel backdrops and huge wafts of smoke; add to this that humongous musical score, including a snatch of

Montserrat Caballé's *Norma* for anyone in need of a familiar reference point, such as a Terrence McNally play, and it's easy to see why Kushner might be crazed. Just as well, too, since Mayer's diamond-clear production may be the last time he'll have a chance to recall the virtues in plain speaking; just as Donnellan honored Kushner with bull's-eye simplicity in London's *Millennium,* so did Mayer in NYU's *Perestroika.* No longer within, behind, beyond, or above his handiwork, Kushner was deeply immersed in the handiwork—and mischief—of all the others. One mercy for him, anyway, is that neither Wolfe nor the producers pressed him the way Elia Kazan once pressed Tennessee Williams to put Big Daddy into the third act of *Cat on a Hot Tin Roof.* Appearances notwithstanding, Broadway no longer demands wholesale textual changes, or so it seems from this example; instead, these co-conspirators merely rearrange tonalities, emphasis, balances, and meaning: loudness and sentimentality are in, politics and sex are out.

Now: my own subtext should be clear enough. Try as I'd like to keep up the fairness game, I'm not positioned to offer anything but comparisons, some of them invidious, which can hardly come as a surprise. If I had to guess, I'd say that if a review of Bach's *B-Minor Mass* in 1749 declared that it was "the most thrilling German Mass in years," I might have turned from devout Lutheran to confirmed doubter. Luckily for Saxons at the time, and surely for the diligent, unexpectant Kapellmeister himself, it was only when the *Credo* was performed in 1786 that some loopy Hamburg critic fell from his pew to write that it "was one of the most excellent pieces of music ever heard," high praise, indeed, and not a moment too soon. Hyperbole on behalf of Bach was no more common than performances almost a century later, and then the first shout came from the Zurich music publisher Hans Georg Nägeli that "for such things we have indeed a small public." Not for want of trying: Nägeli was surely right and sober in 1818 when he called the *B-Minor Mass* "the greatest musical work of art of all times and nations," though I hate to think of how this claim might have affected Beethoven and Schubert, then pursuing their trade without prizes, without much praise—and with not many performances for that matter.

It was my good fortune, then, to come upon *Millennium* in the spirit of a passerby slipping into a Leipzig church long before Nägeli had launched his lavender prose. More to the point, I saw it during a long London weekend featuring Paul Scofield's baleful, basset-hound Shotover and Vanessa Redgrave's delirious, flying-saucer Hesione in Shaw's certifiably masterful *Heartbreak House.* I was entitled to guess that, whatever the obvious merits of Jonson's *The Alchemist,* Pinter's *The Caretaker,* or Kushner's *Millennium Approaches,* no performance could match Trevor Nunn's production in the full grip and majesty of Shaw's appalled vision of the modern world's final blast. Nor—or so I allowed myself to think—would anyone dare to try.

But you know the rest: I had not reckoned with young Kushner, wrestling, like the aging Shaw, with his own version of apocalypse, undaunted by both history and the history of playwriting, so intensely involved in contapuntal narrative and what, at first glance, appears to be a sweeping command of Swiftian irony joined to an unyielding Jacobean anguish. As much as anything, I added *Angels* to my short list out of curiosity about an American play gaining its early renown in London, much like Albee's *The Zoo Story* in Berlin more than thirty years ago. Furthermore, as a card-carrying skeptic when American vowels trip not-so-lightly off British tongues, I was entertaining the complacent notion that the actors would be resorting to broad rasps masquerading as A-murkin speech.

By the fourth scene of *Millennium,* in which Louis Ironson and his lover Prior Walter chat about the funeral of Louis's grandmother and their missing cat, both discussions emerging quickly as metaphor rather than small talk, it was clear that Kushner's gifts are at once novelistic and theatrical: not for him the niggling domestic quarrel or joking insult; instead, he races over a psycho-political landscape with the laser beam that has already eluded Bill Clinton, juggling a half-dozen tales daringly into an epic horror story about gays, Jews, Mormons, right-wing power nuts, endemic American racism, abandoned women, fiction truer than fact meeting documentary fact (Roy Cohn) overwhelmed by lies and self-deception—all of them converging on the most abandoned adoration of theater doing what it does like no other written form, density shining out of translucent vision.

The British actors, too, were another surprise, Henry Goodman's Roy Cohn having transformed Whitechapel into Flatbush, the others mostly in charge of an unself-conscious, never-illustrated idiom, Salt Lake City or New York, that was usually graceful, proportioned, and never arch or outlandish. Best of all was Marcus D'Amico's Louis, the young Jew (at last!) as hunk, light years away from Woody-Dustin nerdhood, the best and the brightest without a doubt, but no more in sight of leadership or sainthood than any other hero manqué. D'Amico is noble in carriage and demeanor while retaining the fragrant intensity of the self-appointed victim looking eagerly over his shoulder for his next ravisher. Louis can't bear responsibility for another's pain, yet D'Amico gives him the intelligent presence of Hamlet, the lightning wit of Mercutio, and the spluttering fury of Hotspur. With D'Amico, that peculiar achievement of actors at their best begins to take over, lifting the play from our customary expectations about sympathy into a realm where reality can have full sway: Louis is a god who behaves like a shit.

It was in New York, however, that I began to understand the full measure of D'Amico's—yes, and Donnellan's—success with Kushner's precarious balancing act. For one thing, George C. Wolfe turns every scene into a chorus line of quips and demonstrations. Ron Leibman's Roy Cohn is encouraged to take toothsome bites out of the moving scenery, literally hijacking attention from the central miseries in the American century in order to make claims on a raucous display of sympathy for the biggest shit of them all. Here, indeed, is the rasp and unfocused energy I feared from the British, not just a matter of caricatured accent or cartoon violence but an unmannerly display of antic disposition gone haywire, selfish, and stupid. Worse, it's highway robbery of Louis's centrality— Louis, the other Jew, the one who doesn't give a damn about clout or power, the talented, princely intelligence whose unspoken text is that he could be the lawyer that Cohn has become, but some miserable doubt survives that prevents him from pursuing ambition of any kind. Instead, he works as a word processor in the court system, nowhere to go but down into the interior of his constantly examined life. Broadway's Joe Mantello makes an honorable accounting of Louis, the embittered clerk, but he's not part of a production that seeks any further news from the text.

On the contrary, his is a dutiful, on-the-line version of Louis being merely disloyal, unfaithful: a cowardly kitten rather than a lion in heat.

But, as I've come to realize after NYU's *Perestroika,* Louis's mysterious reticence, his incapacity to seize feeling from reason, his refusal to dwell in the house of his instinctive wisdom, is Kushner's stalwart unhappiness, too. The play's ambitious reach is the mirror image of Louis's retreats. Like so many in the audience of *Millennium,* whether in England or America, I had every reason to guess that the Angel's arrival in front of Prior's sickbed was the signal of his imminent departure, death at last having dominion over the simplest and saddest of characters. "The Great Work begins," she declares, only to reveal in the next play that it's beginning more for Prior than for the others. To my astonishment, then, *Angels* may be an AIDS play after all, with Wolfe heading for the slobbering jugular because he knows that current events are better box office than Louis's cosmic battles and failures, most especially current events that dwell on effect rather than cause.

The kicker here is that if Kushner wished merely to be current, he would have to be more inclusive, offering a rainbow coalition of supershits and sappy saints—more WASPs, surely more fundamentalists, one real lesbian at least, a Native American to go with the Eskimo who passes through the Mormon wife's fantasy, and no doubt some country-western twangers, Hispanics, CEOs, students, seniors, and maybe even a token president or Supreme Court justice or car salesman, real estate agent, talk-show host, or perhaps David Schine, the forgotten man in the real Roy Cohn saga. That Kushner is selective is a sign of a practical dramatist, not given to pageant playwriting, wholly committed to the power of image, metaphor, and resonance. Then, too, if he had wanted to write an exclusively gay or AIDS play, his models could run the gamut from those early Gore Vidal and James Baldwin novels in which the horrified gay man was on a long suicide trajectory, to *Boys in the Band'*s self-laceration, *As Is'*s romantic grief, or *The Normal Heart'*s rage against gay trimmers and closeted politicians—in short, a play identifying itself with pioneer clichés and journalistic agitation.

Millennium, however, is its own model, even if *Perestroika*—and Wolfe —are jerking it back to more familiar territory. Kushner, if I may try my own shortcut, is stalking big game in country already charted by those distinctly un-American types, Jean Genet and Michel Foucault, acknowledging the extravagant sexiness of the hunt, the famished need to fill oneself up with defiance and experiment. True, Louis is only a beginner, not likely to get more than a C in Foucault 101, but he's on the edge of always testing the unthinkable, which, like it or not, is how gays can make meaning out of a universe that forbids choice. In Central Park he finds momentary adventure with a leather-clone who can't take him home because he lives with his parents. Kushner pushes swiftly past this irresistibly funny reversal into the briefest erotic encounter. (*Stage direction:* They begin to fuck.) Louis has sought both sex and humiliation, even surrendering to the possibility that the rubber has broken. But the ultimate disgrace comes after the man pulls out, Louis getting slapped for sending his "best to Mom and Dad."

"It was a joke," he says, left only with hapless truth and forlorn grace. Kushner's mastery here is complete; time could scarcely be more compressed, tension more breathless, danger more severely linked to sex itself as the most contingent symbol available. Even more, perhaps, this is Kushner's encounter with every kind of limit, even including what can be shown and dramatized, not least to an audience of straight men, especially, unwilling to look at men holding hands in public. If this is a dare, however, it's not one that escapes Wolfe's soft touch: where Donnellan gave the fuck its own expansive time in what amounted to an act of unforgiving presence, Wolfe throws a literal spotlight over Louis's agonized face as he jolts up from the first thrust. Louis admits he can't relax; Wolfe is admitting he has to relax all those tight-asses out there so ready to be disgusted by what they're unwilling to know. This is a spotlight on gay clichés disrupting a play fighting to be gay in ways undreamt of in old theologies, gay or straight.

The signals, are, however, that Kushner's most challengingly dangerous instincts are losing the fight. What we know now is that Louis, like the rest of us, had greatly exaggerated Prior's death. Kushner eventually lets the ghost of Ethel Rosenberg say *Kaddish* with Louis over Roy Cohn's corpse, but the joke is on both of them because Cohn, too, refuses to die, at least for a moment. As in *Millennium,* the other stories keep colliding with one another: Roy Cohn's protégé, Joe, the Mormon abandoner of his wife, has become Louis's lover and a literal gay-basher, his mother abandons Salt Lake City, soon finding orgasmic ecstasy with the Angel, and Louis (well, the actor playing Louis) turns into his dead grandmother playing cards in a heaven that sounds like the old Grand Concourse. And, if you're still following me and can credit what I'm recounting, the suffering survivors end up on a Central Park bench proclaiming that Hope, if not the thing with feathers, is at least a glimmering on the otherwise bloodied horizon. In short, Kushner, for all his prodigal anger, enjoys seven hours of first-rate storytelling that fizzles into a short commercial message telling couch potatoes what they always clamor to know.

Have I reason to be disappointed? You bet I have. Not merely because Kushner is a dramatic poet settling for less, but because he hasn't given Louis the full sway of his own tragical-comical-historical imagination. Instead, he punishes him with a more punishing affair while rewarding Cohn with a sardonic last laugh (very funny, indeed, and Kushner should have stopped right there) followed by the dignified death no AIDS victim ever enjoys. But if it's only natural to be enthralled, as Milton was, by the powerful lure of an omnivorous devil, it's not necessarily the only goal for an energetic playwright, especially one who has found a protagonist capable—as D'Amico revealed—of living in the full, consequential glare of his own lighthouse intelligence.

Suddenly, it looks as if Louis, on a course with destiny, has been thwarted by his playwright into a course with triviality. Think of what would have happened if Peer Gynt had been shoved into his own play's sideshows, the onion never peeled and his fate allied to Oswald's in *Ghosts,* leading everybody to conclude that the play is really about a disease that dare—or dare not—speak its name. This transparent absurdity is surely no more Kushner's subject than syphilis was Ibsen's. Yet with Wolfe ferreting out the sideshows—and who can wholly blame him for leaping at the bait?—Kushner's dark rendezvous with stratospheric gods slips into footlight follies.

You'd be right to surmise by now that I've begun to jam all these experiences into one giant Kushnerian stewpot, mixing Donnellan's seasoning with Wolfe's heavy dousing of sugar and honey, unable to rescue the true wonders of *Millennium* from the still-rewritable detours in *Perestroika*. It's Louis, of course, with his dynamo mouth and tortured sin-tax, who keeps on insisting on his right to a play of his own. The life at stake here is the retreating conscience of the nation, not only a gay man claiming space while rightly screaming from the rooftops that it's about time, but a life grappling with loss even before it happens, unable to cruise neatly and completely past the murmuring adjudicators within his heart. God spare him from the slaphappy claims of those, including myself, who love him too uncritically and more than he can ever know.

(1993)

Shakespeare and the Brits

British Theater: The Fight Against Situational Chat

London. A week spent in London's theaters is a week spent in the company of words. As a consequence, it is also a week spent in the company of too many actors who rely upon a definition of acting as an interpretive art occurring somewhere between the throat and tongue. Only the great British actors—and fortunately, many of them are currently at work at the National Theatre (NT), the Royal Shakespeare Company (RSC), and in the West End—have been able to avoid total captivity to the voice.

John Gielgud is an acknowledged master of words, who nonetheless fills the stage with personal texture. Several years ago, he confessed, "When I listen to my old recordings, they sound to me very voice-conscious, and I'm rather ashamed to think that I was so contented with that kind of acting." Sensitivity to the problem is not uncommon among other English theater artists. Before opening the fan-shaped, thrust-stage, raked-seat Olivier Theatre in the NT complex, its director, Peter Hall, expressed his wish that the space itself would change "the way we act, the way we design," perhaps giving the actor "a greater awareness of the body rather than the head...a more physical approach to acting." And a young playwright-actor-director, Steven Berkoff, whose London Theatre Group performed as guests at the National during the past summer, described his search for material in terms quite definitely opposed to the theater he has known in England: too many plays that are "simply a mass of dialogue, with no resonances of inner life, where the actors hurled situational chat at each other."

As director of the NT, Hall stands quite naturally at the center of the problem. His position cannot be anything but uncomfortable. British playwriting, good and bad, is inescapably verbal. The British have given us our best playwright, of course, and in this century dozens of extraordinary actors. But they have never offered a great teacher: no Stanislavsky or Vakhtangov, no Brecht, no Grotowski, no Michael Chekhov or Stella Adler. To the director of a major theater, such as the NT, falls the teacherly responsibility not only to the public in terms of repertoire but also to his actors. Like it or not, British theater will feel the Hall-mark for generations to come. On the one side, he will push for that awareness of the body to which he referred. On the other, he will be working with a body of plays that can suffocate the actor in situational chat.

For the moment, all English theaters are running full steam ahead on chat. Striking a balance between the body and soul of experience and the verbal expression of it is a mystery still unsolved by most British directors and actors, though the exceptions are striking and often more gratifying in England than anywhere else. There is not one *place,* unfortunately, where the exceptions might be found: to see Gielgud, for example, it's necessary to brave an astoundedly shapeless production by John Schlesinger of *Julius Caesar* at the NT; to see Ralph Richardson, there's only the fundamentally depressing West End performance of still another numbing amble with crusty upper classes by William Douglas Home, this one called *The Kingfisher.* Richardson in Home is better than Richardson retired, but it is a pity that London so often offers vintage champagne as if it were bottled beer.

One reason may be that a theater ruled by the casual pragmatism of the marketplace will always be a theater without passionate identity and a clear performing profile. Joan Littlewood's Theatre Workshop had both for many years, but she—and it—are not working anymore. It *is* a strange National Theatre that can calmly hire Schlesinger to do Shakespeare while Littlewood sits in a French village, probably too hurt to ask for the dubious honor of an invitation. Otherwise, Peter Hall's management of the NT uses its new home on the banks of the Thames as richly—and pragmatically—as anyone might imagine: all three theaters are humming with activity, while the lobbies and squares outside have so many pre-performance concerts and exhibitions that for a dizzying moment one almost believes that the Thames has become the Mediterranean. Unlike the rest of England, the building never seems to sleep, and it is relentlessly, almost self-consciously, populist in spirit. Understandably, perhaps, it is a theater devoted more to the undefined crowds who buy its tickets than it is to any singular idea of what theater might be as an art.

Laurence Olivier was Hall's predecessor as director of the NT when it was performing a similarly extensive repertory in close quarters at the Old Vic. He is a difficult act to follow, even for a director such as Peter Hall, who had so much success earlier as director of the Royal Shakespeare Company. The new building is not really a solution, anyway. Any new theater building—as we have learned at Lincoln Center and in other performing arts complexes all over the country—can only bring new problems, such as maintenance, while setting patterns for production that might well stand in the way of the best artistic choices. Hall was painfully aware of this when he observed in a 1975 interview that by 1967, "the present generation of radicals of the theater decided they didn't want the National Theatre after all." Nor, indeed, did they show much interest in or support for Joan Littlewood.

The profile of the NT under Olivier was plain enough: Olivier chose plays for actors, particularly for the Big Ones, like himself. Hall's inclination, on the other hand, is to choose plays that make Big Statements in an avalanche of words. Most of the plays he is currently choosing to produce are grandly impersonal. They draw their energy from public forums, as if life could be viewed mainly as a rehearsal for a House of Commons debate. *Julius Caesar* is the most obvious example of such a play, with Brutus showing only the most tentative reach toward a complex interior life. But plays coming from all directions, different periods, and opposing genres all seem to assume a similar, stentorian stance.

Ben Jonson's *Volpone,* directed by Peter Hall himself with minimum repose and maximum rhetorical surge, was as funny as it is ever likely to be because of Paul Scofield's ready, bluff, deadpan dignity in the title role. Scofield has a marvelously paranoid style of acting, stealing around the dialogue as if he isn't quite sure that some alien word won't pop out from behind another to slug him. He wrestles with words, showing them sounds they never thought they could make. His confident speed and precision are matched by Paul Rogers, as Voltore, one of the best ensemble actors in the world, always a bit querulous about the amazing events threatening to overwhelm him, but always clear and personal in the images he selects. Lady Would-be is Elizabeth Sprigge, totally absorbed by her own many obsessions and daring in the windblown way she presents them. John Bury's design puts Volpone's bed and courtroom on tracks while flapping panels from one side to the other in order to keep the production marching to the insistent rhythms set by Hall. It is no surprise that all the actors cannot define themselves as clearly as Scofield, Rogers, and Sprigge manage to do: impersonality follows so easily from Hall's driving, declarative thrust. In the end, Jonson's embittered, superbly unreasonable comedy looks much like the other plays in the NT's repertory—a weighty, moral argument more interested in its rhetoric than in the people behind it.

Harley Granville-Barker's *The Madras House,* written in 1910, is better suited to this task. For those interested in the genre, it is a remarkable rediscovery. Prescient about both the lure of women's liberation and the Middle East, it is shaped like a Bruckner symphony that has been invaded by a Rossini gremlin. The production at the NT by William Gaskill is immaculately detailed, presenting the stately wit of Barker in rooms thoroughly furnished with Persian carpets and late-Victorian chairs and tables. It is clear at once that these are rooms where confrontational discussion is more common than emotional or physical passion. That is what some of the women don't like. For the men, however, the business of living is the business of business. Except for Constantine Madras, the exiled leader of the clan, who has chosen to be a Mohammedan. His entrance is delayed by Granville-Barker until the third of the four acts. Scofield (again) strolls through the door while an American merchant is talking—and talking. He is casual, unobtrusive, yet bearing an authority that steals attention instantly from the others. It is one of the minor ironies of the occasion that, in the enveloping, voluptuously commanding presence of Paul Scofield, this silent entrance is the most compelling moment in the play.

Another irony is that the most banal play in the NT's current repertoire, Robert Bolt's *State of Revolution,* received from its director, Christopher Morahan, and its actors—particularly Michael Bryant as a demonically incisive Lenin—the most loving and continuously energetic attention. The play carries the Bolsheviks from their Capri exile to the Finland Station, Lenin's acquisition of power, his semi-paralysis, and his aborted frantic decision to have anyone but Stalin succeed him. So long as one remembers that such history plays are always, at their best, charming fantasies, the play can be enjoyed unseriously for its skill in telling lies with so much assurance. As long ago as 1839, Friedrich Hebbel wrote in his *Journals* that "most writers of historical tragedy don't give us historical characters but parodies of them." Bolt writes neither tragedy nor history. His Russians talk like Oxford professors because his prose is locked irretrievably into the clipped rhythms of cultivated Englishmen: Gorky accusing Lenin of being "possessed by vanity and crude excitement," or Lenin announcing that "history is devilishly hard." Ralph Koltai's splendidly hard and mobile design helps Morahan drive the play in a swift, forward motion. The headlong rush of the prose is arrested only by the sharp, angular performing wit of the actors. They possess a sensitivity to pause and breath that is otherwise missing too often in the NT's productions.

The NT is not, of course, the only culprit. A production of Ibsen's *Hedda Gabler* in the West End, directed by Keith Hack at a pace that would frighten horses and in a style more suitable to the prowling melodramatic antics of Frankenstein's Monster, is still another example of a production more responsive to what the characters say about themselves than to what they are. There is only one idea visible: the portrait of Hedda's dead father, General Gabler, is spotlighted on occasion, no doubt to suggest that his spirit lives in Hedda. Which is hardly news. Meanwhile, the actors fret, frown, and drape themselves around the heavy furniture as if they were inmates playacting in order to keep out of trouble rather than inhabitants of Ibsen's ambiguously tender, precariously balanced, and—above all—highly intelligent world. The production is fashioned with spectral lights, the sounds of pigeons offstage, and a real oven for the burning of Lövborg's manuscript—all accompanied by a heaving style of performance that would look outsize in the trashiest silent film.

Ibsen always deserves better, and at the RSC's London headquarters a first preview of his rarely performed *Pillars of the Community* (1877), directed thoughtfully by John Barton in a simple, spacious, and useful design by Michael Annals, revealed the master playbuilder in his most expansive, if moderately confusing, mood. Teapot Dome and Watergate have made Ibsen's contemplation of corrupt leaders appear more antique than one might have expected. The play threads its way laboriously through bewildering plot developments that make sense only if you listen dutifully in the first act to the sewing circle of upright ladies who are there really to provide information about what happened years before. In that sense, it is apprentice work; and in the sense that we know that the corrupt counsel, Karsten Bernick, would probably be just as unrepentant as Nixon, the play can be faulted for naïveté. Its sophistication lies else-where—in its broad ambition, its majestic sweep, and its frequent pauses for soft, ruminative, awkwardly gentle encounters. The consul's sister, Martha, has the best of such moments, in a confessional scene that looks forward to Chekhov. It is played by Paola Dionisotti with a quiet inten-sity and spiritual glow that proves once again that English actors don't have to talk fast and loud in order to be gripping or real.

Steven Berkoff's *East,* a brilliantly impressionistic piece for five immensely physical yet verbally adept actors, was only a guest in the house of Peter Hall. Yet in the small bear pit Cottesloe Theatre of the NT, it had the urgency, raciness, and authentic modern grip that isn't found often in London's theaters, National or otherwise. Berkoff may be fighting against situational chat, but he isn't denouncing language. His text is slangy but eloquent in its brash mix of Cockney blather and Shakespearean allusion. There is the "Longing Speech" of the girl, beginning sweetly with a mocking plea: "I for once would like to be a fella, unwholesome both in deed and word and lounge around one leg cocked up and car keys tin-kling on my pinky." The images keep threatening to cancel each other, simply because they are so extravagant, so lush and demanding: "cave mouths"..."scrubber-slag-head"..."knife-worn splatter and invective splurge." But since they are placed so firmly within a performing frame that never lets the actors lounge their way lazily from one word to the next, the work acquires a listenability that usually eludes plays that are merely intoned reverently and acted without physical presence.

The British are too quick to banish plays like Berkoff's to what they condescendingly call "the fringe." The Establishment center is a bit of a snob. There must be other Berkoffs in the wings, just as there are actors in the center who could perform in their plays, given a chance. The great, superbly refined stars of British theater continue to be its most reli-able glory. But they need roles, more personal plays, and more devel-oped, cooperative ensembles.

When Peter Hall refers to the "point of command" that he would like to see on the stage of the NT's Olivier Theater, I'm afraid he may really mean words, words, and more words. He should look to his stars, as he did when casting John Gielgud as Julius Caesar, shifting the stress of the play back to where it probably belongs—with Caesar as the inspiration for all the actors, both before and after the assassination. One's heart sinks, of course, realizing that Gielgud's voice will be silenced, leaving the others to drone on. His instrumental elegance has obscured the fact that he listens as well as he speaks. When the others are blasting their lungs, his lips are already forming eloquent answers, hurling themselves into apostrophes, question marks, and lemon-soaked periods. When he is insecure— as he is in the role of Sir Politick Would-be in *Volpone*—he never fakes security with a mouthed, shouted audibility. If only most of the younger actors would really listen to him and watch him listening. They will need the help of plays that will discourage their chatter while wrenching them into occasional silence. Which means that Peter Hall might consider some new point of command.

(Summer 1977)

Neocolonial Puns and Games

Nicholas Nickleby's charms notwithstanding, let us at last bury the dumb, craven idea that British theater is the best in the world. For a start, there is no best, only the good emerging in one country or another—Germany at present—when aspirations and subsidy manage to coincide for a passing moment. Americans envy British theater people largely because we are impressed by actors curling tongues around consonants, playwrights supplying them with more consonants and story in one play than we are likely to find in a hundred plays, and directors who could unsnarl traffic on the Long Island Expressway. We like them for being verbal and orderly, which is no reason for charging them with genius.

What they are is clever, making imitation look new and resourcefulness look like invention. An entire generation is now making a living from the works of the past—not merely the classics but the ways in which plays were put together by all those directors named Peter during the floridly experimental 1950s and 1960s. *Nicholas Nickleby* was not my first marathon day in the theater: that was Peter Hall and John Barton's *The Wars of the Roses*. A bold merging of Shakespeare's *Henry VI* trilogy and *Richard III*, it was nine and a half hours of ravishing engagement in politics and warfare, a project made not only to test endurance and our capacity to check our brains with our coats, but designed and executed to illuminate the folly of power and the lunacy of war. As one London critic said to me, today everything manages to be long at the National Theatre. Which means that much of the purpose has been left behind with the Peters while much of the muchness seems here to stay.

Of course, this isn't entirely fair. Peter Hall is still a leading figure, more visible as an NT administrator than as a director. Meanwhile, Peter Brook is in Paris pursuing mystery and wonder, a near-genius who haunts the young with his concentration and dark concerns. They are right to be haunted, since so much of their work reveals only frivolity and physical energy: British theater today seems to be directed by gymnastic instructors who find delight in tossing words on trampolines.

Michael Bogdanov, one of ten associate directors of the NT, is momentarily notorious as part-defendant in the unbelievable suit against the National for presenting simulated buggery in *The Romans in Britain*, still another marathon. If only his work with Molière's *Le Malade imaginaire* (called *The Hypochondriac*) and Calderón's *The Mayor of Zalamea* was stimulating enough to be offensive, whether legally or not; what hurts is that it is so tame, so insular and unidiomatic. Bogdanov's ideas have that neutrality common to much art today: they could apply to anything, they could belong to any old play.

Not that he doesn't talk in a radical idiom. "I can see no reason to involve myself in a medium as powerful as theater," he said in a recent interview, "unless I can make it help people formulate ideas for a change." He is seeking Molière the "outcast," the "rough man of theater, battling against the capitalist, exploitative, mercenary forces." Fighting words, true, but not riddled with conviction in his production. Instead, Bogdanov stages a uniquely unfunny Molière in which actors who can't sing, dance, or juggle are made to sing, dance, and juggle. Daniel Massey plays a character named Argan, though it is clear that his chopped phrasing and bleated, upward inflections are really about a character named Laurence Olivier.

The Calderón play moves in a similar limbo, with Massey offering the plummy, posh Olivier this time, speaking as if he had a querulous potato in his mouth. Bogdanov trots out his raucous processionals, standing a marvelous comic-tragedy on the shoals of High Fashion directing. His Spanish peasants might just as well have drifted from his French commedia: the raped peasant daughter of the protagonist seems to be at a Swiss finishing school where nasty boys put bugs in her bed. She's been violated by Givenchy, not by experience, just as Bogdanov's social conscience seems to have stumbled unwittingly into the Spain of Vincent Minelli's *The Pirate;* Judy Garland and Gene Kelly are missing, of course, and that's only part of the problem.

The other part, and probably the larger, is that the National is enthralled by a weird combination of verbal fireworks and elaborately staged dumb shows. Every production begins with an Overture, as if to soothe the nerves of Verdi and Wagner freaks who don't know how they have managed to stray into a space where thinking might be allowed. They needn't worry, however, since directors and adapters have taken such care to make every play look and sound alike.

Tom Stoppard has plundered that popular source, Johann Nestroy's *Einen Jux will er sich machen* (the progenitor of Thornton Wilder's Dolly), calling it *On the Razzle,* and using it as a structure he can decorate with puns and other forms of verbal double take. At the National, however, much of the pleasure disappears seamlessly into the stream of National play experience: Stoppard's Nestroy makes jokes out of German ("the wurst is yet to come") while Adrian Mitchell's Calderón sounds no less modern and localized ("Let's retreat, hopeful that we may meet...some meat") and Alan Drury's Molière is coy about French. ("Here's a sample," says someone about urine, to which the doctor replies, "Oui, oui, oui.") None of this should be surprising in a theater so obsessed with getting its own surfaces polished while making a mess of national and individual difference.

While it can be fun to see plays with more than two or three characters, or to hear words honored in the observance, it's not so much fun to see actors and plays that have been mashed through the same national psychic machine. All plays are not cushioned and restful, but you'd never know it here. Equally, all peasants don't come from Yorkshire, and all classy people don't have to sound like trainees for the BBC: England lost its Empire, so its theater people—taking up the slack as usual—seem to be colonizing other nations' plays. Despite what Stoppard, Mitchell, and Drury may be trying to contrive, it isn't likely that Vienna, Madrid, and Paris will agree that their favorite playwrights were British all along.

(December 1981)

Uneasy Lie the Crowns

Acting may be the least accountable of the performing arts because so little of the best is ever really seen. Imagine audiences at the opera unable to measure the passing Callas comet against the exquisite Tebaldi mineral, or ballet fiends unaware of Ulanova's Giselle when viewing Fracci's. At the opera or ballet, the past is always sending startling information to the present and the present keeps passing bulletins about the past. But an actor with Callas's power may wear a crown at home while remaining obscure abroad. It is only too easy, therefore, for pretenders to arrive as if they deserved the throne.

Alan Howard, now floridly decorating C. P. Taylor's *Good* (Booth Theatre) with a kind of bad acting that the play's rottenness has probably earned, is only the latest in a group of English actors whose nominal success in England and America seems to depend on the short memory or deprived experience of the audience. Once upon a time and not so long ago, the standards set by Laurence Olivier, John Gielgud, Ralph Richardson, Michael Redgrave, and Alec Guinness were enough to set an American audience tingling with anticipation when younger upstarts such as Paul Scofield or Albert Finney came along. The crowns in those days seemed to be passing securely from one deserving generation to another.

Suddenly, however, another type of actor emerged, adept at borrowing surfaces from great actors while shoving substance aside: there was John Wood offering Gielgud's elegant babble without the wounded soul, Ian McKellen suggesting the rational bleakness of Guinness without the dark despair, and Alan Howard presenting Olivier's machine-gun mouth without any of the lion's pride and kitten's humor. No one among them had learned, or ever knew, that acting is finally what Ralph Richardson once called "a controlled dream."

It isn't clear yet why we are getting the controllers rather than the dreamers. Over the years any seasoned traveler could have reported on the performances of English actors who rarely, if ever, jumped the Atlantic. One of the great favorites in and out of the profession was never a knight at all. Known mainly now for his appearances as Alfred Doolittle in the filmed *Pygmalion,* the late Wilfred Lawson was surely one of the most amazing actors who ever lived, that breed of deep, textured performer perfected by the Moscow Art Theater who makes one realize why Chekhov left Firs to hold the stage at the end of *The Cherry Orchard.* He wasn't what is sometimes patronizingly called a "character actor." Rather he was a character who acted people suddenly allowed to live beyond a playwright's bookish imagination. Unlike the sinewy flyweights sounding one bleated sheep's cry throughout the plays coming from England today, Lawson had a body that inhabited the world and a ravaged voice that seemed to be echoing down the corridors of history.

Lawson offered what all great actors possess—a shock of recognition marked by a presence and weight belonging to nobody else. Among other major English actors who remain virtually unknown on our stages are Peter O'Toole, Michael Hordern, and Dame Peggy Ashcroft; it is difficult to believe that had they been seen here often in past decades, the stars of the Howards and the McKellens could have risen quite so high. The young O'Toole once played Petruchio to Ashcroft's Katerina in *The Taming of the Shrew.* She was 53 at the time, and as the performance moved on, the years kept "sprinkling off her," said O'Toole. Now almost 75, she is finally scheduled to appear in New York next spring for the first time since *Edward, My Son* in 1948, this time in the Royal Shakespeare's *All's Well That Ends Well.*

Hordern, too, just seen on Public Television as a remarkably lucid but diminished Lear, has always been an identifiable presence, more sane, surely, but almost as craggy and quirky as Lawson. In one Stratford season, he played Sir Politick Would-be in *Volpone,* Caliban in *The Tempest,* Menenius Agrippa in *Coriolanus,* and, most wondrous of all, Jaques in *As You Like It*—the latter described by Kenneth Tynan in a manner that, perhaps unfortunately, might also describe his Lear. Hordern, said Tynan, "played him with a marvelous sense of injury, yet beneath the shaggy melancholy you felt a finely tempered mind, drawn still toward wit and beauty...a great performance: rooted in self-disgust, but with a tattered plume of merriment capering always over its head." In England, once, an actor didn't need to be a star to be superb.

With Howard gawking over his neatly arranged spectacles, worn by him as uncomfortably as he wears relationships with other actors, the ground rules seem to have changed. Now, it seems, an actor doesn't have to be superb to be a star. He need only do as Howard does: lope into something like a toilet-crouch for most of the performance while carefully ticking off each querulous glance on the computer that stands in for his imagination. Not much can be at stake with such a noisy actor. He's so busy congratulating himself, he can't spare a moment to have an experience. In Howard's performance, a good man doesn't really slide into Nazism, since he is coming not from a state of mind but from a state of acting. That state, and the world that accepts its dubious credentials, is a lot less than good.

(November 1982)

Richard Unbeckoned

"Gangsters glorified by titles and blank verse." That's how one superb Shakespeare scholar, Northrop Frye, describes the nobles surrounding Richard II. And bloody thugs and monsters they are, even Richard himself, deposed by Bolingbroke for his incompetent kingship but redeemed more than the others by his command of words. Not that he's alone in poetry: this is the strangest of all Shakespeare's plays, the only one written entirely in verse. Frye sees this as Shakespeare's effort to keep "the dueling ritual" unbroken by the usual bawdy or mundane interruptions; even the gardener speaks in couplets. More likely, Frye was right the first time: Shakespeare can't resist giving the nobles a crack at eloquence.

How little they deserve it is aptly illustrated by the murder of the language we're witnessing from our own political gangsters, unlucky enough to speak for themselves, no Shakespeare around to dress their horrific transgressions in gorgeous cadences and lively rhythms. Not for Richard the cringing petulance of Nixon or the Clint Eastwood quotation chanted by Oliver North so often in the Irangate congressional hearings last week—"I'm telling the truth, the good, the bad, and the ugly." Richard's fall guys, Bushy and Bagot (and what a law firm they would make), are "the caterpillars of the commonwealth."

If only Joseph Papp's production of *Richard II* made a stronger case for drama over reality. With so much going for it, especially Richard's solo flights into a musical ozone layer all his own, the play ought to bring the day's news into startling focus, improving on the muddling interpretations and surrenders made by congressmen and media boobies anxious to find good in everyone. Papp's *Richard,* unfortunately, is about little more than processional memory, a long, yawning march through a land of wooden soldiers.

Chief stick is John Bedford-Lloyd's Bolingbroke, whose only claim on the crown must be that he's taller than Peter MacNicol's diminutive Richard. Otherwise, how did he get there, much less on a stage? True, Shakespeare doesn't give the usurper much time for interior reflection, but surely there's more to Bolingbroke than long hair, hulking stance, and gruff tongue. Like so many in the cast, Bedford-Lloyd never raises the stakes by genuine action or reaction.

Banished by Richard, he seems no more moved or indignant than a halfback given an F on his term paper. When Richard says, "how high a pitch his resolution soars," it's impossible to believe that MacNicol has watched him. Similarly, Freda Foh Shen's Queen, shunned at first by Richard and then torn from him, parcels her words in dainty pseudo-English tones like a child learning elocution, a perpetual teenager hurt by a broken date. This is the kind of production where Bolingbroke and the queen can announce the arrival of oncoming characters without showing the slightest sign that they've heard or seen them. Papp's most subtle, if unintended, political comment may be the image he purveys of leaders reading cue cards.

Shakespeare doesn't make it easy to understand the action, most likely because his audience understood the premises implicitly. Even so, it ought to be possible to recognize a major modern issue raised by Frye when he asks, "What kind of law does a lawful king represent who resorts to illegal means of getting money?" or even more tellingly, "who resorts to means that are technically legal, but violate a moral right?" Papp's program note is as wan and unilluminated as his direction, merely referring to the play as "a study in loyalties broken and sides changed." What sides? Loyalties based on what?

Richard's colossal error is tunnel vision, his consistent incapacity to judge the power of his potential enemies. Shakespeare knows his nobles: what really gets them going is property; threaten it, as Richard does, and you might as well kiss your crown good-bye. What lifts the play into a rarefied realm is Richard's extended farewell: unlike today, his resignation becomes his finest hour. Acknowledging Bolingbroke's mighty right, Shakespeare nonetheless gives Richard all the glorious cadenzas, as if to say there's nothing more noble in life than the leaving it. Sly conservative that he is, Shakespeare's advice to leaders would be mass resignation.

Papp's mass confusion reveals none of this, though MacNicol might one day make more sense and poetry than he does here. He listens more imaginatively than he speaks, starting well as a bored executive squatting lazily on his throne, scratching his feet with his scepter. With his high-pitched southern drawl—"Ah do salute you mah hand"—he could be Truman Capote flirting with the public. That he brings so little weight and heft to the long good-byes is only partly his fault: too often, he's working within undefined relationships, never revealing why—for one example—he's drawn to Bushy, Bagot, and company instead of his more powerfully dangerous cousins. It may be that neither Papp nor MacNicol is willing to explore the sexual undertow once examined by such distinguished Richards as Michael Redgrave and John Gielgud. But if not sex, there has to be something palpable and present to enlist such defeatist loyalties.

Gielgud, incidentally, showed immense sympathy for future Richards when he referred to the character's "utter lack of humor and his constant egotism and self-posturing." Yet he saw the role as offering a rare chance to luxuriate in language while "shielding himself, both in words and movement, from the dreaded impact of the unknown circumstances which, Richard feels, are always lying in wait to strike him down." None of that is here.

Edward Sang's Scroop is alone in joining character to precisely heard verse, and Judith Malina brings a completely delightful bounce to her brief appearance as the eager, nagging mother of Richard's slippery best friend, Aumerle. But any production of *Richard II* that can't compete with the rising full moon over Central Park or the occasional bicyclists in the distance has only the most most fragile claim to our attention. Gielgud urges a performance that is "finely orchestrated, melodious, youthful, headlong, violent, and vivid." For that, I'm afraid, turn back to the hearings.

(July 1987)

Et Al, Brute

The good news about Stuart Vaughan's otherwise clunky production of *Julius Caesar* is Al Pacino's fiercely serious, sharply spoken Marc Antony. A small man, almost unrecognizable in the beginning, he merges into the fabric of the play like a prowling beetle, one of those little ones you should beware. His face is a mask, rarely talking for him, the only giveaway his darting, cavernous eyes. Modest to a fault, Antony claims a lack of wit and absence of "utterance." Pacino, however, knows otherwise: husky in his middle register, this Antony can still find a trumpet in his voice when the crowd must be swayed. That tiny frame, fighting for the size he ought to have had, can barely contain his malevolent energy. Pacing up and down the steps where a calmer orator might choose to cover ambition, he's inventing the next ruse as he goes along. He may not be a hero—*the* hero—but, by God, you'd better notice him.

If he were surrounded by equally grainy performances, he'd still stand out. Popular as the play may be in high schools, it needn't be so foursquare and processional. Vaughan punctuates or prefaces each scene with Lee Hoiby's brassy "announcements," using music to cover up the production's sagging momentum. Pleasant as it is to look at the brick and marble surroundings designed seamlessly by Bob Shaw to present a spotless Rome, it takes only a few moments to recall that the play is not meant to be a smooth journey to nowhere: this may be Shakespeare raw, uncertain, not fully in command of what Harley Granville-Barker calls "the drama of inward struggle, triumph and defeat," but surely it's not a weightless, strutting succession of pompous confrontations.

More to the point, even when those senators and conspirators blend into one another, it should still be possible for the play to shine with texture and character. Vaughan's actors look interchangeable—and foolishly, sometimes, they are: Cinna the conspirator and Cinna the poet are played by the same actor, thus making nonsense of the latter's brutal murder by the crowd, who are out to kill anybody by that name and are *not* suffering from mistaken identity. But it's really all those pageboy haircuts, those self-consciously worn togas, that keep getting in the way of the play's dark identity. Many of the actors look as if they'd feel better stripped and on the beach, perhaps calling less attention to their knocking knees.

Apart from Pacino and the splendidly direct, clear-voiced Joan Mac-Intosh as Portia, this is one of those respectable Shakespeares, not without an intelligent moment or two—John McMartin's Caesar making much of the games played with the word "will," or Edward Herrmann's Cassius frequently mixing driven rhetoric and meditative brooding—but looking as if nothing much is at stake most of the time. Martin Sheen's Brutus is a striking disappointment, not only because of his ravaged voice but more because of his withdrawal from the inside track of every scene, as if unwilling to meet Portia's passion on her own terms, or too shy to show his young servant, Lucius, his true tenderness. (Not that he's helped by Vaughan putting Lucius to sleep behind a wall in the first act.) Sheen's Brutus shows no reluctance in stabbing Caesar; all the more strange that he shows so much reluctance in doing anything else—most of all feeling something about Portia's death or his own.

What a wonderful, complicated play it could be, especially with those plain, offhand phrases Shakespeare uses whenever it looks as if decoration is taking over: Cassius's first farewell to Brutus, "Think of the world," and Antony's dazzling, "Passion, I see, is catching." Vaughan stands in the way of what can be heard, but he rarely gives the word its space or time. The play feels cantankerous rather than angry, like a spoiled child impatient with politics instead of a young titan battering the world.

(March 1988)

The Abbey Theatre: Speechless at Last

It's not difficult to guess what the contradictory Yeats would have made of the Abbey Theatre's hemi–semi–demi–modernist production of Tom MacIntyre's *The Great Hunger,* based on an epic poem of Irish rural misery by Patrick Kavanagh (1904–1967). Yeats loved "poetry" in the theater, but by that he meant his own. When O'Casey submitted *The Silver Tassie* to the Abbey, with its expressionist second act plunged between the naturalism of the other acts, and its robust antiwar passions standing so far outside Yeats's dreamy ideas of what theater should do, it didn't take long for Yeats to send his foolish rejection. The *Tassie,* however, looks like taffy next to MacIntyre's experiments with abstracted narrative, minimal language, and maximum gibberish.

The Great Hunger confounds any number of expectations. It's not about the Potato Famine, and it's not about the Irish gift of the gab. Instead, it traces the life of an impoverished rural community hungry for sexual and spiritual life it will never know. Patrick Maguire (Tom Hickey), a beanpole farmer, is tied to a hopelessly fallow land and mother image that won't let him go. Whatever Kavanagh's poem may have been, MacIntyre and the Abbey have "workshopped" it into more than a hundred lines which, so far as they go, don't add much to the ecstatic series of movements, grunts, and sighs that attempt to push the story along.

Under Patrick Mason's patient, often imaginative, direction, the seven Abbey actors tear into their scenes like jazz wizards enthralled by a mysterious spirit. Three young women smear lipstick on their lips in gleeful circular motions. A priest caresses a large statue (the program tells us it's a mother "ikon"), and later Maguire's sister embraces the "mother's" head with her hands and arms while her sweater covers its shoulders. Maguire pumps a leather bellows frantically as if masturbating. When he removes the rope from a sheet over the ikon, he wings it like a lasso. Over and over, he moves his head and body like a chicken furious with its own dumb noises.

For the Abbey, no doubt, all this removal from traditional verbal fuel must seem like revolution. The few real phrases that emerge seem to be like great showers on a parched landscape, even though they don't strive for the flourish or delicacy found in Synge and O'Casey. This is Irish theater laying claim to the century, abjuring what we think it does best. And when MacIntyre speaks, he often resorts to odd inversions: "We mustn't want too much to know."

Placing half-verbal confrontations against the background of songs like "Isle of Capri," or a scratchy recording of Dietrich's "Lili Marlene," is not so daring by now, yet it's easy to see why the Abbey might wish to catch up. Britten's *War Requiem* makes a mighty noise during an Easter procession that would look at home in a Buñuel film, yet by the end the images look tame – not least the predictable sight of a young man standing on the farm gate as if crucified.

Best of all are Maguire and two other men, caps on their heads, swilling pints of Guinness back to back, oohing and ahhing as they rub their backs against one another in that subsexual state of mind such men usually deny. Surprising – and funny too – is the way the actors make three syllables out of the word "whole." Are they dying to get back the symphonic blabbing they do so well? Hickey's Maguire may leave me cold by the end, but it's fun to see him move around the stage like a shadow Clov, shuffling or trotting in spastic steps, reminding the world that the Irish made Beckett before Beckett did. There's rage in this event, unforgiving, wounded by an inheritance that should have killed the creative urge long ago, willing to initiate a freedom that doesn't come easy, unashamed to be tedious, yet charged by an insatiable desire to live.

(March 1988)

Out, Out Loose Canon

Shakespeare deserves a rest, especially if he's to be rescued from English teachers who think him better read than said. Let them have their way for a time so we can argue, confer, and suffer a little while trying to discover how these plays might come alive again in the theater. Surely, pick-up casts, whether on Broadway or at the Public, are the worst kind of answer. If I differ in any way with Michael Feingold's devastatingly fair review of *Macbeth*, it's in his generous tribute to Papp, whose love for Shakespeare has rarely helped him to produce or direct an indispensable Shakespeare performance. There has to be something more than unguided goodwill and cultural pretense.

Certainly, this is not a new problem. When Henry James found Henry Irving's 1875 Macbeth "the acting of a very superior amateur," he was only one of the earliest to recognize that Shakespeare demands more than arbitrary, whimsical choices. James had been astonished by an Italian production of the play where, in the scene after the murder of Duncan, Ernesto Rossi reeled out "red-handed from his crime...to give 'imitations'" of Duncan's terrified grooms. None of Rossi's tricks, he said, "can be called acting Shakespeare." What would he have made of Christopher Plummer in the same scene, emerging with two bloody daggers like a funeral director advising you to choose between pine and walnut coffins?

Lucky James, spared the work of inferior professionals, not forced to see the most chilling scenes in Shakespeare reduced to routine blithering. Plummer is hardly the worst offender this year. He may look like the laziest actor in town, but at least he knows how to delegate rhythms and emphasis, and unlike most of our inexperienced Shakespeareans, he's not afraid—sometimes—to be quiet. Most of his performance, however, fits comfortably into what is rapidly becoming an American tradition of butchering Shakespeare by doing nothing real at all.

Not that the territory should be surrendered wholesale to the British, busily confusing Shakespeare these days with Andrew Lloyd Webber, spectacle and imitation taking the place of ideas and personality. Good performances still happen—Judi Dench's recent Cleopatra at the National, for example—but even then they're within a tediously processional context or against a partner such as Anthony Hopkins, matching Plummer pound for every flaccid pound. The great danger, anyway, is to cast a star with credentials—Glenda Jackson, for one—who knows only how to do rigidly what she's done in the past. What point can there possibly be to Lady Macbeth's astonishing pleas to be unsexed when she's already more macho than anyone else on stage?

I know the old arguments: the kids have to see Shakespeare, each generation needs a crack at the canon. Yet, with few exceptions—the delightfully rambunctious Pyramus and Thisbe scene in A. J. Antoon's Brazilian Dream at the Public—what they're hearing are voices without color, verse without poetry, and an antique vocabulary that constantly disrupts what little meaning has been found in the action. What kid or modern grown-up can figure out quickly that "I doubt some danger" really means "I *fear* some danger"? Years ago, Robert Graves provided some three hundred clarifications on that order for the National's *Much Ado About Nothing,* undetected by most critics, probably because they were understanding the text for the first time.

Which is to say that the heresy of emendation would be better than the heresy of aimless performance. Shakespeare is feared by the young precisely because their elders are so damned sanctimonious about him. Papp's current plan to shove all thirty-six plays down our throats in six years can only be a way of colonizing our minds with Shakespeare's dubious goodness. But he's not good for us, not in deadbeat productions sporting fashionable concepts or no ideas at all. Shakespeare isn't an artifact, he's an amazing dramatist with a slashing gouache technique that defies all the rules. A master of light and darkness, startling shifts and counterpoints, mischievous flirtations with unanswered questions, he's an authentically difficult, demanding playwright who can be clarified with impunity, but never simplified.

Yet what we're sure to get from Papp are more of the same "inexplicable dumb shows" costing millions by the end of the canon, none spent on educating the actors and most spent on flags, spears, cardboard castles, bodkins, welkins, boots, and tights. Composers will be commissioned for new alarums and exeunts, designers will fall over themselves to provide swift moves from Venice to Cyprus, London to Agincourt, as if technology can make up for absent drama, and directors will give interviews about the stunning new meanings they've unearthed. Troilus will moan and drone, Rosalind will woo us instead of Orlando, Lear will lose his voice, and no doubt Meryl Streep will trot out another accent, maybe Lady Macbeth sleepwalking with a bagpipe instead of a candle.

Does the Philharmonic, with instrumental skill most of our actors lack, bother to play all forty-one symphonies of Mozart? And if so, would audiences be content with only an odd slow movement or minuet truly well played? Why, then, must we put up with unskilled, phony "completeness" in the theater? Think, too, of our abused, neglected playwrights, thirty-six of them *not* getting a production in the next six years. Papp's taste in new plays may be limited—gregarious affirmations usually winning out over introspective doubts—but at least he's been committed to the new.

When Glenda Jackson pukes at the end of the current *Macbeth's* first act, she's trying to be startling and original, though it's quite possible that she's an unheralded ironist, staggering into an act of dramatic criticism. Papp, too, gives the game away by offering a T-shirt to hardy survivors of the canon, which says "I've Seen Them All," possibly one of life's most meaningless achievements. If that's as you like it, so be it. But seeing them all is bound to be much ado about nothing.

(March 1988)

Brevity Is the Soul of Grit

When William Hazlitt saw Edmund Kean's Shylock, he was surprised not to find "a decrepit old man...sullen, morose, gloomy, inflexible, brooding over one idea." Only afterward did he realize that he had drawn this notion "from other actors, not the play." Glory then to Dustin Hoffman, who, like all gifted actors, takes cues only from himself. It isn't even too farfetched to see him as a Kean incarnation: the short actor who breaks all the rules about heroism, showing Shakespeare in lightning flashes, yet never pandering to expectation or display. Unlike Kean, however, Hoffman has been a stranger to Shakespeare, which, apart from Barrymore and Welles, may be the real American tradition. How wise of him to hazard acquaintance first with Shylock, where brevity is the soul of all its grit. In five scenes only, Shakespeare packs a lifetime of experience, calling from an actor the most swift-footed emotional shifts, anxious swings from sardonic humor to what can only be called severe, reflective genius. Hazlitt, as always, got it right when he concluded that Shylock moves beyond stereotype and genre: "He has more ideas than any other person in the piece."

The others are a prodigal mess, easily recognized when Shylock implores Jessica to keep "the sound of shallow fopp'ry" out of his "sober house." Shakespeare's dazzling counterpoints tell a different story from what might be expected: both Jessica and Lancelot Gobbo are nasty about their fathers, while one scene after another turns out to be shivering with sub- and supertextual obsessions about money. Shylock the lender is easily outclassed by strict constructionist law that bends in an instant for anybody with cash and clout. Assuming Venice and Belmont are stand-ins for Shakespeare's London and the Cotswolds, this is still another fable about English rapacity run riot. Centuries later, Oscar Wilde would pursue Shylock's error in his own way, trusting the law to prosecute its letter rather than its own class interests.

Peter Hall's production, sober as Shylock's house, makes no special effort to "interpret" the play, preferring instead a straightforward account, alternately fabulous as fairy tale and austere as document. Shakespeare doesn't judge; he gazes at lives caught in the dispassionate logic of their momentary, driving passions. Like everyone else, Portia stops at nothing to get what she wants. Only Shylock fails, because he's the nominal villain, and also because the others are privileged to be charming in their villainy.

The Hall-mark here is the continual forward motion of both verse and prose, in which key words are lit upon like rafts in a storm. Hall once told Simon Callow that he had "a tendency to fall in love with the wrong word." Callow learned that he had to phrase by the line rather than the word, which is another way of saying that meaning resides in exhaustive thought: the actor must grasp the architecture of an idea even as he or she lets feeling swell up into instantaneous behavior. Most of Hall's actors, including Americans, are master builders in this vein. More than anything, they are intoxicated by narrative sweep, as if they can't wait to show us everything they're finding out as they go along.

Too bad Hall doesn't go for broke, letting the story burst into consciousness without intermission. His actors are burning with energy: the young bloods—Nathaniel Parker's Bassanio, Richard Garnett's Lorenzo, and Michael Siberry's Gratiano—have an extraordinary confidence in their own light-headed readings of events. Gratiano charges Antonio with a sadness that can only be role-playing, and Leigh Lawson confirms this in the fluent way in which he slips from sentiment to the dismissive violence he heaps on Shylock. He's a languid, eloquent lout, unaware even to the eleventh hour that he might be in real danger. Hall doesn't bother to underline the locker-room affections of Antonio and Bassanio, though like every other transparency in this production, they're out front to see. When Portia tells Nerissa that she's eager to pretend she's a man, if only to enjoy for once the "thousand raw tricks of these bragging Jacks," it's clear that she's responding to male bonding stronger than Shylock's bond. She's in love with an affectionate gold digger, and that's good enough for her.

Geraldine James is an astonishingly vigorous Portia, with all the "affection and pedantry" Hazlitt found in her but awash with gleaming goodwill just the same. With a sharp-edged profile that would dress any coin, she's in command of all the action, moving without pause from bigotry to tenderness. Somehow she becomes the play's blunt mercantile center, smart enough to know power is her money. Her Portia is the first career girl, Carole Lombard crossed with Rosalind Russell, smart enough to know she's smarter than all the men combined.

Not smarter, really, than Hoffman's Shylock, even though he can't possibly win. His performance is best when resisting bombast: the famous apostrophe to his own reality—"Hath not a Jew eyes?" etc.—emerges pitilessly from true thought, newly coined as if he's hinting that this is only the beginning. Hoffman may be an outsider in this largely British company, but he proves himself to be a Shakespearean who can heft a phrase with the best of them. He may not have the demonic intensity of the young Peter O'Toole, or Morris Carnovsky's dark, Talmudic authority, but his quiet, gnomic assurance is no less magnificent. In a better theater, he might go on now to Iago, Jaques, Caliban, or Lear: no longer in need of stumbling on feelings before he speaks, he's suddenly in the front rank of Shakespeareans—an ironist unafraid of being wise on stage.

(December 1989)

Ardent Sex Change

In Christopher Grabowski's cunning adaptation of *As You Like it*, Rosalind is not only a male actor as she once was for Shakespeare, she's also at one time or another Silvius to her male Orlando who's momentarily playing Phoebe, and just as suddenly she's Jaques or Touchstone as Orlando becomes Audrey while her female cousin, Celia, switches from Phoebe to William and back again to Celia. Nor is this all: with only four actors to play on the round, raked mat, Orlando must wrestle with an imaginary opponent, the bad Duke is a voiceover, the good Duke never appears, and Rosalind gets his best lines; by the end a previously addled Orlando admits that the young man calling himself Ganymede can be only what he really sees—"If there be truth in sight, you are my Rosalind"—so he strips to the waist, Rosalind does the same, and we, too, see only what we see: Rosalind with a hairy chest. The women playing Oliver and Celia also embrace as women; the circular, spinning images converge on what may be the proudest, most romantically gay self-assertion I've ever seen in the theater.

Grabowski's take on the play, including his interpolations of sonnets and lines from *A Midsummer Night's Dream, Love's Labor's Lost,* and—not to be outdone by Lee Breuer—*King Lear,* is playful in the most winning sense, as if he's refusing limits even as he shapes a new, more compact work than Shakespeare's. Some of us in the United States, and Peter Brook and Peter Stein in Europe, have long since claimed that same pleasure in reimagining Shakespeare that was always admitted to Verdi, Berlioz, Prokofiev, José Limon, and others. Grabowski is doing only what ought to come naturally to any good director who loves Shakespeare so much he can't part with a word of it—or rather, whose adoration translates unaggressively into a desire to tell his own tale with Shakespeare's magical words.

If there's any difficulty here, it may be that, in his headlong rush to hit the high points, Grabowski is neglecting the transitions that usually help an audience to follow the story. He's almost as intoxicated with his idea as Rosalind is with Orlando. It can't be an accident that the first sonnet he uses, giving the lines to Celia, is "My love is a fever," though if I'm not mistaken what she actually says is "My thoughts are as a fever." Either way, Grabowski is "feeding on that which doth preserve the ill, Th' uncertain sickly appetite to please," at times falling into obscurities that only a much stronger group of actors could define and clarify.

While it's a relief to watch young Americans in either an exhilarated or a pensive attack on Shakespeare's mighty lines, unafraid to switch interior realities as swiftly as they exchange genders, it's less satisfying to see—and hear—them dash past the grace notes, or shout their most tender observations as if trying to reach the outer limits of the Met. "Speak you

so gently?" asks Michael James Reed's Orlando of Michael Liani's raucous Rosalind, which only makes sense if one or the other is dead.
Between the miked voices losing distinction and color in Breuer's *Lear,*
and the abrasive noises made in *A Forest in Arden,* it looks as if we're
headed for rock 'n' roll Shakespeare, with technology and actors doing
whatever they can to drown out the poetry.

That said, I'd not like to hint that daredevils like Breuer and Grabowski
might be discouraged from carving out idioms all their own. Even if *Lear,*
for example, has less to say about gender than it does about American
ways of death, its final passages, in which the Jukes and Kallikaks comedy
gives way to the gathered horror of a wrecked universe, capture a
requiem grandeur usually missed by genteel, conventional productions.
Grabowski's more modest invention may be the sharper stratagem—a
frank use of only what he needs from his source, and a clear banner-
headline idea of what he wants to say. There's nothing in *Arden* to match
the sure, poetic touch and quiet wisdom of Isabell Monk's Gloucester, or
the aching magnificence of Karen Evans-Kandel's Edna (Edgar), but on
the other side, *Arden* celebrates and protests the giddy, youthful joy only
Shakespeare finds so consistently in matters of love. Even better, it's
warming testimony that despite an indifferent universe, sex is one, clear
political act that can always be done as you like it.

(February 1990)

Cracking the Code

The second act of Hugh Whitemore's *Breaking the Code* begins with a
long, impassioned address by Alan Turing (Derek Jacobi) to the boys of
Sherborne, the school he had attended twenty-five years earlier. It's 1953
and he's comparing the human brain to "a bowl of cold porridge," a
casual, if provocative, observation meant to lead the students into his real
subject: the description of the computer, a machine than can think. The
audience has already learned that Turing—as the mathematical wizard
hired by Winston Churchill to break the Nazis' Enigma code, essential if
the British were to win the war—is the kind of man who thrives on paradox and complexity. For him mathematics cannot be reduced to right

and wrong any more than the human heart can be confined comfortably to socially acceptable behavior. Cold porridge or not, his own mind is luminous with possibility, if only his unapologetic gay encounters don't get in the way.

They do, of course, automatically shifting attention from Turing's brain to Turing's cock. Imagine Brecht's Galileo without the adversarial intelligence of the pope, the play suddenly turned from serious argument into less serious, though tantalizing melodrama. Based on Andrew Hodges's biography of Turing, Whitemore's play takes its cues more from domesticated fact than from the intriguing playfulness of Turing's dreaming imagination. According to an interview with Jacobi, Turing "was a very taciturn man, very internal...the eyes would glaze over, and he'd be gone...a group of numbers had come into his head." Not exactly God's gift to a dramatist, so Whitemore offers Jacobi in almost nonstop talk, most of it in encounters with mother, colleagues, lovers, a detective, and a government watchdog, and, in what little time is left, in three long speeches where he explains how he's lit upon computers by way of Bertrand Russell and Ludwig Wittgenstein.

The talk is good enough as far as it goes, teddibly British in its delicate, tippy-toed traversal of indelicate emotions and intractable theorems. The English are never more odd than when they're trying to be internally true without the slightest interest in internal psychology. When Turing tells his mother, Sara (Rachel Gurney), that he's in trouble because his affair with a boy has been discovered, she moves within three seconds from disgusted outrage to decorous concern, conveniently calling upon a reminiscence of a time years ago when Daddy went trout fishing and Turing had to return to school; shrubs hid him from sight, and "for a moment," she "was quite breathless with panic...wanted to jump out of the taxi, run back, and hold" him in her arms forever. Sara closes the scene a moment later with one of those drawing-room remarks meant to get them both through without further injury to their upholstered feelings: "Do come and look at the guest room. I'm so pleased with it."

Turing asks that favorite question of his colleagues, "Is God a mathematician?" Whitemore's crafty setups inspire a similar question: "Are all classy English people playwrights at heart?" Everything is so neatly arranged in their lives, it's a wonder they run into troubles at all. When Turing meets John Smith (Richard Clarke), the watchdog worried about his reliability with secrets, it's only a hop, skip, and a jump to Smith's remarks about the brain as cold porridge, a coincidence explained by the news that he has a nephew who heard Turing's speech at Sherborne. Whitemore's facts keep losing their credibility as he maneuvers life into so many implausible equations. Turing, surely, was more than brilliant: he was a branch bent against the wind, an abstracted intelligence floating in what, for others, would be a void, a brain—ironically—that no computer could possibly unscramble. Whitemore, on the other hand, is mostly wind—smart, certainly, but devoted to unscrambling everything. He's feeding his word processor limited information.

Luckier in his colleagues than Turing, Whitemore's seventeen scenes move seamlessly out of chronology, between 1929 and 1954. Clifford Williams shifts actors back and forth with the appropriate virtuosity of a director in total command of his resources. Using Liz da Costa's gigantic gray hangar, with its angle-poise lamps flanked on both sides by lights and knobs suggesting that the entire set may be the inside of a mechanical brain, Williams gives the play a hushed grandeur that it might otherwise miss. One or two characters occasionally hover on either side at a great distance as scenes progress, urged like the ominous chords heard at the end of scenes into the service of a suspense only glanced upon by Whitemore. Inevitably, the actors look lonely in such vast, inarticulate space; like moths, they float into Natasha Katz's shafts and pools of light, eager to obtain warmth, more eager to infuse Whitemore's shorthand psychology with the quick-witted heat of their own headlong imagination.

More than anything, they're all good listeners, pointing the way for the rest of us, so that when Turing springs into celestial celebration of logic and ideas, we too shall listen with equal attentiveness. Michael Gough, as the overseer of Turing's pioneering work, is particularly good at suggesting a life hidden from Turing and everybody else. He's like an aged Puck, gingerly playing with the ambiguity of his own authority, sure of himself, but then again just a bit clumsy, not so sure. Evidently straighter than a programmed arrow, he makes sense of a character later revealed as a former lover of Maynard Keynes and Lytton Strachey: Gough is an actor completely in charge of the surface; underneath, always, there has to be another man.

Game, set, and match, however, for the classically assured Derek Jacobi. A natural soloist, he's unabashedly present in his partnerships. Before anything else, he gets the outlines right: nails constantly chewed, a stammer that threatens always to destroy, and laugh caught short by snorts a pig might envy. None of this technical certainty would mean a damned thing without Jacobi's dead-on emotional grounding. His hands and fingers keep reaching for light like emblems of his vaulting brain. When he jams his hands into his jacket pockets, letting them lift the jacket-ends like winged chariots, he's signaling another flight into territory unknown. He seems to love Turing but with no more ego than Turing had; here, it's simple affection, a gravitational pull toward incandescent intelligence, creepy and bone-chilling in its ecstasy. Jacobi supplies all the resonance, all the essential privacy missing from Whitemore's prosaic orderliness. With him pressing life into Whitemore's keyboard, the porridge feels like a brain in heat.

(November 1987)

Theater Mania

London. Wagner may have invented the performance as religious pilgrimage, but the British have perfected it as a long, swooning, major event in anybody's day. True, directors outside of England such as Robert Wilson, Ariane Mnouchkine, and Peter Brook are more commonly identified as auteurs who will go to any lengths to command—or lose—your attention, but surely London has domesticated the phenomenon, making the long evening or half-day seem normal, the definable guarantee of an occasion profound.

Years before the RSC's eight-hour *Nicholas Nickleby,* it had produced Peter Hall and John Barton's revision of Shakespeare's *Henry VI* trilogy and *Richard III* as the nine-hour *Wars of the Roses.* Hall has since done a five-hour grouping of Greek tragedies for the National, and there were others—a cycle called *The Romans in Britain* and, most recently, a version by Michelene Wandor and Mike Alfreds of Eugène Sue's epic novel *The*

Wandering Jew, directed by Alfreds and advertised by the National as "a complete serial in a single evening." Sure enough, catching the spirit of the hype, one reviewer called it an "exciting, new 5-hour spectacle... more twists and turns than *Dallas* and *Dynasty* put together."

And there's the clue: what may be a Good Idea has already been turned into a defensive insistence that theater can be as good as T.V. Strange, isn't it, that the infamous source of short attention spans should also be used as an excuse for epic evenings in the theater. Or not so strange, if a night out at a play can be sold to the public as a convenient way to obtain the emotional equivalent of fourteen weeks with the Raj in India, a paradoxically brief encounter with melodramatic kicks.

Length, then, may be one line of defense engineered by London's theatrical paranoids frightened of losing middle-class couch potatoes forever. That there are others—good plays and superb performances—goes without saying. Yet long evenings continue to be the order of the day, the best of them better than *Dallas* because they're unapologetically smarter. Thatcher's London, with its sharp divisions and brutal landscape—the views from Waterloo Bridge look like Hitler and Speer's dreams of a fortress city—is not much fun anymore, yet it's still the city where a varied repertory is often ambitiously performed.

There's nothing better in London now than Mike Alfreds's latest five-hour evening, a version of Carlo Goldoni's 1761 *Villeggiatura* trilogy called *Countrymania,* still another of those resurrections that calls into question the endless recycling of drama's fifty easy pieces between *Hamlet* and *Hedda.* "Writers struggling for ideas for a comedy should come here," says one of the servants in part 2 (*Country Hazards*), and no better advice could be ordered. A more hapless collection of parvenus, greedier and more subtly defined than their desperate counterparts in *Serious Money,* would be hard to find.

Part 1 (*Country Fever*) is Goldoni's warmup: two households—Leonardo and his sister Vittoria's, Filippo and his daughter Giacinta's—are in a frenzy to uproot themselves for the gambling and mating season in the country. Leonardo's broke, Vittoria must have her new gown anyway, Giacinta can't decide between Leonardo and Guglielmo, her gloomier suitor, and Filippo can't decide about anything except his need to pair Giacinta with the richest man—so he thinks—Leonardo. Both families are trailed by the waspish Ferdinando, gossip and leech, for whom the burning issue is always who will feed and house him best. Add to these Costanza's household in the country—"She cuts a fine figure," says her servant, "You wouldn't know she's a shopkeeper's wife"—and Giacinta's aged aunt, Sabina, either seduced by or seducing the awful Ferdinando, and you have maneuverings for what must be one of the darkest comedies ever written.

Alfreds and his company are on top of the details all the way. Entire passages seem like those glorious, exhaustively stretched ensembles in Mozart where, alone and together, characters discover that events have escaped their control. Whether playing viciously at cards—four tables in distant isolation from one another over the enormous Olivier Theatre stage—or revolving in languid parade to a café where they plague the waiters with ten different orders (Giacinta complaining about the service), they are viewed by Goldoni and Alfreds with laser-beam precision. Alfreds bridges scenes with deliciously funny recorded madrigals by Ilona Sekacz, written to an explosion of Italian musical terms—"sostenuto, agitato, subito pianissimo, etc."—that mirror exactly the dizzy comings and goings of the plot.

Good as they are together, all the actors are assured soloists, no one more so than Mark Rylance as Leonardo, a delicate tenor trying with utmost seriousness to be a masterful baritone; he's a wispy pocket version of a leading young man, extraordinary in his balancing of manner and miserably real substance. Sian Thomas is his sister Vittoria, all splayed, elongated vowels, helplessly eager to make her arranged engagement to Guglielmo work. "Maybe when he's my husband, he'll wake up," she says, capturing the plaintive zaniness that threads its way through Goldoni's hard-edged satire.

Alfreds's actors are more natural conversationalists than Peter Hall's in a play I feel like calling *Enobarbus and Cleopatra*. Anthony Hopkins is merely lazy as Shakespeare's Antony, staggering through his scenes like an aging, stoned hippie, no match for Judi Dench's constantly prowling Cleopatra. Michael Bryant's staunch, crooning Enobarbus—a lieder singer giving each word its weight and measure under the Egyptian sky—quite believably says she "beggars all description," remembering her hopping forty paces through a street: between them, Dench and Bryant make Shakespeare's bitter romance vivid by sheer force of belief and a powerful hold on the "word" as instrument.

Hall's productions these days—including David Edgar's sprawling *Entertaining Strangers* in the tiny Cottesloe Theatre—always seem to be aspiring to opera, as if he were bored with logic, detail, or anything that can't submit to noisy interludes or aimless pageantry. More drill sergeant than director, he even uses follow spots for his stars. Both productions are long, not from necessity but from his compulsion for processions and technology. His recent work is the National's prevailing, flaccid arrogance at its worst, grinding out productions like new models on the automotive assembly line.

It's probably just coincidence, but my friend Peter Shaffer is *not* presenting his latest play, *Lettice and Lovage,* at the National under Peter Hall's direction. Instead, his delightfully ramshackle comedy—all three easygoing hours of it—is in the West End, directed with loving care by Michael Blakemore, with Maggie Smith offering one of her extravagant comic visions, a fantasist named Lettice ("as a vegetable, obviously one of God's mistakes") who wants only to blast London's hideous new buildings into well-deserved oblivion.

This is Shaffer relaxed and passionate, disgusted with those who value gray reality over eccentric imagination. Rambling over three sets and acts, using thirteen actors for what is essentially a two-character play, he's single-handedly reviving a type of leisurely English comedy that expired when Oscar was crucified. Lettice would be a great character even without Maggie Smith, though it doesn't hurt to have her animated-cartoon arms and screwball comedy eruptions to push the plot along. Quietly and surreptitiously, the play reveals itself as the story of an emerging, unlikely friendship between two women who begin as natural enemies: Margaret Tyzack's reproving Lotte, supposedly the voice of dull bureaucracy, transforms herself magically into Smith's tart and tender accomplice, both actors making a meal of Shaffer's bubbling wit and verbal twists.

Length has never mattered less. London's wisdom these days may be the wisdom of our easily forgotten past, when it was possible to enjoy live performance not for brevity but for its honest delight in telling stories authentically felt. If Goldoni-Alfreds and Shaffer have anything to say about it, the long attention span will never be defeated by the commercial break.

(February 1988)

Serious Money

She won't be liked for it, but with *Serious Money*, Caryl Churchill is offering news that rarely hits print—not what we already know about Ivan Boesky and his comrades in sleaze but what fuels their greed, the overheated intensity that keeps them breathlessly alive, immune to the unnatural disasters they're dumping on the rest of us. A serious poet, Churchill lets her free-market monsters talk *molto vivace* in free verse—in one stroke giving them a dignity they don't deserve yet at the same time making their appalling cruelties worth listening to. No wonder we miss the news in real life: Churchill's theatrical imagination is so much better than journalism, insistently present tense yet, like all superb theater, severely condensed, selective, about resonance rather than message. Funny-laconic, rarely ha-ha, she's as brutal as her targets.

In her visions and loathings, Churchill is the complete democrat: nobody escapes her slashing brushstrokes—young, old, men, women, Jews, Africans, Americans, and the British. If the New York audience turns to ice at the first sign of collective guilt, as they did at the last preview, so be it. This isn't a play about Soviets, Germans, or Japanese, or even for the poor in the subtext who keep voting (or not) for the next wholesale theft of their rights and patrimony; this is about central casting —the players on both sides of an Atlantic easily crossed by computers, phones, and the Concorde who have jumped into the chaos to seize what they can. If Churchill is right, Marx didn't dream the half of it. In little more than two hours, *Serious Money* bombs supply-siders out of their bunkers. Churchill has found out that capital is not about need, product, or sensibility—it's only about money, paper, and the endless supply of horror in the human heart.

Like her enemies, she's a demon possessed. Distributing twenty roles among eight actors while adding a chorus of eight to cover runners and

jobbers in London's Exchange, she's seizing any number of theatrical risks
—that we may not always know who's playing what, that we'll lose sight
of what little narrative there is, that we won't quite know what she feels
about any of them. It's not a play about domestic concerns or bedroom
feelings. Characters here scarcely have time for sex, let alone romance.
Jacinta, the Peruvian wheeler-dealer busily betraying everybody, finally
has a night reserved for Zac, the London-based American caught in the
middle of everything. "My feeling for you is very deep," she says. "Mind
very much if we go to sleep?"

Exactly right. Churchill captures all the displacements, the way in
which children update their fathers' crimes, the styles of work that keep
everybody in doubt about everybody else. Out of the hastily traversed territory of her confusing exposition—where the same actor plays betrayer
and betrayed—she concocts something like a detective story: Scilla Todd is
determined to find out why her brother Jake is an apparent suicide; by the
end, she doesn't care any more since she's interested only in discovering
where Jake put his winnings. Like Michelangelo Antonioni leading us to
forget what happened to the missing Anna in *L'avventura,* Churchill allows
the likely fate of Jake—murdered by Thatcher's election-hungry government—to fade into the background. Scilla's quest binds the frantic episodes
and the act-ending choral songs into one pile-driving force.

Churchill's penultimate scene lines up her eight leads for a swift summary of their various fates—Marylou Baines, the Wall Street operator second only to Boesky, "ran for President in 1996"—and it's a clue to how
Churchill might have made her exposition easier to follow: a similar
lineup at the beginning might easily have relieved the first act of its
murkiness. Good as she is, Churchill seems to be presenting a first draft,
written in white heat but not yet organized or edited to say what she
really means.

Even so, she's wondrous in her presumptions and seriously amusing.
Lucky, too, in her production: Max Stafford-Clark gives his actors space,
light, and freedom to make their transformations part of the fun. Peter
Hartwell's elegant design turns easily from stock exchange floor to champagne bar and plausible hound-hunting territory with only the most minimal changes. With its central Norman arch framing Marylou Baines's

upper-level New York office, it's the perfect image for the play's vaulting reach—a visual equivalent of Churchill's ambitious linkages, the old, the new, and the flashing screens and telephones all shouting for equal attention.

The actors are similarly merciless in their dispassionate etchings. Paul Moriarty has trouble with Zac's American vowels and presence, but he's got the smarm in place, that loose, querulous don't-know-what-I'm-doingness. Linda Bassett is more comfortable with Marylou, perhaps because she shifts so strikingly from her English banker, the prune-lipped Mrs. Etherington, delicately advising the biggest crook of them all—Billy Corman, a corporate raider—how to play his shifting cards. Best of all are Joanne Pearce as the self-proclaimed immoral Scilla, Meera Syal as the slippery Jacinta, and Allan Corduner as Jake and Scilla's father (and four other roles). As cabinet minister Gleason, Corduner assumes his most effective disguise: summoning the raider at the intermission of the National's *King Lear,* Gleason is particularly impressed with "Goneril, Reagan, and Ophelia" (a nice Churchill touch, this), but wishes the play could be cut; Corduner drapes himself in stretched vowels and slapped consonants, the very picture of the languid killer who wins elections while losing our bankrolls.

A warning, however: this production runs only another four weeks, and you may hear, also, that much of the language is either obscure or offensively dirty. More power to Churchill, anyway: when Scilla castigates Daddy—"You're trading like a cunt"—Churchill's making her perspectives painfully clear. This is theater, not solace. Like a bitter parodist of the Greeks—"Count no man decent until he's dead"—Churchill uses rhythms, rhymes, and a wicked tongue to display the biggest cover-up of all: our systemic refusal to believe that things can't get worse.

Just to prove that British playwriting isn't always up to Churchillian snuff, Louise Page's *Real Estate* reveals that some playwrights know only how to reduce all possessive relationships to family feud. This must be the 9,000th play in this century to grapple with earth-shaking issues surrounding mothers, daughters, pregnancy, and neurotic loyalties. Page sets up a tearful symmetry: Daughter returns to Mother after twenty years, insinuates herself into Mother's home with Stepfather, manages to lose the father of her child, plans to bring the newborn baby into Mother's household, thus forcing Mother to leave home. This is the sort of "liberated" landscape where the men prepare cake or peel sprouts while the women argue over honor in real estate.

I'll spare you the details. Enough to report that Sada Thompson's quietly contained Mother represents an intriguing contrast in acting style to Roberta Maxwell's self-conscious, totally unspontaneous daughter. Not that it's smooth sailing for any actor when called upon to speak to the unborn in the tummy. Thompson, however, is what she has always been — one of our treasurable, emotionally available, unfussy performers. Give her the provocation, and her face and eyes will balloon into feeling. Would that Page had shut up more often or that she might take a cue or two from Churchill, opening her family experience to the world.

(December 1987)

Sublime Neglect

Wasting no time, George Chapman's *Bussy d'Ambois* (1604) opens with Bussy's astonishing soliloquy bitterly describing the outrageous, illusionary politics that have reduced him to abject poverty. (Has there ever been a more daring stage direction than Chapman's "Enter Bussy d'Ambois, poor"?) With an almost embarrassing prescience, Chapman describes how shallow, upstart phonies can be transformed against all the evidence — "Fortune, not Reason, rules the state of things" — into imitations of "unskillful statuaries." Bussy has noticed that the spin-doctors surrounding him believe they can forge a hero by making him "straddle enough, strut, and look big, and gape." "In their affected gravity of voice," they then congratulate themselves that "their work is goodly."

I hope I can be forgiven my narrow response to Chapman's marvelously unmanageable tragedy; he's more than just a pit-stop on the way to transitory relevance. Yet that opening moment in Jonathan Miller's production at the Old Vic last month came as a startling reminder that, for the most part, we don't see the plays that deserve to be done, and we don't get the plays we need. Bad enough that armies of American playwrights are reduced to fobbing off dead-end staged readings as their contribution to the new; even worse are the endless, droopy recyclings of Shakespeare and

Chekhov, usually mugged by arrogant directors or unprepared actors. Much as they'd like to believe it, the British aren't always better, but their playwrights languish less than ours, and their repertoire—at last—is beginning to expand.

Miller's *Bussy* production turns out to be one among many resurrections. The National will be opening Ben Jonson's *Bartholomew Fair* on October 20, having recently closed Dion Boucicault's *The Shaughraun,* that riotous nineteenth-century Irish play anticipating Synge's *Playboy of the Western World* and O'Casey's *Juno and the Paycock* and *Plough and the Stars.* Chances are that some of the RSC Stratford productions of Restoration rarities will soon appear in London: Farquhar's *The Constant Couple* is there instead of the moderately more familiar *Recruiting Officer* (available anyway at the Royal Court), Wycherly is represented by *The Plain Dealer* instead of *The Country Wife,* and Etherege by *The Man of Mode.* To tie a modernist ribbon on the package, they're also producing Edward Bond's *Restoration,* evidently an acerbic comment on the tradition. Finally they're "reviving"—what a joke on us who've never seen it—Seneca's *Oedipus* in the Ted Hughes version produced by Peter Brook twenty years ago.

The British press, bless them, still seem to think that drama has an authority unmatched by its media clones. Few of these plays are directly about us in the vulgar way I've adopted *Bussy* for our election miseries. They're better than relevant: alive with consequence, responsible to cruel realities, superbly uninterested in dippy identifications with sentimentally sympathetic characters: crazy enough to put the universe onstage, they take charge as if no other form existed. Living without this vast repertoire is to us what the absence of Haydn's quartets, Mozart's piano concertos, and Beethoven's symphonies would be to the world of music. One long weekend in London was enough to remind me that New York has become the capital of theatrical deprivation.

Bussy wasn't the only revelation. Proving that Mozartian diversion may lead to Proustian meditation, the RSC's production of James Shirley's 1632 comedy *Hyde Park* was, if anything, the more satisfying surprise. Shirley's Mistress Carol and Fairfield needn't defer to Beatrice and Benedick or Millamant and Mirabell: working out a contract not to marry but to separate, they are the only couple of four who are finally successful in their alliance. The play's early scenes celebrate a wedding that is doomed because it's revealed by the end as bigamous. The ceremony is a masque designed to herald Bliss, Fertility, Fidelity, and Prosperity, all of it illusion. Meanwhile, the vicious, languid Lord Bonvile attempts a rape—"the place were good enough if you were bad enough"—only to discover that "I do not like myself."

This charming, melancholy comedy has been directed by Barry Kyle to fit a concept that actually makes sense. Carol, Fairfield, and their friends are viewed as so many succulent Bloomsberries, passing gently from studio life to parkland games and romance. Carol (Fiona Shaw) is a totally "new woman," an Ottoline Morrell refusing to be pinned down by anybody while harboring a tear she doesn't wish to be seen. Shaw, swooping on vowels and dipping into exalted question marks, must be one of the most instinctively witty actors alive. She's exposed nerve-endings, appalled muscle spasms, bereft soul in search of an examined heart, easily compared—to her credit—to Maggie Smith but very much her own generator. It's not surprising that one of Carol's numerous suitors should love her face "as heavenly prologue to her mind."

Fairfield calls her "Madame Jeerall" and says "I will not endure the imagination of your frail sex." Remarkable how this play—indeed, most plays before our monolithically sexist century—uncovers the furious courage of undaunted women. Few of the men in Chapman, Shirley, and Shakespeare can endure women's imagination, another word for independence. In *Bussy d'Ambois*, Bussy's sponsor and ultimate nemesis, Monsieur, remarks upon "the infinite regions between a woman's tongue and heart."

Chapman, however, is exposing the infinite regions between a man's tongue and his soul. Like most of the men in *Bussy*, Monsieur is a frivolous presumer, described aptly by Bussy as having "a breath that will kill to the wall a spider...utterly without soul." To this obliterating remark, Monsieur can only say, "Why, now I see thou lov'st me." Familiar Jacobean territory, yes, but not to be casually dismissed merely because it delights so much in nasty reproach. Monsieur's manipulations lead to Bussy's downhill seduction of Tamyra, another courtier's wife, and that in turn puts Tamyra on the rack—an amazing scene in which her vengeful husband slices her arms, forcing her to write an accusation in her own blood.

Miller's production doesn't flinch. David Threlfall's Bussy may be shy of the flash and shine in Chapman's rhetoric, but he rises to the wondrous final pages where he insists that he "will die standing." As Irving Ribner puts it, Chapman is seeking "a basis for morality in a world in which the traditional bases no longer seem to have any validity." Miller offers a dispassionate display of everything, and Sara Kestelman suffers Tamyra's torture with an angular, quiet dignity.

The same can be said of Geraldine James in the National's production of *Cymbeline,* directed by Peter Hall. I realize that Joseph Papp will soon be offering the same play with Holly Hunter, directed by JoAnne Akalaitis—one of the few alluring combinations he's managed to muster in his monotonous cycle. Hall, however, brought *Cymbeline* into a retrospective presentation of Shakespeare's valedictory plays, including *The Winter's Tale* and *The Tempest,* which he mounted as his farewell from the National's leadership. I hadn't time enough to see the unit, but *Cymbeline* qualifies sufficiently as neglected repertoire, though you'd hardly know it in London, where the Hall version can be compared to a concurrent RSC production with Harriet Walter.

Hall's dramaturgs have decided that the heroine should be known as Innogen. By whatever name, and especially in James's blazing presentation, she's a woman far ahead of the men—indeed, far ahead of most twentieth-century women. With Tim Piggot-Smith as her would-be seducer, Iachimo, it looked for a moment as if we might be witnessing a classical rerun of *The Jewel in the Crown.* Perhaps we were, after all: James and Piggot-Smith headed a cast that positively gloried in the plotting—all those crazy, twisting adventures resolved by Shakespeare in a final scene that must be the summit of his lunatic virtuosity, a display not outclassed by Verdi's fugal finale for *Falstaff.*

If London renewed my crankiness, so be it. What it also renewed is my trust in theatrical art. Hall's actors, like the others, can't hide their playful delight in heroic, lyrical, totally confidential performance: fools that they are, they insist on sharing that delight with the rest of us. Surely they're discovering that there are more roles in heaven and earth than Hamlet and Juliet. Words alone seem to enchant them. These neglected plays offer a way out of the general torpor. They set their hearts not on image but on

truth. About *Bussy*—and she might have been writing about all these plays
—the late Una Ellis-Fermor said it well: "The long, weighty passages of
imagery fold themselves about their limbs so that they go forth clothed—
to form part of a pattern, to create with others a sustained harmony of
color and mood which runs through the play almost as a plot within the
plot." London's recovery of theatrical history, its recognition of our complicated past and signals to the future, may be part of a broader recovery:
theater, surely, need not be Bush-whacked by the impulse to forget.

(October 1988)

Hare Today

Would it were not so, but David Hare's *The Secret Rapture* reveals him as
a closet Tory. This current National Theatre success, headed for the Public next fall, pretends to tell the story of kind, easily victimized Isabel,
coping bravely with the death of her beloved father, despite pressures
from Marion (her Thatcherized sister), Irwin (her dependent yet way-
ward lover), and Katherine (her father's young, bitterly alcoholic
widow). Isabel is good, the others are bad—or at any rate, they are
arranged by Hare to do bad things to Isabel. She, in turn, accepts everything that comes her way, with the notable exception of Irwin's need and
love. Naturally—and who can blame him?—he kills her.

Hare says that his title refers to "that moment at which a nun expects
to be united with Christ...in other words, it's death." Maybe so, but
how hard that is on sad-sack Irwin, never realizing he's been set up, not
by that great playwright in the sky but by smart, trendy Hare craftily
pushing pawns on his pseudopolitical chessboard. Evidently, Irwin didn't
know what Chekhov could have warned him about: when playwrights
hand you a gun, they're also going to make you pull the trigger.

No one in Hare's world has a fighting chance for independent life.
He's probably trying to say something nasty about Thatcher's England,
with everyone playing out some government-sponsored role. Marion
won't bail her family out of trouble by offering the hapless Katherine a
job. "Don't be ridiculous," she says, "I'm in the Conservative Party."
Meanwhile, Katherine declares that good people are "here to help the

trashy people like me." Later, she asks, "Why has God made me so fucking mediocre?" With all this evidence before her, Isabel nonetheless decides to abandon Irwin in favor of Katherine—and I don't mean hanky-panky, which would have certainly meant checkmate for Hare's immutable scheming.

Isabel's condemnation of Irwin is that he wants "to be saved by another person." Yet she's staying with Katherine because Katherine "has no resources...it isn't her fault, it's a fact." Hare slides past this seeming contradiction like the expert playwriting bully he really is. Far be it for him to give Irwin any argument but the gun. Hare's hermetic universe is about nothing less than his own generalized cynicism: goodness wastes its energies on trash, and Marion's greedy party—"in power forever"—is left to pick up the pieces.

Hardly surprising, then, that the best arguments are Marion's, anyway —or at least, the best lines. She reports that she told a delegation from the Green movement to "come back to see me when you're glowing in the dark." Left alone with her husband at the end, she at last admits that she's been angry all her life "because people's passions are so out of control." Which sounds like Hare complaining about the kinds of characters he's unable to write.

Deep down he scorns them all. As he himself admits—even citing *Pravda,* his collaboration with Howard Brenton—"modern plays have seemed, perhaps unintentionally, to end up celebrating malign energy." And it's true that with the special charge given by Penelope Wilton to Marion—a particularly elegant teakettle on perpetual boil—the devil gets more than his (her?) due. Hare doesn't seem to notice that he's battered the life out of Isabel, letting her emit only passively cruel gush from one scene to the next. By draining her of anything but personal sullenness, he moves *The Secret Rapture* squarely into the enemy camp, her goodness no more than an apolitical trance.

(October 1988)

Playing with Ire

Not easy to put to rest is the myth that protagonists in plays ought to elicit sympathy. That this would be news to Athenians and Elizabethans doesn't daunt those tyrannical sentimentalists who persist in judging plays as if they were making up a guest list suitable for charming dinner parties. I'm reasonably certain that Medea, the Macbeths, Tartuffe, and the whole Orgon clan would make lousy companions, even as I'm equally clear that it would be hard to compete with their gift for the fine-tuned phrase. My choice, then, would be to exclude them from dinner but catch them anytime they're doing their act.

If the myth seems less evident in London, it's only because the entire British theatrical contraption would fall apart without audience complicity in nasty behavior. Whether digging up neglected classics or recycling the familiar, the London theater, for all its cushioned traditions, revolves around a silent agreement that giving a damn about characters is less important than watching them squirm away from their destiny.

Indeed, the source of the best modernist acting is the actor's willingness to make the performance itself more important than sympathy; far from commenting on the character's situation, the actor is now offering no-comment, another kind of distancing in which the character is laid out before us like Eliot's "patient etherized upon a table."

The best British actors, however, are on a genuine high, enjoying the events in their plays as if coming upon them for the first time. For Alex Jennings as Dorante in Jonathan Miller's Old Vic production of Corneille's rarely produced comedy *The Liar,* the precedents have to be few; for Peter O'Toole in *Jeffrey Bernard Is Unwell,* a new West End play by Keith Waterhouse about the very much alive alcoholic columnist of *The Spectator,* the relaxed, naturally boozy style of the play is almost an appeal for the actor's most spontaneous invention; but for Mark Rylance in Ron Daniel's RSC production of *Hamlet,* the precedents are exhausting, too many of them embalmed in the kind of sentimentality that barely permits actor or audience to see the play as the remarkable document it is —always available to the pressure and temper of another age.

Having seen the diminutive Rylance several years ago as the stud in *Kiss of the Spider Woman* opposite Simon Callow, and more recently in the amazing Goldoni *Countrymania* at the National Theatre, I was prepared for what had to be a new take on Hamlet. Rylance, even more than Dustin Hoffman, is the little guy triumphant, Harold Lloyd and Buster Keaton suddenly combined into an unlikely matinee idol, handsome yet just this side of mocking boyishness that threatens always to disturb the peace. Dwarfed by a floor-length black overcoat with upturned collar, he makes his first entrance carrying a giant valise: draped in unfathomable sorrow, all alone in his outcast state, this Hamlet has packed for the only occupation he's suited for—scholarly retreat. His back to the audience as he begins his first soliloquy, gazing at the Turneresque seascape beyond the gigantic crooked twelve-paned window of the court, he offers modest elegance rather than unaccommodated man, an absurdist gentleman waiting for the next flight on the runway.

The cursed spite is that he's surely too gentle, too meditative, to set it right: what follows, however, is the emergence of mounting excitement, a brilliant seizure of every opportunity to be outrageous and exotically mad within a quietly antic framework. Roaming the court in striped flannel pajamas, he's a *Marat-Sade* inmate ready to bare a buttock to the prying Polonius, slam Ophelia to the ground with a violence that turns infuriatingly into softness and light, and paint Gertrude with the blood smearing his face and body after the murder of Polonius. When Claudius jams Hamlet's head under water, it's a clear, if momentary, demonstration of how a real—and more sympathetic—murderer can act.

That, of course, is only half the story: Rylance never forces anything, and he speaks with a hushed persuasion that never lapses into rant or aria; by the time he returns to meet Yorick's skull and Ophelia's funeral, he's found something like unbrooding peace at last. It's characteristic and oddly right for him to revise the famous remark about heaven and earth to apply not only to Horatio but himself—"our philosophy," he says. It's a nice touch, too, that he carries Yorick's skull into the duel with Laertes, placing it lovingly on a mantel, the only "god" looking on this appalling occasion his old and loving clown. Despite his cruelties, all of them as unashamedly displayed as that buttock, he's the first Hamlet in memory who truly warrants Horatio's encomium—the sweetest if most hair-raisingly complex prince I've ever seen.

Corneille's disreputable hero may seem less existentially modern, especially in Miller's jolly, white-costumed production, but he would surely recognize in Rylance's Hamlet a kindred outsider spirit, even if he could never understand Hamlet's devotion to truth. Corneille gives the funniest lines to Dorante's valet, Cliton, who (in Ranjit Bolt's bracingly wicked translation) refers to Dorante as "primed and cocked for amorous action." This is a familiar society where "lying is in vogue," and Alex Jennings could scarcely be more ingratiating as the "callow, impish boy," playing "trick after trick, fiction after fiction." Like Rylance, Jennings is eager to be in the moment, caught in the intoxicating rhythm not only of the verse but of his obsessive desire to "fascinate and thrill." Tall, suave, and dashing, he's also Rylance's stylistic obverse, vocally forward, brashly himself, a thoroughbred proud of his actorish breeding.

Nobody is more thoroughbred than O'Toole in any role, but without Shakespeare or Corneille conferring bruised innocence or the weight of ages upon him, he's left with only his own majestic charm, effortless as technique but not quite able to disguise the ashen emptiness in Jeffrey Bernard's heart. Waterhouse is playing smartass dumb in this brazen star vehicle, parading cynical oneliners and breath-defying, heaving reminiscences as if they were newly minted by some weird Celtic clone of Oscar and Dylan. But they come from the graveyard of cynical playwrights out of touch with theater as a forum for reason and ideas. Perhaps this is an accurate reflection of an alcoholic's mental drift, a light mist spinning out of dense fog, but what's funny about that? O'Toole's razor-edge timing and posh blah-di-dah inflections, dipping and swooping from baritone to tenor at the slightest encouragement, could raise laughs from the dead. But this is an archaeological achievement, a reminder that acting used to be about lavish effects more than spiritual adventure.

I keep coming back to Hamlet padding around that ageless space in those shabby pajamas. Rylance may have less obvious presence than O'Toole, but surely he's the future, likable and sympathetic finally because he's eager to be so unaffectedly loathsome, honest putty in an honest playwright's capable, remorseless hands.

(January 1990)

Operas and Musicals

That True Phoenix, da Ponte

Prima la musica e poi le parole: first the music and then the words. This ancient issue, decaying from overexposure, can be settled at once by agreeing that, in opera, in *musical* drama, the words bear a less central position to artistic results than does the music. This is not quite the same as saying that words stand beneath music or that they have no significance at all. When Richard Strauss joined with Clemens Krauss to fashion a speculative romance around the sophist comedy of *Capriccio,* he was writing music to a libretto prepared not by a poet but by a musician. This was surely part of the joke. Two rather wry musicians, with years of operatic experience almost literally draped over their endeavor, were pretending to present a neo-Socratic dialogue, a theoretically balanced and fair debate, on the subject of Words vs. Music. Even as the Countess seems to waver between the worlds of poet and composer, she is always wavering to music. It is this casual irony that unmasks implicitly the argument for what it is: a battle won before its beginning. In the end, Strauss and Krauss had the audacity to suggest that the only resolution available to such a question is a trivial one. And so the operatic dialogue, this *Conversation Piece for Music* (my italics), ends elegiacally with strings and horn, little doubt remaining that Madeleine will choose the composer for her lover.

Lorenzo da Ponte, who in life would have moved a rakish heaven and a scheming earth to make the poet—himself—the chosen lover, would nonetheless have deferred to the composer in the operatic situation. Little as we know of his direct working relationship with Mozart—and external evidence is almost as shadowy as what we possess on Shakespeare's life—we have by now surmised from the evidence of the three operas themselves that da Ponte had an instinctively sensible, professional view of his proper role.

Not that he loved either music or Mozart more than he loved himself. Indeed, his biographer April FitzLyon says that the only evidence of music in his soul is that he played the violin in his own brothel while still wearing his priest's cassock. Moreover, Mozart was neither his favorite composer nor the source of his proudest collaboration. Measuring artistic success by box-office returns as he did, it was *Una cosa rara,* which he wrote with Vicente Martín y Soler, that pleased him most.

With da Ponte, in fact, we are forced away from romantic gush, from portraits of the artist as a chained spirit, a soul in torment. Love, whether of Mozart or music, was not at issue. Living, however, the complex business of staying alive, was. Poets today are distinguished publishers (as was T. S. Eliot), doctors (William Carlos Williams), or university professors (almost all the rest). In da Ponte's Europe, they wrote odes and sonnets to potential patrons, and they vied for the few jobs available as Poets to the Opera or Imperial Court. In short, they wrote words to music in order to survive, just as most of our contemporary poets write criticism. Da Ponte had only to realize in his infinite cleverness that the best way to serve himself would be to serve his composer first.

His own story was preparation not so much for service as for adaptability to emergency situations. Da Ponte's energies, his darting will for work and play, were only a shade less prodigious than his astounding talent for inventing new forms of survival. He was like a man sentenced to umbilical life on a tightrope, never to come down until severed by death, balancing himself for almost ninety years on two continents, in four countries, and in four major cities.

It's small wonder and a special blessing that Hollywood has up to now overlooked his life's story. Da Ponte would no doubt have loved nothing better than writing the screenplay, embroidering it, as he stitched his *Memoirs,* with innumerable patches of fictional adventure. The moguls, with da Ponte's accommodation, would cast Rock Hudson in the leading role. A more fitting choice, however, would be an actor combining the buckling swash of Douglas Fairbanks, the incredible daring of Laurence Olivier, the brooding cynicism of Richard Burton, with all three capped by the rough suavity of Ezio Pinza in his waning years. Who but this chameleon, this quick-changing Pulcinello, this actor's actor could ever hope to embrace the shifts, the brazen elegance, the gentle vulgarity, the blinding ego of da Ponte—a Jewish merchant's son who in one extensive lifetime was a Catholic priest, a Venetian seducer, a small-town teacher, a court poet, a librettist to fourteen composers, a friend to Casanova, a London bookseller, a devoted husband and father, a theater manager, a Pennsylvania grocer, a distiller, and the first professor of Italian literature at Columbia University? Yet it is certain that for all the skill of this ideal actor and for all the technicolored features of da Ponte's life, the central achievement would be missed.

One of the teasing ironies in any man's life is that, grounded as he is in the shifting sands of domestic survival, he may himself die without an awareness of his unique moment, his passing instant of personal glory. While he struts and frets his hour upon the stage, searching for means to express himself or, less grandly, for a profession or, more philosophically, for his identity, the guiding fact of his life may well have been there all the time.

For us—and quite rightly—the fact of da Ponte's life is that he wrote the libretti of *Le nozze di Figaro, Don Giovanni,* and *Così fan tutte* for Mozart. Listeners today, it is true, scarcely think of da Ponte when faced with these operas. His moment misses them no less than it missed him. Perhaps this is as it should be: first music, then—somewhere in the background—the words. But the fact persists that Mozart wrote three of his five major operas to libretti by da Ponte. And, unless one believes in accidents, magic, or the divine unimportance of the librettist, da Ponte deserves placement and more than a grain of appreciation for his part in these transcendent works of dramatic imagination. To serve so well the mind of Mozart was to reveal in turn, whether he knew it or not, a mind touched by genius.

Genius, as we are constantly reminded, is *una cosa rara*—a rare thing. In the libretti of most acceptable operas, it is conspicuous by its absence. This might well be a contradiction in terms. It is better to say that an opera of genius must perforce be set to a libretto touched, at the very least, by the same brush that inspired the music. The society of honored opera librettists could scarcely be more exclusive: da Ponte, Arrigo Boito, and Hugo von Hofmannsthal, with a grudging, critical nod to the heavy labors of Wagner. Clearly, such a tiny circle of talented librettists suggests that the few who have succeeded—however inharmonious a group in most respects—shared some peculiar quirk, some odd mole of nature, some twist of spirit, that enabled them to submit to the special discipline of drama for music.

The mole, however, like all creative forces, resists definition. One assumes, for a start, that any writer has what can only be called a chemical attraction for his particular form. Great poets are almost always poor dramatists. The thumping verse and sweet melodies of Byron and Shelley sailed headlong into drama and promptly sank. Indeed, in the English language, there has been only one poet who crossed the frontiers with ease, and for Shakespeare a nondramatic form such as the sonnet represented only a sideline job.

A useful rule, in fact, informs a writer that he is wise to find his form and hold onto it. Novelists invariably write better novels than plays. The broken drama of Henry James, Joyce, Hemingway, and Steinbeck should be testimony enough. In like fashion, playwrights such as Arthur Miller and Tennessee Williams have written indifferent novels. And—lastly—the dissimilar, unlikely, less than holy trinity of da Ponte, Boito, and Hofmannsthal stands clearly for the justice of the rule, the conditioning of the mole: they are remembered today not for poems or novels but for operas. And opera, like it or not, prescribes a form.

That da Ponte was first a careerist and then an artist takes nothing away from his instinct for the form. Mozart, it would seem, had an equal instinct for da Ponte. In May 1783 he wrote to his father from Vienna:

> Our poet here is a certain Abate da Ponte; he has an enormous amount to do in writing pieces for the theater and he has to write per obbligo an entirely new opera for Salieri which will take him two months. He has promised after that to write a new libretto for me. But who knows whether he will be able to keep his word—or will want to?...If he is in league with Salieri, I shall never get anything out of him. But indeed, I should dearly love to show what I can do in an Italian opera!

Mozart undoubtedly knew what everybody else knew: that da Ponte was far from being an experienced dramatist; that, in fact, he had arrived in Vienna with little more than his social ambitions to his credit. To the Emperor Joseph II he was "a virgin muse." The virtue of da Ponte's virginity was that he knew his models (having been weaned as a young man on Pietro Metastasio's texts) and that he had the joy of spirit and the quick imagination to make any new experience very much his own.

Mozart, as we know from a 1781 letter to his father, was searching for "an able poet, that true phoenix," someone who understood that "in opera the poetry must be altogether the obedient daughter of the music." Some scholars are persuaded that by the autumn of 1783 he was already in collaboration with da Ponte on an opera that was to remain unfinished, *Lo sposo deluso* (K. 430). Whatever the story of that aborted effort may be, it is clear that by 1786 and their first finished collaboration, *Le nozze di Figaro,* da Ponte had already suffered the kind of apprenticeship—translating, adapting, and inventing for Salieri and Martín y Soler—that fitted him admirably for the needs of Mozart. In the same year, he adapted Shake-speare's *Comedy of Errors* for Stephen Storace, the exploration of which, says the musicologist Alfred Einstein, "would be tantamount to writing a short story of the dramatic technique of the opera-libretto."

Da Ponte's reputation today suffers less from detraction than it does from indifference. At one time, clearly, his standing was higher. Hof-mannsthal linked him with Goethe and Wagner. Shaw saw the libretto of *Don Giovanni* as "an odd mixture of the old Punch tradition with the highly emancipated modern philosophy of Molière." And Mozart him-self, not likely to be satisfied by a disabled poet or a disobedient daughter, demonstrated by the frequency with which he collaborated with him that he had found his man.

Detractions ranged from the moral outrage of Beethoven and Wagner, most clearly expressed by Ruskin (the *Don* is the "foolishest and most monstrous of conceivable human words and subject of thought"), to Ernest Newman's understandable, if no less arguable, formal view (the *Don* libretto is "one of the sorriest pieces of stage joinery ever nailed together by a hack in a hurry"). More typical, but perhaps even more bizarre and unjust, is the opinion of da Ponte's biographer FitzLyon, who, while crediting him with "good craftsmanship, willing subordina-tion to the music, verse expressed in the contemporary idiom,... wit, sound plot construction, good characterization, and elegant verse," con-cludes, nevertheless, that da Ponte's real contribution is only "the frame-work and the frills." Mozart she calls the active partner, da Ponte the pas-sive, with Mozart, finally, the source of "the works' intellectual depth and thought." Worse writers than da Ponte, genuinely content with hackery, would be happy to manage such "frills" as good wit, craftsman-ship, plot, verse, and characterization. But the habit of treating him dis-missively appears to have caught on even with his admirers.

Da Ponte, as I have implied, suggested the habit first, by treating this part of his career so casually, and often insensitively, in his *Memoirs*. In this, he was only a child of the eighteenth century. A truly obedient daughter of music was then only a lackey of the state, little more than a footnote in an emperor's notebook. Even so liberal a monarch as Joseph II would have traded all his composers for one good soldier, and there is no way of know-ing how many librettists he would willingly have burned for two. Given such status, it is no wonder that Mozart had so much trouble finding a da Ponte and that da Ponte had so much trouble appreciating himself.

Nothing is easier, therefore, than to speak of Mozart as if da Ponte scarcely existed, as if, in fact, a daughter, obedient or otherwise, is not necessarily a person. The latest to do so is Brigid Brophy in her extrava-gantly psychosexual analysis called—with no apologies to da Ponte—*Mozart the Dramatist*. Scarcely necessary as it is to agree with all the con-clusions she draws from the impotence, castration, repressed homosexu-ality, and incest woven into her thick texture, it is still possible to accept her formative assumption that psychology was Mozart's revolutionary contribution to opera. What is missing, again, is da Ponte's likely share in that psychology.

First, of course, two psychologies must be distinguished: that of the operas and their characters, and that of the two men who created them. The three operas have in common one theme or subject that imposes on them a specific psychological atmosphere, more severe, intense, ironic, and highlighted in these operas than in *Entführung aus dem Serail* or *Zauberflöte:* an atmosphere of seductive intrigue. To the end of testing the fragile constancy of men and women, the sources of true personal free-dom, the tremors or doubt people have about themselves—to this end all three operas revolve around schemes, deceptions, masks, and masquer-ades, utilizing most of the trappings of mistaken-identity comedy which can be pressed into quick service.

The play—which is to say *playing*—is the thing, the comic dramatist's oldest metaphor for the psychology of feeling behind words. Characters in such comedies serve a double action: the movement of the drama and the movement of their games, each action dependent on the other, both expressing the manner in which men fool themselves while pretending to fool others. This playing within the play becomes at once the source of comedy and the expression of an idea. A man in fear of attack tries to attack first. In gaming comedy, his sharpest weapon is whatever illusion he can create, if only for an instant. Through illusion—through playing at life—he finds momentary relief and protection from demons within and without. The identity he mistakes in the rush of events propelled by him is really his own: for men and women masked are men and women running from themselves. This is as true of the Count trying to exercise his droit du seigneur over Figaro's Susanna as it is of Don Giovanni running from the masked trio of Anna, Elvira, and Ottavio.

As intrigue links the operas, so does its psychological corollary—fear of attack—link librettist and composer. Shrill, sometimes desperate strains of imminent danger pervade da Ponte's *Memoirs* and Mozart's letters—da Ponte's haunted by rogues after his jobs and money, Mozart's by fear of imagined inconstancies and even, toward the end of his life, of being poisoned. How easy and natural it was, then, for these two to make drama together from such a powerful, shared response to the world. Phantoms from life became figures in the living dream called theater. If drama is the enactment of fantasy, the dynamic presentation of an image in the mind, then Mozart and da Ponte—however else they differed—were ideally suited to each other.

Mask and play, then: Mozart putting a face on drama, covering intrigue with the abstractions of music, shadowing sensuality with sound; da Ponte giving intrigue its first rhythms, its orders, shapes, directions, its concrete humors and impulses; Mozart expressing, da Ponte impressing, both serving the whole, like comedy and tragedy in the best plays, as one: unromantically, beyond the regions of conscious will, both of them imagining, and then conjuring drama for music.

To speak of these linked impulses, these twin psychologies, is not to say that Mozart and da Ponte spoke of them. When artists collaborate, they speak not of art but of craft. Once each is assured of the other's talent and temper, art can be assumed. It was neither the fashion then, nor is it even a necessity now, for artists to share psychologies openly. All that was required was a sharing of forms, the way to build blocks of action that suggested varieties of music. While Mozart and da Ponte were never aggressive reformers in the Beethoven or Wagner mold, they did, in fact, blur the inherited lines of opera to make something at once richer and more expressive; no longer *seria* or *buffa* alone but, in their place, a blending of forms and atmospheres pierced by irony.

Da Ponte's predecessor, the high priest of librettists, Metastasio, described himself as "a bird of court, used to ease, comfort, and repose." To him, drama for music was foursquare and immutable; action moved forward by blank verse set as recitative, lyrics set mainly for arias or duets, the chorus used sparingly, and larger ensembles almost unknown. Heeding their own free spirits, Mozart and da Ponte built upon more flexible forms. But—and perhaps here I am suggesting a minor heresy—for all the skill, boldness, scope, and grandeur of their adapted works, *Figaro* and the *Don,* it was not until *Così,* when they built upon a tale of their own invention, that all the elements cohered. Here, at last, was balance, the perfect ordering of material ideal to both of them.

For subject: an intrigue again. For manner: serious comedy placed against comic seriousness. For characters: six types reaching beyond type, evenly compared to one another, unevenly matched. For dramatic line: economy, a spare directness, superb timing, and the most ingenious placement of situation. For musical challenge: a first act moved almost entirely through ensembles, the second by arias, both mounting inevitably toward extended finales that use all the voices and orchestra almost symphonically.

And finally, for the single element that uses and bridges operatic inheritance while reaching forward to operatic future: the astonishing, ambivalent, sometimes absurd, sometimes heartbreaking figure of Fiordiligi. As she crosses centuries, threatening at moments to break the balances, she almost upsets the carefully wrought and contained shapes of both the music and the drama. At once satirical of the indignant, stentorian sopranos of *opera seria* and deeply serious within her precarious, temptingly dangerous dramatic situation, Fiordiligi is the logical touchstone to Mozart and da Ponte's extraordinary collaboration. With her, nature appears richer and more various, bending backward, glancing ahead, perfect and sublime in its touching imperfections. In concept and through music Fiordiligi blows dark winds of change softly and dramatically into the once circumscribed world of opera. Suddenly, for opera, there is an end and a beginning.

But neither end, beginning, nor serene coherence could have been found by Mozart alone. Less than justice is done to Mozart—so human, hardworking, reasonable, and perceptive—when we try to make him into a god. The wonder of art on earth is that it is made by humans, and in the theater, made by people working together. Words alone do not a drama make. Were the librettist's task only a matter of word spinning, then, indeed, music could make the miracle alone. But it's never so simple.

The poet's importance lies less in actual words than it does in the events lying behind them. Words, as such, are only the outward signs of text, the necessary filigree before drama can be developed—the most obvious indications to the audience that the singers are, in fact, *saying* something. Without them, only abstraction would exist, and we would have neither opera nor drama. Yet used as competently, often imaginatively, as da Ponte used them, they become what they must be: bricks placed upon a firm and considered structure.

Art often plays strange tricks with artists' ambitions. Some, like Wagner and Hofmannsthal, begin by climbing mountains, touching peaks, yet often as not just missing summits. Others, like da Ponte, are content to nestle in valley and city, wine on the table, a woman in one arm, and a wild intrigue spawning in the mind. In the end, each type—the profound planner and the modest schemer—may well produce as effectively as the other. Talent finally represents an unreasonable confluence of instincts, the true artist making discoveries only as he works.

Mozart's able poet may not have had a deeply philosophical mind. But as he worked and developed, he became the right man at the right time for Mozart and opera. No one else was doing what he could do, and indeed few after him did half so well. His is not a moving or inspiring story. He did not tear passions. He did not scream ritual rage to the world. What he did do, however, in serving Mozart, was quite enough. The phoenix, as Mozart feared before he met da Ponte, is the emblem of immortality that rises all too seldom from the ashes. To the composer's credit, he found in da Ponte material for his emblem. And to give a minor poet and major librettist his equal due, da Ponte brought the splendor of craft to the emblem and helped beyond measure to make it sing.

(November 1965)

Emotional Weather: Notes on Alban Berg's Theater

That Alban Berg took so many years to write only two operas, leaving one not quite finished, ought to be one clue among many that the stage was not an easy medium for him. Even allowing for the disruption of military service between 1914 and 1917, a disruption, in fact, that shifted Berg's views about both war and the oppressive nature of the army, *Wozzeck* still took another five years to complete, in 1922. Berg first saw Büchner's play in 1914. He had seen Wedekind's *Pandora's Box* even ear-lier—at its first performance in 1905 when he was twenty, having read the version published as *Earth Spirit* several years earlier. Even so, he was still searching for a subject to follow *Wozzeck* as late as 1927 when he wrote Schoenberg that he was seriously considering Paul Raynal's *The Grave of the Unknown Soldiers,* a work that would have led him back to a military setting. The rejection of that text, however, was still not the end of his search: his negotiations for Gerhardt Hauptmann's *And Pippa Dances* fell apart some time after he had already begun sketches for an operatic adap-tation, so it wasn't until 1928 that he began to talk seriously with Wedekind's widow about the *Lulu* plays.

Two years later he had still not finished the first act. In a breathtaking understatement, he wrote Schoenberg in May 1930 that "these long interruptions are the cause of doubts in me." He wondered if he could "still remember how to compose." This was nonsense, of course, since he had just completed the commission he had undertaken in 1929 for the soprano Ruzena Herlinger for a concert aria. Using three poems from Baudelaire's *Fleurs du mal,* he wrote *Der Wein,* frankly making use of the soprano and the idea as a rehearsal for his first (and last) extended music-drama written entirely with twelve-tone techniques. Unlike Büchner's *Woyzeck,* which had emerged out of its early-nineteenth-century obscu-rity as a series of arbitrarily linked fragments, Wedekind's plays did not suggest an immediate cutting and arrangement for a libretto. *Wozzeck's* fifteen scenes culled from the surviving twenty-nine of Büchner's could be selected around some straightforward notions of spare musical form. Where Büchner's words are clean, opaque, and economical, Wedekind's were thickly textured, rhetorical, and many. Berg complained that he had to "cut four-fifths of Wedekind's original," and "the selection of the remaining one-fifth is causing me enough trouble."

He added that "the libretto as a whole has, of course, been clear to me for a long time." Which was probably the point all along: Berg's invention of patterns that could sustain his infinite capacity for delay was far more developed than his invention of music, especially music for the theater. He could know "for a long time" where he was traveling, but he was not likely to go there on the most obvious road or in the swiftest vehicle. Something kept getting in the way of operatic inspiration.

Why opera, anyway? Great composers don't always make great operas—think of Haydn and Schubert for a start. Meanwhile, good plays don't transform themselves automatically into even half-good operas. Just to add further insult to the mystery, bad plays have a disturbing way of looking talented when tenors and sopranos are seducing each other and the rest of us with their intoxicating sounds. Of Berg's two teachers, Schoenberg and Zemlinsky, only the first attempted an assault on the stage, and the stage fought back: *Moses und Aron* is, at its best, a marvelously theatrical oratorio, longer than Stravinsky's *Oedipus Rex* and just as unyielding as theatrical drama. Mahler and Brahms kept their theatrical ambitions under famously severe control, suggesting that a gift for voice and song may have little or nothing to do with a talent for the lyric stage. Berg took more time getting around to his two operas than most composers took to write much more music than he ever wrote. In short, opera may have been Berg's ingenious way of delaying music.

I do not mean to suggest that Berg was misguided in his quest for the theater within himself. We are luckier than Berg and can see how that quest was worth making: *Wozzeck* and *Lulu* loom in the repertoire of this century as *Falstaff* and *Tristan* stand in the nineteenth, all of them endings and beginnings at once, deeply intimidating to composers that followed but completely liberating to the art. Berg's commitment and persistence is at last the most fitting response to Wagner, just as Composer X's work in the next twenty to fifty years will be the answer to Berg. If it took Berg twenty-three years to remember the *Lulu* plays as a possible source, then it must certainly take as much or more time for the most prodigiously gifted composer to cope with the staggering finality and suggestiveness in Wagner and Berg. There is, after all, less need now for opera, just as there is virtually no mass public need for theater. Serious composers and dramatists are scolded today for writing without an audience in mind, but if they don't write first for themselves, then how can they fool themselves into pretending that there is any audience at all? Wagner and Berg seemed to know that work of size, detail, and scope can be written only against the audience. Their eccentric, stubborn writing habits were part of their armory. Great work cannot be scolded into existence.

Berg adored secrets. Just as he lied to his future father-in-law about his schooling, so did he finally lie to his wife and the world about his love for Franz Werfel's sister Hanna Fuchs-Robettin, leaving the traces of that affair buried in the tonal rows of his *Lyric Suite*. (These have emerged only recently in the detective work done by George Perle after Helene Berg's death in 1976, and also recounted in careful detail by Berg's latest biographer, Karen Monson, in 1979.) Mrs. Berg's revenge was to be just as protective about the last act of *Lulu* as Berg was about his secret love, perhaps suspecting that the sordid conclusion would provide more evidence that the blissful domestic life she liked to boast about was only a myth cultivated by both Bergs, separately and together.

Good drama is always as much about its subtext as it is about the words characters say, which may be another way of saying that good drama contains secrets waiting to be unearthed by actors and director. By putting secrets in instrumental music—as Berg did in the *Lyric Suite* (using Hanna's initials to enclose the principal theme of the first movement, or repeated C's in the Rondo that point to Hanna's daughter, known as Dodo)—Berg was using his own subtext as a way of impelling him into the work itself. One need not play the game with Berg. Indeed, it's scarcely possible to follow it, even with signposts provided, any more than it is advisable or possible to follow Wagner's drama by trying to hang on to the leading motifs.

When Monson observes, too, that the Rondo itself is something of a clue because Berg "associated the form first with the manly Drum Major in *Wozzeck* and then with the composer Alwa Schön (who represents Berg himself) in *Lulu,*" then one can be forgiven for feeling unenlightened, thrown off the scent by the musical and dramatic events themselves. Berg would have made density a part of his work even without secrets. Individually they mean less than they do as a phenomenon: they made work possible. More than that, they are the dreamy stuff that drama is made on.

Why opera, then? Because Berg's drama every day of his life was never entirely acted. Just as actors will frequently confess that they feel more alive, even more themselves, onstage than they do in life, so was Berg an instinctive actor-dramatist. The secrets of the *Lyric Suite* are in the end the secrets of an inspired pedant. The secrets in the operas are the secrets of a life otherwise half-lived.

In October 1931 Berg wrote in one of his many secretly sent letters to Hanna that he saw himself as "a...play-acting person." He described his public life (now we call it "image") as that of an "exterior person" who "would never be able to compose *Lulu.*" If he hadn't had letters or the stage, he might have been compelled into divorce and remarriage. Fortunately, drama came first.

Berg told a friend that Ibsen was his "living ideal." Even before Wedekind's *Earth Spirit* in 1904, he had seen *Hedda Gabler* and *Ghosts,* high points in Vienna's 1903 season. That year, too, he most probably became the father of an illegitimate daughter, and though Perle prefers to ask for more evidence, he apparently attempted suicide. The daughter remained another of his secrets, though he kept her photograph, identified later by his nephew. Monson records remarkable similarities between Berg's life and Ibsen's— both sons of fathers whose businesses failed, both fathers themselves of an illegitimate child, and both academic failures. It is even probable that Ibsen considered suicide at one time, though Monson doesn't add this to her list.

Neither does she make much of what these associations might suggest about Berg's dramatic impulse. Noting that Ibsen's plays are often about characters "who harbor secrets of what society call sin," she drops the observation where she finds it. As she says, there is no way of knowing if Berg held Ibsen as his ideal because of Ibsen's biography, though certainly there was a world within Ibsen's plays that he couldn't help noticing as he retreated into late adolescent playacting, brooding around the summer house, describing himself dramatically as only "a tentative seeker! Finding nothing."

More nonsense, then: he was finding everything a writer of theatrical work might need. Lies, deceit, self-deception, and secrets give all the encounters in Ibsen's plays an energy and resonance they would not otherwise have. Revolted by the well-made play handed down by Scribe and Sardou, Ibsen turned the arranged plotting in on itself, letting the characters say almost anything but what they really mean, constantly ascribing feelings or views to the others that the others (and the audience) know they don't possess. Ibsen's characters tiptoe around the truth, exploding into resolute disaster by the end as singers explode into resolute song to express the otherwise unknowable and unsayable.

It is one gift to master musical form—as Berg did—and quite another to find the dramatic form to contain the music. Ibsen appears buried in one letter Berg wrote in 1910 to Helene Nahowski as he was waiting anxiously for her father to give his consent to Berg's proposal of marriage. It is a burial not unlike the clues found late in the *Lyric Suite* and in the variations, passacaglias, harmonic cells, and what Perle calls his "well-known preoccupation with the symbolism of numbers" found in the operas. Berg was telling Helene that the fear that haunted him most was his "fear of nature," referring to "frightening ecstasies...sexual or drunken orgies or morphia dreams." Without Helene by his side, the only retreat was his room, where he could read books and music. Here, at least, he was in his "own realm; anywhere else I might fall ill, and in nature I should disintegrate and be submerged..."

To be submerged by what he called nature was evidently more terrifying for him than rejection by Helene's father or marriage itself. Marriage: the ultimate retreat, the dream that was as sharply etched in his imagination as any of the musical embodiments of escape and obsession that he would bring to the stage in the next twenty-five years. Marriage: his momentary only hope, where he could see himself as "a man, intoxicated by delicious wine, leaning in rapture on the breast of his beloved, with vine leaves in his hair...transformed from a drunken beast into a sublime singer."

Seven years after seeing *Hedda,* he was alluding to himself as Eilert Lövborg, Ibsen's portrait of the artist as raffish, indulgent failure. We cannot know if Helene recognized the vine leaves planted in Eilert's hair by Hedda's imagination, but her obsessive "protection" of the whole *Lulu* for more than forty years might be construed as her way of tossing Eilert-Alban's manuscript into the flames. (Fortunately, she was less of a playact-ing dramatist than Berg.) What registers once again is Berg's image of him-self: a romantic, wasted Ibsenesque suicidal type, yet unlike Ibsen's artist, "a rake" who "looks into the eyes of the beloved and sinks back into holy adoration." Since he was incorrigibly musical, he was also listening to Mahler at the time, seeing himself as "a man shattered by Mahler's Third Symphony." Music and marriage were among his ways of not being sexual.

Ibsen provided subtextual power, but his concentrated encounters, most of them tidily arranged, all of them essential, could not provide the sprawl or fragmentary breathlessness Berg needed for his musical shapes. The epic form was too difficult for Ibsen to pursue once he had exam-ined and conquered it with *Peer Gynt.* The example of Büchner, so much earlier than Ibsen but so unknown until after Ibsen's death, was simply not there for him to thrive upon. *Peer* was exhausting, unproduceable at the time, too large and expansive, too uncomfortable as a dramatic dwelling, too unpredictable and breathless. Not until the end—the last four plays—did he begin to venture out of doors again. *Hedda* and *Ghosts* kept the outside world offstage. Mrs. Alving, Hedda, and the others stayed in their parlors.

Berg needed a form that could spread and splice in one breath. In a word, he needed the epic.

Like Shakespeare's plays, most operas are derived from sources, but few libretti are actually written by their composers. Mozart kept searching for the perfect librettist as much as he was looking for the perfect story, and much the same can be said for Verdi and Richard Strauss. More recently, Benjamin Britten turned to adapters of plays, poems, and stories that appealed to him as sources, and Stravinsky turned to W. H. Auden and Chester Kallman for *The Rake's Progress,* an opera that placed itself defiantly in the eighteenth and twentieth centuries at once, deliberately ignoring the daunting example of Berg. Britten and Peter Pears did indeed shape *A Midsummer Night's Dream* into a libretto for themselves. On balance, however, only Wagner and Berg shunned the collaborator, with Wagner just a bit more original and a lot more prolific than Berg, if a great deal clumsier in his dramatic technique. How strange to think that, as Berg was clearing his mind for *Lulu,* Weill and Brecht were deep into their work together while Strauss and Hofmannsthal were finishing *Arabella,* the last of their perfumed, nostalgic collaborations. Among composers, Berg and Wagner must surely be the most confident dramatists.

Berg's splendid isolation at the time was unique. Where Strauss could only look to a musical and dramatic past in *Arabella* and (later) *Capriccio,* and Weill and even Paul Hindemith were consciously part of the Weimar political world, Berg was alone in his turn-of-the century drama, his musical enactment of sexual guilt. He could not be locked into place or time. Delivering opera into an idiom that would release it from the necessity for a kind of song that had, in fact, been absorbed and captured totally by operetta and musical comedy (just as the well-made play belongs now mainly to the media), Berg had to ignore the old and new surrounding him. Weill was brilliant, original, but dramatically he was Brecht's creation. Strauss wasn't writing operatic dramas for the stage so much as he was writing operas for sopranos. Unlike Strauss, Weill, and Hindemith, Berg was bringing tonal disruption into the opera for the first time, the kind of break with tradition that he, Schoenberg, and Webern had already brought to symphonic form. Perle says that he was "affirming the collapse of the musical language on which the (Mahlerian) tradition is based." Similarly, he was affirming the collapse of dramatic tradition long ago proclaimed by Büchner. That Büchner's innovations went unnoticed is only a description of a peculiar time lag in theater, picked up by Brecht much later but lifted bodily into opera only by Berg. Fortunately for operatic drama, he didn't pay much attention to Weimar's collapse. His work embodied politics without wasting an instant on the political.

Assuming that Othello and Falstaff are self-sufficient in the plays written about them by Shakespeare, then whatever compelled Verdi to give them musical life? Had he another ten years at his disposal, he might have easily added Lear to his musical summits, but that had to be left to Aribert Reimann in this century. Clearly, composers don't ask questions about their own audacity. They seem to assume that no matter how self-contained and perfect a drama may be, it can always be renewed (or improved) by music.

One need not choose. Plays and operas are allied but different arts. I never saw Ralph Richardson's Falstaff (not, after all, the *Merry Wives'* Falstaff) or Tito Gobbi's Falstaff, but I'm certain that I'd like to have seen both. Similarly, I'm reasonably convinced that Verdi's *Otello* is more continually thrilling than Shakespeare's, but only Laurence Olivier's Othello has given me a Verdian thrill.

Figaro, Otello, Falstaff, Wozzeck, and *Lulu* do not replace the great plays of their origin, they simply provide an alternate vision and voice, accessible most likely to a different audience in a different way. Furthermore, if Mozart, Verdi, or Berg could have written plays equivalent in dramatic flair to the plays of Beaumarchais, Shakespeare, Büchner, or Wedekind, then they would have been playwrights, not composers. Confounding the pleasures offered by confounding the genres will not improve either the dramatic or the operatic stage.

In the end, the only comparison worth making is in performance: *Pandora's Box* at the Royal Court Theatre in London some years ago was considerably inferior to Pabst's film with Louise Brooks; on the other hand, Teresa Stratas in John Dexter's production of *Lulu* at the Met (and evidently in Rhoda Levine's production in Holland and Patrice Chereau's in Paris) had an impact not unlike Louise Brooks's. If it felt more anguished, then that was part of the difference between Wedekind and Berg, Pabst and Berg, and Brooks and Stratas. Theatrical performance is the shortest distance between two individualities. A genre is not obliged to justify its presence.

Describing Boito's success with the libretto of *Otello* for Verdi, the late

Joseph Wechsberg observed that "he had to provide his composer with opportunities for melodic expanse and lyrical passages but the action must go on and the dramatic impact must not suffer." As good a description as any for the movement from most plays to most operas, this formula would still not have helped Berg. Melodic expanse was a world apart. Lyrical passages, if any, would appear in the orchestral interludes of *Wozzeck,* those amazing passages on which Berg alights like a hungry predatory bird, starved for respite and release. Berg needed opportunities for contraction, not expanse. Fifteen scenes of brilliantly lit wasteland; voices arid and only momentarily lifted into direct expression; a parched, cruel experience enriched only by strict musical forms and a gorgeously vocal orchestra: playing the role of his own Boito, Berg had to provide his composing self with textual austerity. It can't be surprising that for both operas he chose scenically expansive plays that needed to be cut to the bone.

Why Wozzeck and Lulu? Why characters of such obvious, weighty, indolent stupidity? Pierre Boulez thinks that both are visible primarily as victims, revealing "their gradual enslavement to forces which they are too weak to counter." Effectively imprisoned in the army and in his affair with Marie, Wozzeck is totally unconnected to his illegitimate child. He is the Doctor's experiment, the Drum Major's target, the Captain's slave, Marie's dupe, and his own burden. Murder is the only way to become a complete victim, to relieve himself of life. Lulu does the same, albeit over a longer span of time, sinking into her murderer's arms as Wozzeck sank beneath the pond's willows.

Unlike opera's usual figures, neither Wozzeck nor Lulu lives in high romance or remotely high life—though Lulu flirts with position when she marries the hapless Dr. Schön. Berg couldn't write about princesses and lovers. Instead, he used the crabbed, small lives of tentative, doomed, momentary survivors. He needed a subject that needed his kind of music —not merely dissonance (Strauss had that, after all) or the twelve-tone row, but a music that could defeat his protagonist as they are defeated by life. It is as if the ordinary, unelevated character chosen by Berg would be the only figure likely to succumb to the majestic force of his music.

Theodor Adorno reports that Berg considered his creative drive to be architectural. Hence the continual use of complex, received musical forms. Not only in music, however: Berg's theatrical instincts were also concerned with construction, contrasts, weights and balances, the fusion and awareness of distinctions. His advice for the production and staging of *Wozzeck,* written in 1930 long after his experience of productions, is as precise and demanding as his music. Place and time are his repeated concerns. Marie's room must be completely different from the Captain's, and both rooms, in turn, distinctively contrasted with the Doctor's room. The tavern garden must be seen in a "large open space," but the low dive in Act III, Scene iii, must be in a "narrow corner." He speaks of the sky "with its phenomena" for the landscapes in Act I and Act III, and even the "water in the pond should be recognizable as such." He found in one performance that it was "very effective...to have the water in the pond begin to move gently at bar 275, to have this movement of the waves reach a climax at bars 285/286, and then to let it slowly subside, all movement ceasing completely at bar 302." Even the times of day and night are to be distinguished from one another. Twilight at the end of Act I "must be substantially differentiated...from the other scenes that are played in the same setting, II/iii and III/v." Also, he suggests firmly that contrast must be made between a "fading evening light" and a "morning sunlight in the same setting." He offers the director only a few scenes in which his fantasy can be "given much greater leeway." Even in those rare moments he insists on contrast; for example, between the "harmless fun" of the first tavern scene and "the uncanny, almost daemonic exuberance of the second."

A mistake, then, to link *Wozzeck* and Berg either to the German expressionists or to Brecht. Berg guarded his architecture under an old-fashioned cover of realism, wary of "innovation" that might take flight from specific details as if in response to his flight from tonality. One can sympathize with Perle's revulsion in 1979 at the news of Chereau's production of *Lulu*— "only the most odious example in the current generation of a type whom Arnold Schoenberg characterized almost fifty years ago: 'Producers who look at a work only in order to see how to make it into something different.'" Berg did not leave a similar set of notes for *Lulu's* production, but even if his operatic style had changed between the two works, would it be likely that those architectural details would no longer concern him?

Chereau declares pointless any "arguments about being faithful to the author," a directorial arrogance we have by now come to expect, but it's curious that he talks more of Wedekind than he does of Berg. Perhaps he was suddenly and briefly self-conscious about his ear. Only once in his essay for the recording does he refer to the music, and for a fleeting moment, he points the way to a directorial approach that might actually not need "something different" to obtain its kicks. "Listen to Berg's music at this point," he says, referring to the Paris scene in the third act, "to this forward, rarefied chamber music which tells, beyond 'opera' one may say, of the furtive relationships, of the base and sordid rustlings of those conversations where Lulu fights and suddenly becomes so hard: all the misery of human relationships is here." Too bad Chereau doesn't acknowledge that being faithful to the *composer* is not a matter of arguments, pointless or otherwise, but a matter of listening. For Berg, surely, theater *is* music.

It isn't clear why Boulez finds *Lulu* more accessible than *Wozzeck*. Possibly he finds Berg's "enthusiasm for symmetrical forms" more alive here than in *Wozzeck*. A theatrical response, however, could not ignore the simple, accessible symmetry of *Wozzeck*'s fifteen scenes, neatly dividing the work into three acts, five scenes each. Performed without intervals, as it has been at the Met since 1980, the work assumes a drive and intensity unmatchable in any conceivable *Lulu* production, if only because *Lulu* seems to exist primarily in its protagonist's halting, spasmodic rhythms. That existence is, of course, another kind of symmetry—or rather, a shaping instrument all its own. Unlike with *Wozzeck,* the shape is harder to hear and less visible as a dramatic form.

Take Act II, Scene ii, for example, beginning with an orchestral interlude (as in *Wozzeck*) but continuing first with the film that so deliberately interrupts the action onstage. If Boulez is right—and I think he is—the entire opera "pivots on the hinge of Lulu's imprisonment," yet it is precisely the episode Berg chooses *not* to dramatize. Smart, fashionable thinking might ascribe this to some kind of instinct in Berg for the new media and even the mixed media in this century, but it's more likely an admission of a temporary theatrical defeat. Once the film is over and the characters begin to tumble onstage, one after the other, as they await Lulu's return, it becomes clear that Berg has begun to give up perfect symmetry.

At first the scene appears to be Rodrigo's, with Geschwitz and Alwa as supporting players. Schigolch arrives, leaving immediately with Geschwitz for the hospital where she will replace Lulu with herself. Alone, Alwa and Rodrigo discuss money, and "discuss" is the right word, since they are talking unaccompanied by music. Perhaps this is in the refined, noble tradition of *sprechstimme,* yet somehow it seems to be only dialogue. Symmetrically inclined composers such as Beethoven, Mozart, and even Bizet never seem to be suggesting with *recitative* or dialogue that music has exhausted itself, but in this and similar passages in *Lulu,* the impression is unmissable: Berg is looking for a musical-theatrical idiom that he hasn't, unfortunately, time enough to discover.

The scene plunges headlong into more entrances and exits, the Gymnast and the Schoolboy suddenly arriving, followed by the quick removal of the Gymnast just before Rodrigo goes off to the police. With the arrival of the mezzo-soprano as the Schoolboy, still another operatic tradition is recalled, this time the perfectly respectable one of the breeches role. Even so, all this in one scene?

And it isn't over. Next, after Lulu's arrival, Schigolch leaves to buy the train tickets, leaving Lulu and Alwa alone at last. Lulu comes in to the sound of muted strings playing what seems to be an independent symphonic adagio with the voices used only as accompaniment. Lulu's "O Freiheit" is supposed to be sung, says Berg, "in the most cheerful tone," but I would defy even Maria Callas to find the cheer in that tensile vocal extension.

What it does, however, is quite literally absorb the action into itself. After all the comings and goings, the "Freiheit" is a punctuation, a necessary pause in the action, refocusing attention on Lulu herself. Next, they have another talk without music, followed by Alwa seducing Lulu by comparing her body to "a musical form." Berg, nonetheless, does nothing to illustrate that or any other musical form: the words called upon are *"cantabile," "misterios,"* and *"powerful andante,"* none of them present in those moments in the score. Alwa's last words in the scene are a repeated "Schweig...Schweig"

(Quiet…quiet), both of them sung as a high-pitched cry. It comes as no awesome surprise that Lulu's last words in the scene are merely spoken.

Dense, complex, fearful, and tremendous, yes, but accessible and symmetrical—never. Berg was too good and too sane to be symmetrical a second time.

If he was theatrically uncertain in parts of *Lulu,* it might have been a way of expressing his resistance to opera as a musically accompanied play, with arias (as in the past) and orchestra merely there to illustrate moods or action. Rhoda Levine tells me from her experience directing Stratas's first Lulu in Holland that the film interlude is literally impossible to do in direct correspondence with the music. Some decently inspired director in Zurich once tried to follow Berg's instructions to the letter and found that they couldn't be done. Levine also found that the architecture described in the stage directions makes no sense. Not that any of this should be license for Chereau and his buddies in theatrical sandboxes all over the world, but it is a sign that production might try to unearth contradictions—images and behavior that take arms not against the music but against theatrical cliché.

Levine, coming to our discussion from the theatrical inside, adds that for her the music is "emotional weather." Love, in *Lulu,* is—as she says—anxiety, learned first from Schön, who has given Lulu her sentimental education. An obedient servant until the moment she must save herself from his violence by turning violence on him, Lulu is followed by music that never describes her actions but always reports on her existential undertow. After killing Schön, says Levine, she loses energy, yet the opera pushes on, unflagging in its invention, surviving despite the exhaustion that has been pursuing Berg from the beginning. Berg's great affairs were not with Helene or Hanna but with Marie and Lulu, the women who could be consumed and dominated, as he was, by theatrical gesture and musical form.

(1982)

Don Juan in Hell's Kitchen

Peter Sellars can claim that he's rescued *Don Giovanni* from old age: his cast of young singers, securely embraced by a concept that throws them daringly into what looks like the South Bronx or a hellish Catfish Row, assume the roles as if nothing could be more natural than the mix of Mozart and a life driven by hard drugs, booze, and street fights. Sellars can be trusted not to offer a costume party for miscast tenors and sopranos, but there's always a danger that, like so many committed conceptualists, he'll treat the operatic stage like a playpen for closet playwrights, plundering others for the text he cannot–or will not–write himself. With *Don Giovanni*, he plays with the danger head-on, staging a version that consistently floats above da Ponte's libretto, offering actions and behavior that would normally be accompanied by Bernstein or Gershwin rather than Mozart.

Without reading Sellars's program notes, it wouldn't be possible even by the end to know that his Don Ottavio, appearing bare-chested on the tenement steps where Don Juan has shot Donna Anna's father, is really an undercover cop, but the rest is plain enough: the Don in a leather jacket, a jewel gleaming on his earlobe; Donna Elvira like an Apache Madonna smeared with black lipstick, slamming her oversized bag against the nearest object; Leporello, the Don's black servant-crony, doing a quiet rock 'n' roll riff at the outset, reluctantly accepting a sniff of coke from an appeasing Don as the second act begins; Zerlina's black lover, Masetto, breaking a beer bottle to use as a weapon against the Don and Leporello; the Don stripping down to his undershorts at the party and again before dying; Donna Anna shooting up in the middle of "Non mi dir," just in time to give her coloratura a plausible context; and Leporello bringing a McDonald's meal and a giant transistor radio to the penultimate scene, thus giving the Don a chance to throw fries at Elvira. A slum like this may not welcome Mozart, but Sellars is surely demonstrating that, for him, Mozart needs the slum.

Never mind that it only makes cynical sense for Donna Anna to pull out her syringe in front of her cop-suitor. Sellars is clearly more interested in raw events than textual logic. As he says, "The time and place scheme...doesn't make sense now." Consequently, he makes a detour into Aristotelian compression, holding the action to its blasted street where Con Ed's flashing yellow warnings hover over open sewers, while suggesting that everything happens in "real time," with music the most unifying force of all. He tries to find a story that may not make sense against the test of observable urban behavior (where are all the neighbors and cops who don't take part in the night's rousing murder, thefts, and zonked-out orgies?) but which may well make richly textured sense of the score. Sellars is insisting that the music be heard not as decoration but as dramatic admission that life is often a tragic-comic mess worthy of all that mathematically intricate expression.

Along the way, he is only occasionally frivolous. When Leporello corners Elvira to list the Don's conquests in the Catalogue aria, his slide show of porno nudes is one of those thumb-nosing sensations that doesn't move as far as the music. Leporello gets to the amazing Spanish achievements— 1,003 women—without a change in the slide show. The music takes a turn into quiet astonishment, though Sellars merely continues the same dirty pictures. Similarly, those burgers and fries lead less to the Don's fate than to unintended giggles from the audience when he squeezes ketchup out of plastic packets. Weirdly, too, the Don's serenade to Elvira's maid—"Deh vieni alla finestra"—is performed without the Don playing (or faking) the mandolin clearly heard in the orchestra.

But at its best, Sellars's staging is lovely and oddly traditional. Zerlina sings "Vedrai carino" to a battered Masetto, having come out in the street wrapped in a quilt; gradually, he turns into her, curled like a baby, head in her lap, with the quilt pulled over them as they gently fall asleep—surely an image that melts unforgettably into Mozart's *and* da Ponte's intention. Sellars is less convincing earlier when he has Masetto actually beat her up before she tells him sweetly to do so. But if in his urge to be complex, Sellars is often simplistic, smartassed, or intellectually lazy, he's on to ideas that may begin to liberate opera from its boring compulsion to illustrate music with overdressed linear action.

Much of what he initiates may be more for his singers than for the audience. Instead of generalized rant, they're lured into connections with reality. Kurt Ollmann's lanky Don, for example, would be forced into empty swagger if he had to cope with tights and cloak; here he looks genuinely distressed, a pale lonely figure unable to cope. The women may be made to overdo their commitment to kitchen knives, but at least they're dealing with visible, demeaning choices; best of all, Elvira—shatteringly sung and acted by Lorraine Hunt—actually cleans up her act in the next few hours given to her, the only character to emerge from the persistent darkness to another side.

Oh, that darkness. Odd that Sellars should be so compulsively literal about light. James F. Ingalls's dim lighting may be splendidly wrought in itself, but it does nothing for the actors who sing whole swatches of text with no more illumination than the 75-watt bulb hanging over them or the blinding fluorescent lamp in the tenement hall. Surely the road to hell needs better-lit intentions.

Still, Sellars's courage and his frequent dramatic insights may make a case for opera as theater. By playing fast and louche with the operatic beast's tedious conventions, he's questioning and even destroying the form in order to save it. This time around, most of his choices are sharply envisioned, emotionally true, and respectfully presented. Even if he hasn't yet torn me away from recordings of Ezio Pinza, Cesare Siepi, and Elisabeth Schwarzkopf, and counterpointing images of my own, he has begun to suggest that Mozart's powerful urge for the stage had to be right. Opera will be theater again when it systematically refuses to imitate itself.

(July 1987)

Out of the Woods

Stephen Sondheim nasty, mean, and ready to murder most of us is Sondheim at his entertaining best. Even if Susan H. Schulman's restaging of *Sweeney Todd* were less effective than it is, the reminder would be salutary. Only diehard *Sunday in the Park* and *Into the Woods* junkies could possibly disagree: those one-act larks stretched into two-act monotonies fall all over themselves to prove that Sondheim has a heart, but the effort and consequent banality keep bursting through the seams. For whatever reason—incapacity or musical ideology—Sondheim rarely builds a tune; similarly, he and his book writers usually fashion dutiful second acts, their storytelling just as out of breath as his melodies.

Not *Sweeney Todd,* mercifully. If anything, it's the first act that lumbers a bit, as if Sondheim can't quite believe that a tale fueled by revenge gives him all the liberty he needs. For a while, he gives too much air space to Anthony and Johanna, the putative young lovers, eliciting uncharacteristically boring lyrics—"I feel you, Johanna, I'll steal you, Johanna." But the act is saved by its own logic: with demon barber Todd determined to slit throats while waiting for his real enemy to sit in the chair again, and with Mrs. Lovett giddily prepared to grind and bake his victims into her pies, only ecstatic cynicism will do. Sondheim gets high on ruthless impulses, so that by the second act, even Anthony turns vicious, his dumb baritone lyricism submerged into cascading ensembles. One voice tumbling past another—and another—is Sondheim's natural and most energizing instrument. No disgrace that he can't be Schubert or Richard Rodgers: given the right story, he has the cold-blooded skill to turn any stage into a polyphonic Bach playpen.

Despite the extravagant splendors of Eugene Lee's high-tech environmental design for Harold Prince's production ten years ago, James Morgan's fairy-tale picture-book surround of the Circle in the Square's limited playing space is precisely the kind of reduction *Sweeney Todd* really needs. Prince and Lee played directly into Sondheim's grand opera pretensions; Schulman and Morgan, on the other hand, clear space for the story. With a small cast backed by a five-person chorus, all the voices natural and unamplified, the focus is on (mostly) clear words, incisive actions, and the relentless fury of the plot. The price paid for these virtues is loss of orchestral color, since the score has to be rattled off by several anemic keyboards under David Krane's lively direction. Yet without an orchestra overwhelming their distinctly unoperatic voices, the actors in this version can recapture the drama for themselves.

Bob Gunton's Sweeney Todd is a harrowing presence. His staring intensity ought to be as one-dimensional as the score threatens to be, but it isn't: silent or active, he's always listening to inner voices, as if he can never let a good idea—killing people—slip from his grasp. His love song to razors, "My Friends," is the sensual act of a genuine voluptuary. He's the perfect conduit for the delight Sondheim takes in a motivation truly lived, no judgment permitted to contaminate its horrific purity.

Equally good, and something of a discovery, is Eddie Korbich as Tobias Ragg, the perpetual apprentice who finally works for Mrs. Lovett without knowing how steeped in blood he really is. His beautifully ugly profile— sharp nose widely separating cavernous eyes—is cartoon-etched, Dick Tracy to the life. But his soul is more exposed than his eyes: quicksilver movements can't disguise the weight of pain; add to this a voice that lands on pitch and other targets with unerring precision, and you have a singing actor of uncommon eloquence. If he doesn't exactly hijack the show from the others, it's because most of them are up to his vivacity. With Angela Lansbury's flavorsome example as precedent, Beth Fowler's Mrs. Lovett doesn't always avoid the pandering built into the role, but she finds the marvelously stupid tenderness that is there without making more than a snack out of it. Musically, too, she's especially apt, celebrating "the worst pies in London" by slapping the dough on all the right beats.

Not that the right emotional beats in this work are always easy to find. Sondheim continues to be a superb lyricist in search of an equally good composer. Imagine da Ponte without Mozart, forced to turn Beaumarchais into musical compulsion all by himself. It's wonderful that Sondheim persists in what may be a winning performance likely to remain a losing game. With *Sweeney Todd,* however, he's in reasonably full command of a satisfying Dickensian mode. If he can't keep the momentum going to the end—his act-endings are either trivial (the first) or musically repetitive (the second)—he's nevertheless on top of an idiom all his own: he can't write hits or arias, but he gathers into his musical orbit the bitterness and contagion of an America only too willing to make disappointment look like victory.

(September 1989)

Fats-uosity Triumphant

The great fat and sassy star presence heard but not seen in *Ain't Misbehavin'* is Fats Waller himself. Bowler hat cocked over an ear, eyes brimming with mischief, his belly good-capon-lined, he was the Falstaff of performer-composers, thumbing his nose at the state and all its prissy dignities. Like Falstaff, too, he was more than an overstuffed clown. Not that he flaunted anger or draped himself in melancholy, but beneath the joy there was always his mocking awareness of a darker text made visible and eloquent by his insinu- ating inflections, his aggressive intelligence. The first song he recorded, when he was only 18, was "'T'Ain't Nobody's Biz-ness If I Do," a lyric that could easily be his signature if there weren't so many others that testify equally to a stance that was all about quiet refusal and inner freedom. Even that most famous signature line repeated frequently in Richard Maltby and Murray Horwitz's show—"One never knows, do one?"—is funny not only for its send-up of grammar but for the assumption of detached dignity in that awful, hoity-toity "one." He must have loved seducing the enemy with his fatly disguised imitations of white, classy snobbism.

Oh that glorious fat! If *Ain't Misbehavin'* does nothing else, it ought to rescue big and little chubbies from their nasty outcast status. Three of the five terrific performers—Nell Carter, Armelia McQueen, and Ken Page— have a combined weight and literal beauty that automatically call into ques- tion the standards jammed down our gullets by the fashion, diet, and work- out industries. It may be bad for longevity (Fats died at 39), but worn as they do, it must be a great way to live. Never have I seen chins and bellies so wonderfully in command of themselves. When Nell shakes her shoul- ders, continents move; when Armelia turns her cobalt-blue butt in our direction, she makes the sun look puny; and when Ken lifts his chest to the heavens, it's a statement on behalf of the stomach as the center of the uni- verse. Nothing could be truer to Fats's spirit: one are what one are.

To complicate matters, however, the slighter people have their space, too. Charlaine Woodard may be all mouth and no body, but she's cer- tainly something. In "Yacht Club Swing" she makes roulades of squeaks sound more dazzling than Joan Sutherland's pinpoint coloratura flings at Lucia. With her, flesh seems like an afterthought: she's so narrow she looks more like an animated cartoon than a person. It's as if the entire show were declaring the necessity for surprise and variety. The single holdout for the "normal" look is Andre De Shields, turning his knees and wrists into statements that look suspiciously like irony. Four rings blazing from his hands, he tells us, "I dreamed about a reefer five feet long"—a snake in ecstasy, so confident in every move and glance that it soon looks as if he doesn't need us at all.

Which is part of the show's magic: all the contributions—Maltby's direction, Arthur Faria's musical staging, and Luther Henderson's musical arrangements—are finally about Waller's flamboyant wit, his cocky way of misbehaving despite the claim to the contrary. Henderson, unfortunately, wasn't playing the stride piano at the matinee I saw, but he was there nonetheless in those elegant voicings and tricky counterpoints. Despite the raucous overmiking we're supposed to be used to these days, the show retains a musicality and gentleness rare in our theater. In an odd way, its refusal to "honor" Fats with biographical commentary or story line is a way of hauling musical comedy into modernist sensibility: this is implicitly a narrative of night people enduring the twentieth century in the only way they know how—and a mighty blow against the century's real vulgarities it turns out to be. Real, sexy people enjoying their bodies and themselves is the only text needed.

Having missed the show ten years ago, I can't compare the five performers to their younger incarnations. What they've gained in certainty may be at the cost of a simplicity they had earlier: I kept wishing for fewer illustrative embellishments from Carter, a resistance to lip-smacking punctuation from Page; with Fats, the extra sound or bumptious gesture never seemed like decoration. That said, however, I couldn't wish for a more pungent, sometimes stinging entertainment. Those wonderful, complicated conjunctions—"Fat and Greasy," "Black and Blue"—get all the air and space they need. How the actors manage to stand outside the threatening self-pity of lyrics like "What did I do to be so black and blue?" is one of those mysteries that keeps making theatrical performance more alluring (for me) than the other arts. The audience is taken in by the lyricism. The performers, on the other hand, refusing to smile at the ovation, have evidently noticed that the 1929 song is part of their passage through history. Jaunty as they—and Fats—may be, they're not about to forgive anybody.

(September 1988)

Stratasphere

Any number of statues who happen to sing—Kirsten Flagstad, Lauritz Melchior, Renata Tebaldi, and Jussi Bjoerling come to mind—have demonstrated that supreme voicing of a role can for an instant seem like acting. On voice alone, with line held taut or immaculate placement of expressive tone hefted to the rafters, such singers cast a peculiar spell over the dramatic occasion, as if to say that nothing could be more emotionally real than the human body caught in a moment of vocal ecstasy. Yet even when phenomenal singing seems to say everything, someone— Maria Callas or Teresa Stratas—comes along to prove that vocal splendor is nothing compared to an actor who happens to sing.

That said, Callas's disappointing appearance as an actor without anything to sing in Pasolini's *Medea* suggests that musical technique is the structure needed to organize a singer's acting instincts: pressured by chromatic runs or phrases that have to be taken in a single breath, she can release herself into an utterly convincing special reality. It may be misleading, however, to identify that reality with what is otherwise expected from acting. In performance, singers simply have more on their minds than actors. Writing of Callas's musical virtues, Walter Legge refers to her "use of ornamentation in all its forms and complications, the weighting and length of every appoggiatura, the smooth incorporation of the turn in melodic line, the accuracy and pacing of her trills, the seemingly inevitable timing of her portamenti, varying their curve with enchanting grace and meaning." And all this must be happening while she either senses or watches the conductor, balances her sound against the orchestra's, and picks up cues from the prompter!

Legge's reference to meaning is a clue: some singers make sense out of the words, trills, and melodic curves, others make mashed potatoes. But even that distinction doesn't begin to define what makes Callas an actor and Tebaldi a statue, since Tebaldi's idiomatic Italian and sinuous legato were not exactly small potatoes. Knowing her own vocal limitations surely drove Callas harder into her natural, obsessive perfectionism, a stance that automatically nourished her theatrical presence: what she inhabited on stage was less a role than a contest with herself.

Stratas, on the other hand, is in a contest with existence. Wherever music and narrative may take her in Puccini's three short operas, *Il Trit-tico,* she goes there like a prisoner condemned. At first it may not seem so in *Gianni Schicchi,* where, as a puppy lover, she's all melting allure, soft around every possible edge, an enchanted ice-cream cone looking for the most appreciative mouth; but by the end it's clear that she's been in per-petual motion, the possibilities of love catching her by surprise, gazing at the Florentine sky like an earnest student in doubt about the universe. Her entrance in *Il Tabarro* tells a similar story: for an instant her smile looks as if it could light up Paris, but as she moves down the steps toward the barge where she lives unhappily with her husband, a shadow wipes the smile away. That shadow haunts even the simplest domestic phrase, her "Buona notte" emerging in a reluctant hush. Compelled to listen to her friend Frugola for a moment, she covers up her desire to be anywhere else by combing her hair as if it were her last act on earth.

All this begins to suggest that Stratas seems more actor than singer because she fills silences with action and temperament. In *Suor Angelica,* during the interminable first half-hour of fussy note spinning—Puccini's strategy for the melodramatic wallop he's saving for the last half-hour—she buries her head while sitting on the side or retreats to the outside oven, a diminutive Julia Child with nothing better to do. At last, Angel-ica gets the bad news from her aunt: her sister's marriage means that she must renounce her fortune. But worse is yet to come. She circles the ominous messenger, her hands no longer restrained, one shooting up to her mouth as she tries to silence herself, the other soon pawing her aunt's dress. She's guessed already that her baby son is dead, and when this is confirmed, she dives recklessly to the floor. The harsh scream she utters has nothing to do with singing—indeed, it's more like a declaration of war against song and what it can do. And from then on her tight-fisted little body becomes a symphony of frantic hands and little spins, an unac-commodated creature left with only vision and attack.

Singers like Stratas and Callas spend all of themselves at every per-formance, surely one sign of an actor, whatever the medium. In 1824 Giuditta Pasta is reported to have held "her listeners spellbound...so seized and carried away that she collapsed before the end." Wagner found Wilhelmine Schröder-Devrient much the same way, writing of "the almost demoniacal warmth radiated by the human-ecstatic achievement of this incomparable artist." And Maria Malibran is described by Delacroix as ripping "her handkerchief and even her gloves to tatters." All of this could easily encompass Stratas in full sail on Puccini's high Cs—much the better part of her shredded voice, by the way.

It's no surprise to learn that the earlier divas were just as plagued by vocal miseries as Callas and Stratas. Acting in opera is usually about mad scenes or any emotional state that cries out for lunatic concentration. But it's also about ordinary gestures in extraordinary circumstances. On Lear's heath, an actor can't only respond to wind and rain, he must overreach them as if ready to burst into song. In opera, music is the stretch that makes it possible for the singer to act. Most singers may not know it, but opera is their chance to look like the rest of us; it's the naturalism of the soul.

(October 1989)

Two Cheers for Booing

For one, like myself, who applauds and boos in print, the sounds of no hands clapping and big mouths booing is an assault not merely on the nerves but on my hopes for the critical act. Not for me the raucous outburst and impulsive moan or—heaven forfend—the unpondered analysis of a play or performance. My faith, such as it is, has relied always on the hours or days left to think about what I've seen; with any luck, the business of writing, offering a chance to look more precisely on the event, is the way I come to know what I felt like days or hours before.

Imagine, then, my shock at Germany's Bayreuth Festival this summer when, after each performance of the abstract-modernist *Ring* cycle directed by Harry Kupfer and conducted by Daniel Barenboim, a chorus of boos broke through the prevailing cheers whenever Kupfer bravely took his place before the curtain. This was the third cycle of the season, meaning that his *Rheingold* appearance, while a first for me, was his ninth such punishment. Indeed, by quick calculation, since this was also the third summer of Kupfer's cycle, those boos must have been the thirty-third time he had freely given himself over to the ritual, so that by the time next summer ends, he will have outfaced his faceless adversaries forty-eight times!

Now: I am dissembling when I refer to shock. The sorrows—if sorrows they be—of Kupfer were not my first encounter with an audibly miserable audience. When Birgit Nilsson first sang Isolde at the Metropolitan Opera years ago, she retired two tenors to their dressing rooms in the first two acts before taking on her third in advance of the *Liebestod:* one of the faltering tenors was the hapless Kurt Baum, usually booed even before he came onstage, the mere announcement of his name sufficient cause for mayhem. And who can forget the claques lined up for and against Tebaldi and Callas whenever they appeared in alleged rivalry? Tempers ran high on 41st Street in those days, and only the news from Parma that Cornell MacNeil was the recipient of Italy's freshest vegetables and loudest hoots could make New Yorkers feel that, after all, we were civil disobedients at best—or worst.

Judith Malina, surely an authority on and promoter of audience agitation, once floated the notion that some scholar should do a history of theater riots, suggesting that what we know about the premiere of Stravinsky's *Rite of Spring* in Paris (1913) or of Dubliners' initial take on Synge's *The Playboy of the Western World* and O'Casey's *The Plough and the Stars* is only the beginning of a mysterious story that makes Kupfer's experience—and mine—sound like child's play.

Yet what is common to those riots and the booing at Bayreuth is the strange spectacle of conservatives at such a high pitch of war that they can't restrain their otherwise dignified instincts in public places. At Bayreuth, especially, the fashion parade between the acts is just one sign that this is no casual drop-in affair. Having paid top Deutschmark after being on an eight- or ten-year waiting list for the privilege of seeing the cycle in the remarkable theater for which it was written, nobody is there to have a bad time. The paradox, however, is that they endure the exercise, the advance planning, and the expense knowing all along that, because Wieland Wagner placed the Gods on a floating disc forty years ago, surrounded by light and technology outside even his grandfather's wildest excess, most *Ring* cycles at Bayreuth will be a test of their willingness to accept fresh images and ideas that grandfather might have actually liked. "To avoid change," wrote the grandson in 1951, "is to transform the virtue of fidelity into the vice of rigidity."

This, then, is the scene they choose to enter in between the processions they take to display each night's costume change. They are part of what must be the most devoted audience in the world, at least outside a church: when the lights dim before *Das Rheingold,* leaving the house in expectant darkness, the famous E-flat chord steals into a silence so hushed it can almost be touched, and as the work unfolds, a cough or a nervous shuffle turns out to be as rare as snowflakes in August. Nothing has changed, evidently, since 1909, when Virginia Woolf observed that the Bayreuth "pilgrims...scarcely stir till the last wave of sound has ceased." Kinder than I am about their ritual behavior during the intervals, she thought "they seem oppressed with a desire to disburden themselves somehow of the impressions which they have received." But it would seem that despite her view that "the actual performances have been below the level of many that have been given in London," they did not disburden themselves by booing. Curtain calls were not cues for their own performance.

In New York, by contrast, boos are those August snowflakes, though coughs fly thick and fast. Was I wrong in detecting boredom last winter at the Brooklyn Academy of Music during Kupfer's fussy production of Gluck's *Orfeo?* The set, designed as the *Ring* was by Hans Schavernoch, never stopped moving; it featured the same kind of photographed urban images that are among his least persuasive inventions in the *Ring* cycle, and it never achieved, perhaps for lack of opportunity, the astounding variety of his *Ring* design with its playful use of laser beams, a vast open stage that turns Sieglinde, Siegmund, and Wotan into long-distance runners, and a half-dozen giant constructions that could be moved respectably into museums as major installations.

How to account today for the difference between Bayreuth's attentive, active booers and New York's somnolent, passive receivers? One possibility is that for New Yorkers, Kupfer and Schavernoch's modernism is yesterday's discarded bag of tricks; rather than boo it off the stage, we endure the event with utmost courtesy in deference to some highly gifted performers caught unwittingly in the conceptual crap game. Meanwhile, Bayreuth's pilgrims may be faithful descendants of their parents and grandparents, who frequently greeted radical performances with noisy demonstrations: witness Brecht and Weill's *The Little Mahagonny* (1927) in its first incarnation when, according to John Fuegi, "the audience rose to its feet before the completion of the final number and booed and cheered and stomped and whistled." Brecht, with his customary foresight, had prepared for this by arming the singers and himself with whistles to blow back at the audience, clearly a lively standoff which Kupfer may be advised to consider for his appearance next summer.

Somehow, however, these cultural shards don't add up to a satisfying explanation, especially when considering the state-of-the-art boredom that most theater inspires these days. I have no doubt that the Bayreuth booers were wrong in this instance: Kupfer can be irritating and unmusical when he flashes those lasers during the E-flat prelude or when he trivializes the destruction of Valhalla by bringing on a dumb chorus of T.V. viewers, but for the most part, he infuses every scene with passions and actions that echo Wagner note for note, the singers' beautifully rehearsed, specific choices all the more vivid for being done within Schavernoch's nonliteral evocations. But even if the booers could not find within themselves a more selective form of dissent, their demonstrations are not to be deplored. In New York rude chat and occasional snores seem to be the only weapons available when faced with mindless dramas, inflated musicals with flatulent scores, or comedies of insult trying to elicit canned laughter from live audiences. At least the Bayreuth transgressors are feeling something.

During the second act at BAM recently of John Adams's *The Death of Klinghofer*, with a libretto by Alice Goodman that adds new dimension to the word "opaque," my friend leaned over and whispered, "I *hate* Alice Goodman." Aided by supertitles that confirmed the ghastly maunderings emerging from the singers' mouths, we had been squirming for two hours, clearly in need of voting with our feet (the usual American protest) or waiting for the exhilarating public moment when, fearlessly, we could let Goodman know directly how she has appalled us. But it was not to be, partly because the performers were once again enjoying their deserved ovation, but also because Goodman was nowhere to be seen.

My guess is that we would have been outnumbered and outshouted anyway. This was certainly the case at Bayreuth, where booing is treated as a minority right: Kupfer stands alone for a moment, his hands neatly at his side, taking short, sharp bows as he peers through his glasses without any evident emotion; later, Daniel Barenboim (always cheered) puts his arm over Kupfer's shoulder, calmly ushering him off. And the same ritual was performed after *Siegfried* and *Die Götterdammerung* for Schavernoch. A civilized arrangement, it acknowledges every one's un-Italian desire to leave performers alone. No doubt, too, it's too much to expect that all our theaters, prose and lyric alike, might stage similar curtain calls every night so that cranks like me can finally let Neil Simon and Andrew Lloyd-Webber hear what we think of their carbuncled creations. It's a pity that mere practicalities should get in the way of free expression.

If indolent American spectators aren't likely to panic just because I'm shouting "Boo" instead of "Fire," it's possible that some gallant gentlemen might wish to show off by punching me out, leading me to conclude that it may be advisable to confine my protests to print. Some of Bayreuth's stalwarts can't help giggling at each other after their first bellow, proving that booing may be a mug's game after all. Wiser and cheaper to make oneself scarce.

One last note, however, in the form of an open plea to Americans. Could you please resolve to control your knee-jerky impulse to give every Tom, Dick, and Harry (Kupfer?) a standing ovation? It's one thing to shun the booers, quite another to treat every performance as one more victory for national triumphalism. Or is this your way of expressing relief that the whole damned thing is over? If so, then perhaps you might consider a modest boo—or even two—before giggling.

(November 1991)

Cliff Notes

A worrisome moment, indeed, when Amelia, in the Metropolitan Opera's version of Verdi's *A Masked Ball,* arrives on the top landing of steps evidently carved from a Swedish cliffside: ever so gingerly she negotiates her way down, no doubt praying, as we do, that her voluminous gown and cloak will not betray her equally effulgent girth by tripping her over the edge into a percussive fall onto the hangman's scaffold nestled below.

A cliffside in Sweden? I suppose my geographical information is just as skewed as soprano Deborah Voigt's understandable tentativeness when faced with that special crisis in verisimilitude that seems to mark all operatic productions wherever realism is attempted. Our dear old Met, a reluctant entrant into the twentieth century, is now laboring under the artistic dictatorship of its musically gifted director, James Levine, whose theatrical education must have stopped when Nora slammed a real door on a man with a limited vision. Bad enough that Levine's shutters come down at the thought of a nonliteral design. Worse: since *A Masked Ball* was the official entry in Seville's opera sweepstakes last summer, it is reasonable to conclude that he takes pride in the silly Swedish glen, neither noticing nor questioning the ridiculous image of a distressed young woman clutching what is meant to be a slippery, frigid rock—an episode which in the real world would most assuredly prompt her to return home, slide down step-by-step on her bum, or jump to a quick and merciful death.

At the Met, of course, Ms. Voigt finally gets to the base of the cliff in one piece, sadly at a loss for things to do when Verdi gives her nothing to sing. In one startling moment of crackbrained invention, she caresses the scaffold as if it were her clandestine lover, the Swedish king. Was there a director in the house (or even one of those ushers who know everything about opera) to inform Ms. Voigt that what she *does* is what we *see?*

It's more than likely that Levine is simply the most powerfully placed member of his own audience, content to let opera do what it does most naturally: celebrate the human voice and—in Levine's case—the nuclear-powered orchestra that supports or overwhelms it. Who can deny, anyway, that all theatrical discourse, even about spoken drama, revolves around clashing views of reality—*Waiting for Lefty* vs. *Waiting for Godot?* Yet it continues to seem odd that anyone could take seriously as quotidian reality the central operatic convention that men and women communicate with each other in voices raised in lyric—or maybe not-so-lyric—song.

The Met, I confess, is where I most often drift into Natasha's experience at the Moscow Opera in *War and Peace,* described by Tolstoy (and noted by Havel, Einstein, and others) as a weird detachment from what she is supposed to be observing. Like me, she can't help herself: all she sees is the artifice and patent absurdity. As Havel put it in his essay "The

Anatomy of the Gag," "She ceases to perceive the performance as performance, that is, as a series of events which are more or less functional, and instead suddenly begins to see what is really on stage...cardboard sets, and among them fat gentlemen and ladies in colorful costumes who arrive, scurry about the stage, kiss each other, sing loudly, and leave." Einstein, quoted by Havel, sees her as looking at things "spontaneously and suddenly—outside of their ethical or moral significance, outside evaluation and outside judgment and condemnation...to see them as a child sees them through a burst of laughter."

If I part with Natasha in any respect, it is most probably where the child holds sway. Try as I might, I am always evaluating the absurdity. Music, even when personified or acting as ballast for a dramatic event, is surely the quintessential abstract art, masterful in accommodating those in need of descriptive labels—storm, winter, moonlight, for example—but craftily aware that, before anything, it's a triumph of cunningly arranged sonic logarithms. The storm or Till Eulenspiegel's merry pranks are there only by grace of the beholder's easily duped ear. And that's precisely as it should be.

That I don't slip invariably into a Natasha-trance when attending opera is testimony to the amazing way in which the music urges me into a realm of sumptuously arranged abstractions more real than those cardboard sets or laundered cloaks. Instead of strangely dressed creatures, whale mouths poised to swallow conductors whole, I suddenly see passion made palpable, singing itself the only way to say what must be said. Once, sitting near the stage at La Scala, I came perilously close to witnessing not Bellini's Norma but what appeared to be the upper region of Montserrat Caballé's tingling esophagus. What I heard, however, transformed entirely what I saw: Caballé—vast, proud, ungainly—became tissue-thin, a lily miraculously in voice, lost in transparencies of remembrance moving itself into decision.

Caballé, I suspect, would not be caught caressing a scaffold, nor is she at a loss in her enforced silence. Famously lazy about rehearsal, she's clearly a musician before anything else, an intent listener to what the orchestra is telling her about the event. Not for her the masquerade of fraught behavior: Why should Tosca leap from a parapet when a straightforward stroll to the wings will do just as well, especially when her mournful Puccini-convulsion has already filled the stage with a frenzy of whipped cream in no further need of illustration? Similarly unforgettable was Renata Tebaldi's Aida, a head taller than Richard Tucker's Rhadames, turning tubby Tucker into a prop as she slammed one hand on his shoulder—well-earned support for the climbing diminuendo ahead. At the opera one can be consoled by love and death brought to their knees, little more than high-toned excuses for high Cs. Here is realism all its own.

Maria Callas's Tosca would have jumped from the World Trade Center if convinced that the gesture had to be so immense, thus proving that stand-up yawping is not the only way. Much as I love to swim in cool Tebaldi waters, I'm happier burning in Callas fires. Unlike Gerald Ford, who couldn't ski and chew gum at the same time, the best opera singers do everything at once, not least a type of acting that, far from Bernhardt-operatic, is more like Redgrave-dramatic, loaded with the density of inhabited experience. Jon Vickers in deep lamentation, whether in Handel, Verdi, or Wagner, was nothing less than Job released from bookish, biblical narrative; Elisabeth Schwarzkopf's Donna Elvira, a one-person torchlight parade, was in striking contrast to her Marschallin, ice sighing in the wind. Then, too, we have had bantamweight Teresa Stratas behaving like Wagner giants, even though she's not constructed vocally to climb his mountains.

Finally, there's Maria Callas in Tosca's second act, nerveless yet terrified, desperately marking time as she seeks liberty for Cavaradossi and freedom from Scarpia's bed. Suddenly, as she nears Scarpia's desk, the idea slams into her consciousness: a letter opener! All she has to do is drop a hand casually over it—relief at last, triumph stealthily on the march. Puccini provides the melodrama. Callas provides the war.

But if watching thought steal into a singer's eyes seems a rarified pleasure, too Stanislavsky for open song, other dramatic possibilities have begun to emerge (not, however, at our own grand mausoleum in Lincoln Center). These days most modernist opera directors come in two models, both sharing an unblushing incapacity to read a score. The first reach for their updating calendars, scarcely pausing a moment to weigh the difference between decorative and authentic choice. The second operate outside time and place, more involved in a celestial choreography meant to provide visual dimension to patterns otherwise layered in complex musicality. Patrice Chereau's Brunnhilde does not subdue Siegmund by incantatory text alone; she envelops him slowly in giant reams of winding tape, as if constructing an Egyptian mummy.

Robert Wilson's *Parsifal,* a Hamburg production seen at Houston's Grand Opera last season, is not about massive design or recognizable human relationships. Instead, Wilson presents a legend lit by northern lights, a blinding quest for an elusive, perpetually wounding truth, a wondrous adventure in which music seems to be stalking the primeval emergence of an idea. The realism here is the paradoxically motionless architecture of the music: inexorable, unyielding, endlessly expansive. Words tell one story, music another, yet by the end, it's clear that they've always been a part of the same story—a tale of spiritual doubt lit from within by shining curtains of sounds never heard before and not likely to be heard again in quite this supersonic form. If all art aspires to the condition of music, Wilson is trying to make music aspire to the conditions of art. Or to put it another way, he's not impressed by the insistent presence of bodily reality.

Nor is he likely to impress those wedded to the bodily reality of theater bound by routine conventions. The Met fields the best jet-set singers, but rarely is anyone working there on anything so threatening as a fully rehearsed experience or a challenging idea. In recent years, oddly, the most fully realized productions have been of works outside the usual repertory—*Mahagonny, Wozzeck,* and *Billy Budd*—almost as if the Met is willing to confront its audience whenever the audience is unlikely to be there. As Jonathan Miller puts it, "The fact is that opera as an institution is deeply infected with bourgeois vulgarity." True, Miller is repelled by "something nasty about Wagner," unwilling to give himself over to a belief in "enduring permanent archetypal symbols." For him, the northern gods are "rather like leather-clad Harley Davidson bikers. . . . I like operas about humans, human beings I recognize."

Yet even he might not recognize the Met's *Wizard of Parsifal,* no more convincing than Wagner's careless, unobserved Spanish Pyrenees. Under Levine's tutelage, the Met's Wagner productions are always in thrall to someone's love affair with massive gray stones. Meanwhile, follow spots pick up bizarre characters wandering aimlessly among undimensional trees, fields of paper flowers, and hideous arrangements of impenetrable clashing colors—sickly green on varicose peach. As for behavior, one irony rises from the plastic ooze: this drama with music is really silent film, Kundry as Lillian Gish in *The Wind,* flailing at empty air and invisible walls. The Met's *Parsifal* expires long before the last act from terminal stupidity, while Wilson's *Parsifal* moves securely into its final moments as if nothing could be more natural than obeisance to paradise.

Wilson doesn't let Natasha think about anything except the transformative power of musical lines. While this too might distract her from some part of the event, causing her to wonder if anything is real, surely opera's audacities, treated with the awe and respect they deserve, are reality enough for any lifetime.

(September 1992)

Ideas, Obits, and the Critical Act

The Management Game

Ignorance never stopped anyone from having an opinion, so it comes as no surprise where the performing arts are concerned that Europeans envy American energy, sense of adventure, and untiring commitment to experiment, while Americans envy Europe's commitment to national subsidy. Viewing America from almost any European city (except Berlin, perhaps), I might long for an environment in which I can move blithely every day from Joseph Chaikin to Richard Foreman to Robert Wilson, the Mabou Mines, the Bread and Puppet Theatre, or odd little groups with funny names presenting barely definable configurations of dancers who make bizarre sounds, actors who make no sounds at all, playing stones, trees, giraffes; or machines that behave like people, or, more likely, people who behave like machines. Viewing Europe from America, on the other hand, usually reminds an American performer or even enlightened members of the American audience that an abundance of cash, time to rehearse, and a faithful public must be wondrous.

That neither view comes close to reality scarcely matters. Myths are more alluring. Besides, even if the reports of America's experiments and Europe's affluence are absurdly exaggerated, it *is* true that America initiates much that is original in all the arts despite financial poverty. It is also true that the subsidies so lavishly distributed in many European countries do not necessarily lead to anything but more guaranteed security for more artists, certainly not to daring, innovation, or even something so mild as radical reform. On the other side, however, nobody believes anymore that America's relative impoverishment is the one ingredient we possess that induces good new work: that myth has been given, by now, its long-earned burial. The starving artist is a figure of romance only in Puccini.

While I am not positioned to appraise the effects of European subsidy, I can look back on the past twenty years of American theatrical experiment and locate several probable sources for its occasional glories. Before doing so, though, a nod should be made in the direction of eccentricities in American vocabulary: artistic achievement here is linked persistently to two words—*success* and *failure*. But these words do not refer invariably to what the artist has attempted or achieved. On the contrary, in America more than anywhere in the world, success at the box office is always confused with success in the art. Economics keeps upstaging the real actors.

A legacy from the peculiar formations of speculative investment on Broadway, the idea of financial success has also reached into alternative, not-for-profit, nontraditional theaters in sinister and damaging ways. Poverty in those theaters has never been the source of innovative work, but equally, financial success has never been a guarantee of artistic integrity. Or to put it in familiar—and yes, more sinister—terms: America has limitless capacities for absorbing its adventures and experiments into its traditional economy.

The glories, therefore, can be located with ease. What happens to them, however, is clearly a function of the economy: its premises, its language, and its values. Twenty years after the most significant experiments began, it is not difficult to see what went right and what went wrong. (It is less easy, of course, to speculate on what is likely to happen in the next twenty years.)

What went right was the vacuum that was filled when it had to be filled. In the late fifties and early sixties, young American theater artists knew that traditional theater, especially on Broadway, would have none of them. The best playwrights were Tennessee Williams and Arthur Miller, the one apparently locked into psychology, the other into social indignation, and both of them dependent upon linear narrative, and—not incidentally—box-office approval. (Poor Williams: he experimented with a florid, epic play, *Camino Real;* Broadway hated it, and he never tried anything like it again.) In short, the most visible American theater—Broadway—didn't seem to know that the other arts existed, that narrative need no longer omit density, or that vision could be both comic and tragic at once. Pursuing a career in American theater at that time seemed juvenile and spiritually unrewarding, like going to college and joining the football team rather than reading Joyce or Proust, writing research papers, or working in the laboratories. An alternative didn't lie readily at hand, so it had to be created.

What was created was something that was not quite happening in the rest of the theater world. (We were to discover later that a Pole named Jerzy Grotowski had been playing with similar ideas and considerably more financial support for many of the same years.) One paragraph shouldn't describe an era, but it is reasonable to report the following: absurdist theater began to find its voice and image in a place that came to be called Off Broadway; directors, actors, and playwrights began working together in workshops devoted to improvisation and the building of works from ideas, stories, and speculations; those works became, in turn, the basis for new theatrical groupings in a place called Off-Off-Broadway; some of them spilled into touring arrangements that moved from one university campus to another, and consequently, many of the universities began to train actors and directors for what appeared to be a "new" theater; private and public foundations began to lend some support to groups Off-Off-Broadway; some of the experiments traveled to Europe (one—the Living Theater—was literally forced into exile because of its radical incapacity to adapt to traditional laws or funding arrangements); and much of the work pushed many of the people into various forms of fame—actors finding jobs on television or in film, directors offering "master" classes on and off campuses, and playwrights allied to agents and producers who were endeavoring to "advance" their work to Broadway or Hollywood. The absorption process took no more than a decade to gather momentum.

Such nonlinear, group experiments were by no means the only activity developed away from Broadway. New York, as the tourist is always being told, is not America. Similarly, Broadway and its offshoots, while holding center stage, gave way in those years to institutional theaters built in cities throughout the country. For the most part, these were (and are) theaters devoted to filling still another gap in American theatrical life: namely, the centuries of repertoire from the Greeks and Shakespeare to Chekhov, Ibsen, Shaw, and O'Neill that were otherwise suffering neglect on Broadway while remaining, also, outside the natural and practical interests of the experimenting, improvisational groups. And it was with these theaters, especially, that a new theatrical miniature industry was born, one that has no official name but that could be called accurately the Management Game.

Obviously, where money is involved, somebody has to be responsible for finding, distributing, and controlling it. America had known non-Broadway theaters before, some of them—such as the Group Theatre and the Mercury Theater—operating as alternative enclaves on Broadway itself. But it had become common knowledge that such ventures were always doomed: there were no orderly systems available for floating indefinitely what was, after all, an operation that could never recover enough of its costs from the public's enthusiasms; when the public lost its interest in a particular production, these theaters had to respark their primitive money-raising engines and begin all over again. It was an exhausting business, so most of the actors and at least one prodigious director—Orson Welles—escaped to Hollywood.

Regional theaters, and the development of centers devoted to performing arts in major cities, were the occasion, understandably, for the initiation of more orderly financial systems. The race into the Management Game was the next inevitable development. As usual, Europe provided the early models, particularly the Arts Council of Great Britain. But new models, characteristically American in their arrangements, values, and priorities, caught on rapidly—not least, the idea that theatrical management could be taught as a discipline all its own, leading to a graduate degree in various important universities. A new subspecies was being ripped literally from the dream of stagestruck youth who might otherwise have pursued the customary forlorn and insecure careers of actors, directors, designers, and dramatists: this class of theater animal knew that, with graduation, a job would be found.

But—and here is where this abbreviated chronicle must go off the rails a bit—not a job with the experimental theaters. To be nontraditional in art is also to be nontraditional and even improvisational in organization. When Joseph Chaikin's Open Theater began in the early sixties, each participant contributed five dollars a month toward the rental of the rehearsal space. And that was it. No other system for development, no plan for finding and maintaining an audience, no tortuous schemes for staying alive as a group had been envisioned. And it took many years for just a few elementary systems to be developed. When the Open Theater had a hit Off Broadway with Jean-Claude van Itallie's *American Hurrah,* produced by a traditional management with profit in mind, its own rehearsal work-shop had to be suspended for a time. When the actors were the subsidizers, their real work—the improvisational workshops—could go on. Enmeshed in producing and management systems, they might be able to cease working as waiters or teachers, but—like their exhausted predecessors from the Group/Mercury days—the real work would take a holiday. More sophisticated arrangements did, in fact, develop over the years: the Open Theater, La Mama, and many of the groups that followed hard upon their activity, found some support within the newish federal, state, and private foundations that turned already to giving partial support to the more traditional regional theaters. But newly graduated management teams, to say nothing of the various foundations themselves, never found a will or the means to keep experiment alive.

The Management Game was playing for higher stakes: for big performing arts centers, for the construction of new theater buildings, and for the satisfaction of wealthy people who liked to have their names engraved on the backs of seats in the new theaters, or—if they donated larger sums—to have their names given to the theaters themselves. In short, the big federal, state, and private money was going to not-for-profit theaters that were expected to hold their own in a profit-making world. They didn't have to make money at the box office, but they had to behave as if they did. At every stage of creation, organization, and management, they had to reach certain prescribed levels of success.

All of this is allied to still another American eccentricity: a system of taxation that rewards the wealthy with relief from the full weight of their nominal tax burden by encouraging them to give to the needy in the sciences and the arts. Of course, they give more to the sciences, and so, too —in the form of military spending, nuclear and space research—does the federal government. But the arts have continued to have higher and higher expectations of support. The recent shock attacks by the Reagan administration on all but the military needy have reminded artists not only of a systematic dependency that is bad for artistic health but of just how far in terms of sensibility Americans have yet to go.

Those prescribed levels of success in regional theaters and in not-for-profit arrangements Off and Off-Off-Broadway have developed a vocabulary that, with close scrutiny, has little or nothing to do with the creative spirit or process. Management teams in public and private foundations are telling artists, in effect, to stay alive by hiring management teams. The language found to describe the needs of donors fails to describe the less codifiable needs, customs, and rhythms of the theaters. Here I am not referring only to the mountain of paper that bureaucracies love to consume. (At its most ridiculous, this can often mean that small groups spend almost as much money and time—time being money in America—in filling out forms as they do in rehearsing their work; moreover, the amount of money received doesn't often match the money spent in meeting the foundation's "guidelines.")

I am referring, however, to phrases that were invented to serve a manager's idea of purpose and success: *fiscal responsibility, efficient marketing strategies, efficient fundraising,* a *strong board of directors* with people listed as *patrons, friends,* or *donors* according to the amounts they have *pledged, matching funds* (meaning, the foundation will give X dollars providing X dollars are also coming from another source), *audience development,* and finally—reflecting a paranoid relationship to a potentially scolding public—the issue that is always being raised about how *public funds* are spent.

Earlier, I had suggested broadly that much of what has happened has sinister implications. Perhaps it has always been so where patronage is concerned: few of us would be willing to trade our foundations and systems for even a trial relationship with the Medici, Prince Esterhazy, or Ludwig II of Bavaria. But then few of us are as marvelous, extravagantly gifted, or quite as aggressively committed to our own work as Michelangelo, Haydn, and Wagner were. (Robert Wilson is the exception: a Wagnerian imagination without, perhaps, the matching gifts, and certainly without his Ludwig; even so, he continues to dream, demand, and create, while plundering European philanthropy and performing spaces whenever—and so often—American patrons and theaters let him down.)

No, what is fascinating has nothing to do with conscious deviltry and conspiracy. This is quite clearly the American way. Those who fled Europe and conquered this territory were not searching for a better place to produce art. Theirs was a commercial venture with a lot of piety about freedom of religion thrown in for good measure. The Constitution of the

United States of America must be the most sophisticated afterthought in the history of societies. It is the one miracle wrought by the exodus from Europe, and its almost accidental genius and consequent fragility are visible to all of us all of the time: we never stop fighting over it. Meanwhile, where art is concerned, there are fundamental constitutional protections, yes, but they cannot address the artist's need for protection from the Philistines.

Hence, the sinister. What our new systems of patronage have created is a gigantic network of control over what is actually produced. This is managed by making fiscal responsibility and consciousness of the audience into the central measures of success or failure. What has been called the "edifice complex" is only one instance of the way in which these measures have operated. No artist in the theater ever really needed those huge, stuffy, absurdly overdesigned theaters with their engineering, lobbies, and minimal rehearsal spaces. But to finance the work, to do it all, many of them spent as much time consulting with architects (though often finding their advice ignored by both the patrons and the architects) as they did in realizing their own work.

The result is plain to see by now: buildings too costly too maintain, many of them inflexibly designed and run by a team of managers devoted to selling subscriptions, fixing seasons years in advance, fixing the number of performances, and, thereby, fixing dates for openings that might have little or nothing do with the way a particular play might be developed in rehearsal. America always wanted theaters with the prestige and reputation of Stanislavsky's and Brecht's, but it never wanted to foot the bill for the time it takes to make such productions and build such companies. The one word omitted consistently from the Management Game's vocabulary has been *process*.

Perhaps the directors of regional theaters have simply fallen prey to a system they deserve. Less interested in the new, less devoted to the idea of training or the development of talented actors accustomed to working together in relative ease and harmony over stretches of time, or to the exploration of fresh ways to tell a theatrical story that might differ markedly from the forms and contents popular to the media, they have driven themselves into corners from which the only escape is failure—

death sentences given without trial by well-meaning but ignorant boards of directors.

For experimenters, however, failure (but with genuine distinction) is really a way of life, and it must continually find less expensive ways to be so. It can't really be fiscally responsible, because it is deliberately and by nature outside the accepted systems of industrial production—which is to say that the small group may not always be in an artistic vanguard, but it is always constructed to be in the vanguard of what can never be anything but a cottage industry. *Small Is Beautiful* is the title of a book by E. F. Schumacher popular with young American conservationists desperately trying to survive on the land and through the barter system: it is a phrase that serves equally well to describe the basic research work in performance developed by theatrical pioneers. Obviously, it would appear to be an especially "American" action and creed; also, obviously, it is an avantgarde endeavor fighting with rear-guard means. The managers don't know what to do with it any more than they would know how to handle a small farm.

Neither does the actors' trade union, Actors' Equity. For years, its mostly unemployed members have been stealing time from the restaurants and shops in which they squeeze out a living in order to rehearse with many of these groups, sometimes with a view to appearing in what is finally billed as an Equity-approved showcase. But that activity has been under relentless attack by suspicious members of Equity's council, most of whom spend more time governing Equity than ever working on a stage. They have known, of course, that most of the work is secretive, and that most of the actors are agreeing to lie about how many hours and weeks they have actually worked in a workshop. So the council adversaries have been spending years in devising obstacles to these clever subterfuges that are indispensable to experimental development in America.

Of course, once again, the actors are the real subsidizers, and the union wishes, understandably, to protect them against themselves. But the most recent ruse in the council has been, if anything, more sinister and pernicious than even a Medici or a Rockefeller could have devised: instead of assaulting producers, they want the playwrights to pay indefinitely for the actor's contribution to the original project, asking either that the actor be cast in subsequent production even in theaters that already have their own actors or that actors receive a percentage from the playwright's infrequent and unlikely profits. Having turned artist against artist, they have succeeded only in reducing the number of plays rehearsed, developed, and shown during the past year. And, as a natural by-product, they have kept more of their members out of work. Fewer "showcases," approved or unapproved, merely leads to lower visibility for the actors.

Can it be asserted or demonstrated that genuine artistic experiment is seriously affected by so much perverse, organized anarchy? Perhaps not, though there is little doubt that energy spent on survival is energy not spent on work; nor is every good or even great artist automatically a survivor in the known marketplace, whether profit or not-for-profit. I cannot help noticing that much of what is done can be approached and sustained only by the young, especially the young and physically adept, most of them vigorously uncommitted to equally nourishing personal relationships. The artist-subsidizer can be a damn fool for only part of his life.

Then, too, where is he to turn? If he is in New York, he used to depend a little on the generous vibrations and available spaces offered by Ellen Stewart at La Mama, E.T.C. But she, too, is getting not only older but wiser and poorer. Even before the Reagan cuts were announced for the National Endowment of the Arts' budget, Ms. Stewart's funds had been cut by the Endowment itself. The incredibly jingoistic, censorious reason given was that she was spending too much of the taxpayers' money on invitations to foreign groups—as if that weren't a service to both American theater workers and their audience. She was also not able to demonstrate that she was overmanaged and, therefore, "fiscally responsible."

With Joseph Papp's godfatherly embrace, prospects are nominally better, though perhaps more ominous. Papp's vast enterprise has been praised recently by George Balanchine's Maecenas of many years, Lincoln Kirstein. "Papp," says Kirstein, "more than anyone else, can play both sides of the tracks—Broadway, off-Broadway, and off-off Broadway. He has learned how to operate art and commercial theater by handling real-estate without realtors."

Who has Papp handled, however, but the realtors of Broadway? Work done in his space has not only the breath of *A Chorus Line* and *The Pirates of Penzance* giving it financial ballast, it also has the hotter breath of such commercial success breathing hellfire and possible damnation down its back. Papp's taste and sensibility have never been any match for Kirstein's: there has been no room for a Balanchine in the Papp enterprise (though, no doubt, he would argue that there have been no Balanchines visible in the theater), and so much of what he produces looks arbitrary and unfocused. One year a playwright or director is the darling of the place. The next year he's on his own again. It doesn't seem so accidental now that one of Ellen Stewart's former house directors, Wilford Leach, moved on to life at Papp's Public Theater, soon crowning his princedom with the direction of *Pirates*. An innovator in Papp's busy emporium must always be sneaking a glance at those Broadway successes, vainly hoping that he might be the first to create both an artistic vision and a hit at the same time.

Blame need not be delegated, and predictions would be foolish. There are few saints in the avant-garde, and even fewer sages positioned to give advice about balancing books while doing the hard, lonely labor of crafting an art in the theater. As Steven Marcus put it years ago, in America nothing fails like success. And America's particular theatrical profile is—as I hope I have demonstrated—a very American entity, subject to our behavioral, political, and economic laws, certainly unlike any other country's.

At our best, we are also disturbingly at our worst. Depending upon one's ethical bent, we are either a whirl- or cesspool of contradictions: profligate spenders who are incorrigibly mean, puritanical economizers; groupy and faddish but intensely individualistic; fanatically unwilling to cope with socialist concepts when it comes to the poor and (the same thing) the artist, yet only too quick to bail out ailing industries such as Lockheed and Chrysler with public money. We fund large institutions but rarely the individual artist. Conservatives behind Reagan claim to be against the interferences of Big Government, but that doesn't stop them from threatening interference in all aspects of our private lives. (Where else in the world do bumper stickers keep urging other citizens how to vote, pray, think, or live?) And—as the saying goes—only in America could meager federal funding for the arts come under attack while money for military bands is raised.

Of all the arts, theater is probably the least well-organized to defend itself. Most of its practitioners are confused, bustling from coast to coast with motives no less mixed and contradictory than those held by other Americans. Theater is supposed to be a collaborative art, and theatrical Americans can get sloppily sentimental about their fellow workers when the cameras turn on them at award ceremonies, but the truth is they don't really like each other very much. If they knew how to serve their interests, if they knew how to explain that the spadework done in classrooms and workshops all over America is just as essential to the big, productive movie and television industries as the forging of steel and making of wheels are to the automobile industry, then perhaps they would also know how to stage the greatest show of all: a strike for their right not to fail but to do the best, most imaginative, even radical, work their collective powers can muster.

Deep down, Americans know they can't live without big entertainment, which means they can't live without the small groupings where occasional hits and future stars are born. In other words, whether they like it or not, Americans can't live without the dark, complex visions of real theater. The trouble is, they want the fun and they don't want to pay for it.

(September 1981)

Geraldine Page

Repose wasn't her style. Geraldine Page's natural home may have been Off Broadway's pocket stages, but no space could adequately contain her body and soul sounding their alarms. Who can forget that surprising voice, with its panpipings suddenly interrupted by great, flat baritone wails? Page was identified early with Alma Winemiller's fragile longings in *Summer and Smoke;* then her Alexandra Del Lago in *Sweet Bird of Youth* released the glamorous lion lurking in every Tennessee Williams heroine. At the Actors Studio, she offered a taste of Lady Hotspur and Lady Macbeth, but American theater never learned how to meet the challenges of her idiosyncratic gifts—no Gertrude or Beatrice, no Hedda or Rebecca West, only the astonishing, eloquent silence of the Listener in Strindberg's *The Stronger,* and Olga and Masha from the Chekhov possibilities.

She was that rare actor in America or anywhere else, the impish clown who, given half a chance, could blow the gods off Olympus. That she rarely had that chance is our usual national disgrace; that she leaves so many indelible images of delicate women refusing defeat is a tribute to a woman and actor who always honored her magisterial art.

(June 1987)

The Birth of a Notion

Little did I know at the time, but the 1963 International Theatre Conference in Edinburgh marked the end of drama as theater. I should have realized that the dissonant voices at the conference were announcing a new theater desperate to redefine itself as something more (or less?) than the playwright's art, the theater of conceptual spectacle and high technology we have today. Nobody put it that way, but that's what it was all about. If I think about the conference's extravagant, outlandish, preposterous collection of nonsequiturs now, it's partly because I feel the need for a hard dose of cleansing memory. Accounting for the past may be no guarantee against history's awful repetitions, but it helps on occasion to remember how the old always shadows the new.

Presiding over the four days of discussion among sixty to seventy panelists was Kenneth Tynan, announcing at the start that the Big Issue of the day would be: Brecht or Ionesco—which side are you on? Moments later he had to explain to a confused questioner that the argument was between psychological and social theater. Arthur Kopit wanted to know if Ionesco was to be included under psychology, to which he received the charming, if unexpected, reply that Ionesco was in bed with a fever of 102.

I don't know what happened to Ionesco's cold, but I do know that Tynan never recovered. Within minutes, the conference was turned into a free-for-all, with as many agendas as participants. How could Tynan have imagined otherwise? The year before, Edinburgh played host to a writers' conference which quickly broke down into a series of sexual confessions, led off by the unstoppable Norman Mailer. With any luck, I kept thinking, the theater conference might make similar noises, if only to save us from creepy pronouncements about theater's role in saving the world.

Sex played its part, but not as dominating theme. The big scandal of the conference was a Happening staged by the late Ken Dewey, a San Francisco performance artist who had announced earlier that the conference's tensions were superficial; working with musicians and painters, he was trying to create a studio environment. With the help of Charles Marowitz, already declaring that "the director should be in charge of the theater's future," Dewey arranged the stately passage of a nude woman across the balcony—a perfect upstaging of the solemn rites occurring below, where Poles were talking about dialectics and commitments, Russians were identifying Chekhov, Gorky, and Gogol as "laborers," and our own Harold Clurman was explaining that committed theater was a bewildering term to Americans, since we no longer have politics.

Not to be outdone by the Russians, an Edinburgh citizen shouted from the audience that "the talented people here should build works on greatness and faith." Cries of "Rubbish!" echoed through the walls. While Dorothy Tutin had said earlier that "we shouldn't be bickering…we should be creating something in which we are all deeply involved," most of the participants—twenty-three playwrights, eight directors, eight actors, and eight critics—couldn't be bothered with high-minded unanimity. Edward Albee wanted more to be said about the difference between theater and film, but after trying to explain how a Judy Garland number offered the closest moment in film to "the experience of theater," he stepped back from the podium, murmuring, "I have lost my sentence."

Alone in his honest admission, Albee was sending a signal that should have been more wisely heeded. Rubbish was hardly confined to the hapless Edinburghian committed to greatness and faith. Silliest of all was Wolf Mankowitz, pompously introducing a resolution drafted by legal advisers to the effect that playwrights should retain complete control over the disposition of their texts ("We own and license our wares to the theater"), countered wisely by Peter Shaffer, who "couldn't bear the idea of a union of the imagination." Lillian Hellman reported her own impregnable technique when faced with changes suggest by directors or actors: "I don't hear, as a rule." Judith Anderson begged to differ. "May the actor disagree with the author?…Some phrases stick in my mouth better than they would in another's"—not a happy phrase itself, with echoes of a dental approach to playwriting, but surely just an acknowledgment that Mankowitz was lobbying for the impossible.

The French won the rhetorical battles, despite Peter Brook's *J'Accuse*—"French intellectuals think lucidly and well, but they are missing the common sense that we have in England." Alain Robbe-Grillet replied that, as a trained engineer and biologist, he had "what might be called official common sense." Meanwhile, he wanted to discuss Search, Discovery, and Invention, precisely the tools Brook later came to use when he fled to Paris for his un-English performance research. By now, Tynan had lost his Big Issue, but the conference was clearly staggering undaunted into the future.

Which is why it comes to mind today. If nothing else was settled in Edinburgh, at least the cast of characters was astounding and the right bombs were being thrown. Better four days of agitation than no ideas at all, which is what we get when theater people meet today over real estate and management issues. Worse, most of us don't meet at all, except at memorials for colleagues and friends. Tynan's theater conference was a mess. Even so, it introduced us to ourselves and history. Playwrights outnumbered every other group, yet Brook went away unscathed when he announced "the death of the word." It didn't matter that no one was entirely right; what mattered was that the conference itself meant that the word could never die.

Theater was about to displace drama, but not necessarily forever. Funny now to realize that Ken Dewey's Balcony Nude may have launched Tynan into the assemblage of his only commercial venture, the production of *Oh, Calcutta!* Edinburgh was an unrehearsed Happening that week, four days in which unplanned images were busily ghostwriting prophecies: Ionesco fervently desiring to join the French Academy; Agnes Moorehead, Lillian Hellman, and Judith Anderson banding together gloomily by themselves like the three weird sisters, suddenly out of touch with Macbeth; Laurence Olivier slipping out of the conference on the first day, but not before scaring playwrights and directors alike with his gentle warning that "if you want to know who runs the theater, who to blame, it is I."

Who knows what kind of happening might be produced today when ideas and passion are in short supply? Why not an international theater conference next year, if only to commemorate Edinburgh's twenty-fifth anniversary? Perhaps a John Arden will arise once more, reminding us of Dionysus. Or maybe there will be a moment as touching as Arnold Wesker's simple observation that the differences between him and Harold Pinter didn't matter because "nobody listens anyway." What's wrong today is that nobody talks.

(July 1987)

Cry God for Larry

That master of the chilling death scene has finally mastered the one that counts, dying peacefully, they tell us, in his sleep. But I doubt it. Even if he looked untroubled, he must have been up to his old tricks, searching for a gesture no other actor would imagine, let alone have the lunatic chutzpah to try—Richard III biting the sword that cut him down; a stammering Hotspur choking on the "W" he can't complete so that Hal is left to say "worms"; Coriolanus dashing to a point 12 feet above the stage, speared by the Volscians, toppling forward (as Olivier's Hazlitt, Kenneth Tynan, described the scene) "to be caught by the ankles so that he dangles, inverted, like the slaughtered Mussolini." For color, dash, animal anguish, sheer crazy size, and heroic ambition, there was no one like him onstage in this century. At once modern and ancient, he was a true Olympian, an acting athlete in touch with all sources while protecting inventive corners for himself. Burbage and Garrick would have recognized him as Gielgud and Richardson always did, not as rival but as friend, colleague, secret sharer, guardian of the privileged wisdom that theater—as he put it—"is the first glamorizer of thought."

Olivier was always the first to admit that he was never sure when he was acting and when he was not. Which means, I take it, that he felt more alive onstage than anywhere else, his wicked eye and perfectly pitched ear turning daily life into a continuous rehearsal for what was, for him, the real thing. As a consequence, however, he left himself open to the charge that the deepest truths were rarely his, that with so much artifice behind his liveliness he couldn't possibly reveal anything so tawdry as a simple, troubled heart. If I've flirted with these doubts myself, especially when feeling cut off from the stage actor I've known by the film actor who will forever be the only indelible image, I've countered them by recalling the astounding risks he always took onstage.

Among the most vivid is his Othello, a panther nursing a rash, languid sexuality hanging from his rolling hips, later caught in the whirlwind of Shakespeare's pile-driving images—"the Pontic...Propontic...Hellespont"—then the hair-raising crescendo, "my bloody thoughts...shall ne'er look back, ne'er ebb to humble love," those "ne'ers" stretched into the full-throated neigh of a wild horse. Yet with Olivier there was always more to come, in this case his strangulated collapse into a terrifying epileptic fit. On the lighter side, there was his larkish Tattle in Congreve's *Love for Love,* eyes fluttering, a schoolgirl on her first date, the torso leaning coyly, ready to break into perpetual dance at the slightest encouragement. As Archie Rice in *The Entertainer,* he soft-shoed and sang with true vaudeville awfulness—"Why should I care, why should I let it touch me?"—breaking later into the most agonizing spiritual I've ever heard.

If I have to choose among startling memories—an Astrov in *Vanya* muted in its inner misery, his titanically vicious Edgar in Strindberg's *The Dance of Death* (Olivier never needed to be liked)—it will have to be *Titus Andronicus,* if only because I saw it four times. At one performance, seated down front on the side, I was suddenly witness to what he was doing after Aaron cuts off Titus's hand. There were two separate actions simultaneously, one meant to be visible, the other not: Titus's back is caught in wrenching spasms; meanwhile, Olivier wraps extra sleeve around his hand so that when he finally faces us we see only a bloody stump. Even with illusion broken, the measure of that image was its heartbreaking reality, followed later by the most unforgettable moment of all—Titus parceling each syllable of "I—am—the—sea," and on the last word throwing back his head to reveal only the whites of his eyes as he utters an extended guttural hiss that can be nothing less than waves breaking on rocks.

Last week the British press fell into understandable swoons over the shock that these discoveries beneath the text are finally unrecoverable. Filmed Olivier may be the actor preserved, but it's also the actor disengaged from his ancestral medium, not staring at us with the merciless gaze, no longer filling open spaces with loping or prancing entrances and the grandeur of that trumpet tongue. England would not seem to need more royalty than it already has, but this first and only actor to sit in the House of Lords has long been the country's not-so-secret monarch, arousing in Bernard Levin's ecstatic obituary amazing, yet plausible, comparisons with Drake, Raleigh, Dickens, Elgar, Newton, Hume, Byron, Macaulay, Hazlitt, and Churchill. Levin's lamentation is for "a world awash with...scurvy knaves picking and stealing their way through life...a grey desert world, desperately lacking in figures of size and power and appeal." How much better it has been to have among us an actor with so much natural power turned over to so many peaceful uses, not least the leadership of the Old Vic and the National Theatre when they were at their undoubted best.

Yet who can fail to notice that England also dumped him ceremoniously from those positions? Or that we all too often refer to Peter Brook's *Titus Andronicus* rather than Olivier's? Or that in America we have never bred a protean actor committed as Olivier always was to the idea of a theater: "I believe," he wrote, "that in a great city, or even a village, a great theater is the outward and visible sign of an inward and invisible culture."

Such life and work deserve the best possible poetic finish, and this too he managed to provide last month when he appeared on a videocassette played to demonstrators trying to save from developers the newly discovered Rose Theatre (site of *Titus's* first performance in 1594). "Cry God for Harry, England, and the Rose," he said. "Can a muse of fire exist under a ceiling of commerce?" This wasn't Henry the Fifth speaking, it was Larry the First, irreplaceable, a wondrous theater beast whose best monument would be the salvation of the Rose, if only Thatcher's greedy animals might be willing to surrender one patch of land to the rest of us. The terrible pain at the moment is that Levin's florid impulse to quote from *Antony and Cleopatra* may be all too despairingly apt:

> the odds is gone
> And there is nothing left remarkable
> Beneath the visiting moon.

(July 1989)

Richard Hayes

Richard Hayes's death on January 8 may have been the release he needed from the disappointing years in which he could no longer bring himself to write with the "mandarin eloquence" he once ascribed to Henry James, but to those who cherished him for spoken eloquence, his vigilant reminders that performance standards need not hang back with the brutes, this final defeat is not acceptable. That his work must now be collected goes without saying, though as always with Richard it's a bit tactless that this too must be done by his friends. We had hoped against the evidence for the miracle that would restore him to the critical prose he did so much more majestically than anyone now writing. Instead, he left those heaving messages that taxed the tape on our answering machines—gossip, of course, but also reports of theater, dance, or music performances that, despite his abject poverty, he somehow managed to attend. As one friend put it the other day, Richard didn't know about walls or boundaries.

Except for those he placed around himself. For nine years in the 1950s, he was drama critic for *The Commonweal,* becoming the first critic to win the Brandeis University Creative Arts award (1959). On the committee that chose him were Stark Young, Katharine Cornell, and Eric Bentley, and it's not exaggeration to say that Richard shared something with all of them in style and grace. Years later, I urged him to try a biography of Young, for which he might have been chosen by central casting, but it was too late and he was by then too far from the self-esteem needed to examine another's life. As a founding Obie judge, he must have supplied the throwaway wit needed to leaven deliberations often overburdened by responsibility, the judges weighted by the illusion that the world is really watching. To those meetings, too, he would have brought the gifts of the great teacher he was whenever he showed up for class, capable of making a New York University, Hofstra, or Brooklyn student imagine that Duse, for one, had quietly entered the room to cast her spell again.

But such talent rarely has anything to do with organizational success, and Richard was less easy to place as a tenured professor. To be fair to those unfair to him, he may have given up on himself long before they tossed him on a heap to live alone with his demons. With slow-witted hindsight now, it's possible to see Richard describing his own anguish when writing of others: "O'Neill and Ibsen, finally and terribly, each spent their last years in zones of inarticulate consciousness, hideously resonant—one cannot but believe—with the revenge nature inflicts on those who too audaciously demand it confront its own unspeakable exactions." It was only just that he should temper his sensitivity to O'Neill by noticing with characteristic edge "O'Neill's insensibility to words—to their luster and resistance, their shimmer or weightiness." Soon enough, however, he returned to what he recognized, surely, as their common ground: "Not artifice, nor any solacing reason could mediate the authority of his private pain."

Yet even here, and relying on a dazzling double quote, he had to carry the horror further into consciousness: "'He could not believe,' Nicola Chiaramonte had noted, 'as Rousseau believed, that *it was the fault of others.'*" The authority of his pain notwithstanding, and for all the exasperation he caused in his friends, Richard nonetheless deserves to be remembered beyond fault or blame as a master of line, thought, and unspeakable revelation, a poet-in-prose bruised by the severities of his faith, outside time much of his life yet an elegant, superbly unenvious witness to the good in all of us.

(January 1990)

Theater Without Programs

When a playwright can become the elected president of his nation, as Vaclav Havel did last year in Czechoslovakia, it's time to acknowledge that where theater is, politics cannot be far behind. Yet it can be argued that Havel's triumph as an unlikely politician might have happened had he never written a play. His absurdist comedies, not to the taste of his absurd Communist oppressors, were banished from the stage, but it was Havel's underground essays that sent him to jail. True, Havel and his friends in Civic Forum organized—if that's the right word—the Velvet Revolution in a theater, and on the streets the chant of the day was "Long live the actors!" But by the time I visited Prague in April 1990, it was clear that despite Havel's personal popularity, the real business offstage was once more in the hands of real politicians. If you asked young people if they liked their new leader, they were delighted to say yes, but about his plays, then playing in several theaters, they stared into beautiful baroque-covered space and ordered another cream-covered waffle.

That waffles speak louder than plays might come as a disappointment to those who believe in the power of theatrical art to inform. In the 1960s, the popular word was *commitment*. Either you had it or you didn't; if the latter was the case, you must have been some kind of boulevard playwright, interested only in the foibles or troubles of the rich. Terence Rattigan, popular in Britain after the war as just such a chronicler, used to cite a mythical "Aunt Edna" as his audience, a sweet, contented dowager satisfied with the class distinctions and property inherited from her Edwardian forbears, themselves firm believers in art as decoration. George Bernard Shaw, florid in his disdain, wrote his last essay in 1950 as an attack on Aunt Edna and Rattigan, aware no doubt that his sixty years of agitation about public issues may have been less effective than he had assumed. Had he lived to his hundredth birthday, he might have gloated at Rattigan's theatrical comeuppance when John Osborne's *Look Back in Anger* (1956), aiming at a new audience (probably the sons and daughters of Aunt Edna's backstairs maid), suddenly made issues popular again. It was possible later to view Osborne's work as uncontained fury about postwar Britain's disarray mixed weirdly with contained nostalgia for precisely that Edwardian past. At the same time, however, bursting on the scene as the war cry of a generation, it looked as if the theater had once again discovered a public voice.

Nor was this only illusion. Osborne's contemporaries—Arnold Wesker, John Arden, even Harold Pinter, with his mysterious parables of power and corruption—were seen as "committed" dramatists. Americans like me often looked at these developments with cautionary awareness that Wesker, for one, was mining territory already explored by our own "committed" playwrights such as Clifford Odets in the 1930s and Arthur Miller, famous as a self-appointed public conscience. At London's Royal Court Theatre in 1957, Miller argued that British theater seemed "hermetically sealed" against reality; the discussion, chaired by *The Observer's* stylishly radical critic Kenneth Tynan, was called "British Playwriting: Cause Without a Rebel," as if in early acknowledgment that Osborne's political rage was not beyond its own high-minded, privileged despair. Some years later, at still another conference, this time in Edinburgh, John Arden surprised his committed audiences by declaring that "theater cannot change society, it can only confirm people in what they are beginning to believe."

Such plain speaking was not greeted with delight. Arden was hardly preaching futility; but theater people, battered by their outsider history, a vagabond reputation still clinging to plays and players despite Nobel Prizes, knighthoods, and accumulated wealth, like to hear the good news that what they do is essential. This means that the best contemporary plays are supposed to be those that address themselves to political conscience: Arden's misdemeanor was his implicit admission that most of the time nobody is listening. Worse: there may not be answers; society may have anything *but* plays on its collective mind; and why, anyway, should theaters assume a public duty neglected or disdained by the other arts? Who can forget the image of Beethoven, first calling his Third Symphony "Bonaparte," only to rip the title page in half when he discovered that the first consul had proclaimed himself emperor? Smart writers soon learn that the passions charging their work do not require affiliations.

What is required at any time is an act of imagination. It may be true, as Shakespeare scholars keep telling us, that Shakespeare was a believer in order, his commitment, such as it was, placing him squarely in the company of kings. Why, then, did he keep telling the story of failure and usurpation, making Falstaff, for example, the glorious comic-tragic center of his *Henry IV* plays, the king himself only a peripheral, sickly shadow? Uneasy indeed the head that wears the crown: for all the arguments on behalf of Shakespeare's conservatism, his plays always give strong debater's points to the other side. Coriolanus may be as rotten as—who?— Bonaparte, Hitler, or Saddam Hussein, but so too are his adversaries, citizens and senators alike. Marc Antony comes to bury Caesar, not to praise him; Shakespeare neither buries nor praises, he simply celebrates Timon's embittered rejection of all society, casting him into a blasted world where Timon talks past his visitors, inventing a language that can embrace his titanic despair. And that's the point: neither moralist nor messenger, Shakespeare's only consistency is his mastery of the word—the breathless phrase, the startling image, the transformation of pressured experience into eloquence. His real heroes are those who talk better than the others.

To be fair to message-bearers, political dissent is in theater's legacy. Mimesis, or imitation, lies at the heart of dramatic invention, and ever since Plato, in the *Laws,* cast a bleak eye on the unrestricted ambitions of the imitative mode, dramatic art has had to pay the heavy price of exile in its own realm. A persistent antitheatrical prejudice, documented thoroughly by Jonas Barish in his book of that title, has served mainly to confirm its own hysterical prophecies: as Barish puts it, Plato "fears and distrusts" theater at least as much as "unabashed crime," holding it "responsible for the evils and corruption of the present day." It's scarcely surprising, then, that even the most innocent side issues in plays, whether Molière's doubts about piety in *Tartuffe* or Ibsen's use of syphilis as a haunting presence in *Ghosts,* soon take on an argumentative importance quite outside the mythic splendor of those narratives. "Simplicity," says Barish, is Plato's "goal, and complexity is the dreaded enemy."

The joke on Plato and similar censors of the ineffable and difficult is that the more they would suppress, the more topical and contentious the theater becomes. For the most part, the notion that theater must be recognizably "political" has meant that it must stand in the vanguard of momentary causes usually mobilized by the left. But, as John Gassner writes in his forward to Morgan Y. Himelstein's *Drama Was a Weapon,* America in the 1930s fell naturally after the Depression into an active sympathy for a Marxism "frequently parroted rather than understood" by most of its theatrical adherents. And ironically, New York's Communist press was as critical of Clifford Odets, for all his loyal demonstration in *Awake and Sing* and *Waiting for Lefty,* as Stalin was at much the same time about Meyerhold's theater or Shostakovich's opera *Lady Macbeth of Mtsensk,* though it has to be said on America's behalf that nobody, right or left, set out to murder Odets for his deviations from policy. The irony that really hurts, however, is that the Odets living room, replete with quarrels and insults, soon became the bedrock model for generations of family plays, usually telling much the same story of fathers and sons, mothers and daughters, as if nothing more momentous could be imagined. Odets, the father of politics in American theater, turned out to be the father of T.V.'s situation comedies.

If only theater was ever as dangerous as Plato feared. Conscious citizens, in or out of the theater, grieve for the dead, the dying, the injured—all those traduced by power, whether corporate, government, parent, or lawyer. But it's not likely that playwrights or directors will be able to make much sense of change out of the issues of the day. Give us a war, as presented to us periodically in living color, and there's barely enough struggle left to keep up with the headlines or the highly sophisticated censorship that mobilize public opinion. I may conclude, as I did not too long ago, that Abraham Lincoln was wrong: most of the people can be fooled all of the time. Yet if I were to take that cranky perception into drama, I'm reasonably certain it wouldn't translate comfortably into art. More to the point, I might suddenly remember that Ibsen had already seized it for *An Enemy of the People,* his most topical and least substantial play.

Our own century, no stranger to the urgent issue, has known and even cultivated theaters and plays that often make an honorable case for politics in drama. The Living Theater, at its best, exposed the underside of the drug experience and the Marine Corps long before Hollywood discovered what is sensational in those subjects; and even at their tendentious, hectoring worst, they presented a joy in sensuality and a loathing of repression that would have sent Plato into an apoplectic fit. Rolf Hochhuth, in *The Deputy,* caused some of us to worry more about Pope Pius XII's cozy silence about Hitler. Bertolt Brecht's most popular work, *The Threepenny Opera,* may be his most frivolous, and he's likely to be remembered as much for his stagecraft as for his plays, but who can utterly deny the assurance of his passions, those surprising questions without answers that mark his playful and anguished fables? Cunning as always, Brecht dangled party lines only in his learning plays. Once he threw himself into imaginary Chinas, Floridas, Chicagos, he was no longer bound by topical reality, even as he expropriated the familiar image of Galileo or Hitler. It's almost as if Brecht had to know that when the Berlin Wall would fall, he'd still be there, his East German paymasters in disgrace forever. He may have styled himself the century's most political playwright, but intricate theatrical constructions, densely populated with contradictions and doubts, were his lifeline, just as survival was his daily life.

Theater copes with the present by recalling its roots in a reliable, unaligned past. "I can't go on. I'll go on," is not Beckett suddenly descending to political statement; but a day doesn't pass on the streets of New York or at a glance of the news when I don't mutter that terrible admission to myself. Theater will always be too late to save us from the momentary crisis, yet it can always bear witness, and that is surely enough.

(September 1991)

Othello's Occupation's Gone

Among the ethical pratfalls and linguistic somersaults that marked most of the Clarence Thomas hearings, petty misdemeanors against dramatic literature may leave only a faint stain on the ultimate reckoning; yet surely they demonstrate that great drama, even when traduced and betrayed, has its uses. Witness the spectacular slip, ignorant rather than Freudian, made by Senator Alan Simpson when he was moved to quote Shakespeare on Judge Thomas's behalf. Thomas had not exactly covered himself in eloquence during the initial hearings, and the prose unleashed for his defense against Anita Hill's charges of sexual harassment—"high-tech lynching" and heart-tuggers such as "I died"—might have been effective with the peanut gallery, but it was a long way from the pseudo-iambics we'd like to hear from lips tipped for high-court deliberations.

Enter Simpson. Not about to reveal the substance of the anti-Hill charges that had flown over his transom, he was ready to call on Shakespeare—"the Bard"—for Thomas's rescue. With an argument framed from the outset as Thomas's word against Hill's, Simpson chose *Othello* as his text, evidently counting on two fallacies to make his case inviolate— that characters are always speaking for their playwright's views, and that the wronged Thomas would benefit from close association with the wronged Othello. He could rely, too, on the reasonable certainty that nobody—neither senator, staff member, nor T.V. commentator—would be able to catch him on the astounding association he was really making. In those orotund, southern-accented tones most senators use even when they're from the Northwest or Pennsylvania, he said:

> Who steals my purse steals trash; 'tis something, nothing;
> ....

> But he that filches from me my good name
> Robs me of that which not enriches him,
> And makes me poor indeed.

Far more to the point than "I died," especially since the entire performance was always calculated to send the dead Thomas posthaste into the
heavenly costume of a Supreme Court justice.

Yet if Simpson had been forced to identify Iago as the true source of this
utterance, the judge's cover would have been blown, though no doubt
Democrats would still find a way to kill opportunity with the kindness in
their complicit souls. Iago it is, however, drama's most consummate liar,
resentment gnawing him alive, crafty at only one supreme enterprise—
manipulating the fragile emotions of men, women, and crowds.

Plays, at their best, are an improvement on life, for unlike Simpson and
Thomas, Iago is finally found out. But even if *Othello* is infinitely more
satisfying, the Senate hearings acted as stern reminders that plays today are
letting us down. Not because they fail to be political; rather that they are
like house pets, free from moral conflict as they are of ideas. Simpson's
misappropriation of *Othello* is a sign of more than national cunning or stupidity: it's at once an exposure of reductive politics—the presumption that
the weekend's drama is only about one or another's good name—and the
conceit that great drama itself is merely referential and homiletic. Drama
without ambitious reach into the darkness of experience prepares the way,
however inadvertently, for the surrogate banality of public discourse.
Sham emotions in debased language are what the audience understands
when little else is available. It's the shame of our stage that *Dynasty* and
Dallas set the ground rules. Thomas and Hill appear to be the agonized
protagonists when all along complexity's on trial.

"Mostly," says one political commentator, "it was just theater, hard-
boiled men pretending to be shocked by words like 'penis' and 'pubic
hair.'" Which is not only the common ploy of trivializing theater, it's also
the child's dumb idea that acting is pretending. If we in the theater can't
agree on the need for a drama at least as quarrelsome as our lives, then
how can anybody recognize that good acting, like any art, is deep inside a
reality far more true and present than anybody's public behavior? Harold
Clurman intended otherwise, but his sharp provocation that theater is

"lies like truth" has encouraged thousands of bad actors—Ronald Reagan, Oliver North, Orrin Hatch, Simpson, Arlen Specter, and Thomas among them—to turn their lies into the choked voices, programmed tears, and portentous monotones that real stage actors—John Gielgud, Michael Redgrave, Peggy Ashcroft, and Ralph Richardson, for example —would never admit into their rehearsal, however "over the top" they might be inclined to move from time to time. An electorate in touch with the experience of its own diminished income and impoverished spirit would recognize such distinctions, even in the absence of an enabling theater. But it doesn't help when the vacuum is there to be filled by the tawdry theatricality of the Senate hearings.

If theatricality is all we need, then no wonder the Metropolitan Opera purveys the Disney idea that the twilight of the gods can be encompassed by tumbling plastic rocks that just happen to knock Hildegard Behrens senseless whenever she gets in the way. Or that a helicopter on stage is worth more than the complicated business of actors meeting the argumentative pain and playfulness of great playwrights like Ibsen, Chekhov, and Shaw. Am I simply caught in the downdraft of my semi-annual frustration when I'm compelled to notice that theater is missing still another year when it might have prepared us for the enveloping mendacities in public life? George Herbert Walker Bush admits he lacks "the vision thing," but he has, most assuredly, a directorial concept that warrants more than casual resistance. It scarcely matters that the odds are against good plays and that few in the T.V. audience are positioned to listen, but it does matter when those who know better keep spreading lies like lies.

How terrific it would be if reaction to these hearings were more than an excuse for another *Saturday Night Live* sketch, if plays were around nourishing our laughter and tears in advance of national disasters, and if the terms of the debate were framed by modern Iagos, Angelos, Tartuffes, and Torvalds, so that nobody alert could be gulled by Simpson or walk away quite so easily from such instructive connections. It's only a forgivable exaggeration to say that Thomas is ours for the next forty years because White House playwrights have successfully usurped our territory.

By which I'm suggesting that theater continues to be essential, more so when nobody is watching or listening. Too late now, but the offstage scene in those hundred-plus days before Thomas's disgraceful confirmation were surely more dramatic than anything staged for the cameras — Thomas enduring punishing lessons from the spin-doctors, breaking him into pounds of perspiration as he learns to be silent about *Roe v. Wade,* or practicing indignation and that basso-unprofundo catch-in-the-throat when referring to death and lynching.

> "You remember Ollie, dontcha Clarence?"
> "Ollie who?"
> "Come off it, boy, you know who I mean."
> *(Pinter pause.)*
> "So show your stuff, Clarence. Rage. Tears. Worked for Ollie. Can work for you."

Or Senator Kennedy, trapped everlastingly in the role he's been rehearsing for years — the Chekhov doctor who's forgotten how to treat disease because he's so diseased himself with amnesia, compromise, and alcoholic stupor. Or the three weird sisters, Specter, Simpson, and Hatch, rehearsing bafflement about a woman's anguish while enacting their holy vows to cut her up alive — Specter as Grand Inquisitor, Simpson as Iago, and Hatch barely separating upper from lower teeth as he reruns Joe McCarthy.

Perhaps we're too close to events, but it's not easy to recall a time (even as I mention McCarthy) in which scoundrels were interfering so shamelessly in the balance and civility of our lives. Momentous themes are never in short supply, but 1991 is banner: a useless war, a twentieth-century revolution overturned, and still another closed mind on the Supreme Court. Most of the plays we see, on the other hand, seek to provide solace against the evidence, as void of "the vision thing" as Bush himself.

If I'm counseling anything prescriptive, despite my reluctance to trade in the enemy's coinage, it would lie in the realm of reclaiming the use of drama from those who debase it with the rotten grammar that circumscribes every thought, phrase, and melodramatic gesture their improvisational nuttiness can't cover up. I'd tell those playwrights to read *Othello* again. Get captured once more by magnitude, titanic scope, arias dredged from bottomless despair, villainy *in excelsis* even as it, too, must submit to the crushing fact that we are here only for an instant. Tragic consciousness may seem an extravagant or elusive indulgence when the prose surrounding us is so stripped of vivacity, nuance, and precision. But without it, theater is likely to remain in the cold, outfoxed and undone by public texts written, rehearsed, and acted by the high-tech hacks America keeps electing.

(December 1991)

The Leader We Invented

No doubt about it: Joseph Papp loved to play David armed with grapeshot and righteousness against official Goliaths such as Robert Moses, assorted mayors of New York, and Jesse Helms. The trouble is that once triumphant, he could transform himself so swiftly into Lear, dispensing rage and dismissal at the drop of his latest whim. Only one event reported by Helen Epstein in her honest, uninflected account of his life, *Joe Papp: An American Life,* can come as a surprise to any who knew him near or far, and that is the heroically touching way in which he alternately confronted and denied the cancer that finally smote him down.

One of Epstein's virtues, surely, is that she doesn't fall into the alluring trap of grandiose, organ-accompanied, biblical prose designed to describe a life that always acted its torments on the widest public stages. She admits to the temptation in her introduction, noting that Papp made her think of "Old Testament patriarchs," but that's as far as she's willing to go. Unlike Papp, she knows her limits, but even that doesn't stop her from the over-sized book so common to biographies these days. Someday, perhaps, the publishing industry will return to the idea that heavyweight lives can be told in lightweight books, but that may be as vain a hope as wishing that Papp might have finally learned to turn himself over to peaceful uses.

Evidently, he wavered—over a twelve-year period—before authorizing Epstein's biography, commissioning instead an oral history of Free Shakespeare in the Park and the Public Theater. Although he returned to Epstein, it remained for his widow, Gail Merrifield Papp, to give her "full access to both the vast New York Shakespeare Festival archive and to boxloads of private papers." Familiar with doubt but a stranger to humility, Papp, I suspect, would have preferred to control his biography as he tried to control everything—and everyone—else. Even as he abandoned playwrights, he never wavered in his conviction that with Shakespeare as his God, the writer would always be the guiding force of his theater. It's reasonable to guess, then, that just as he lived through the writing of others, he might have hoped to live forever through a biography marching to a macho, iambic drum, the book that he most assuredly couldn't write himself, and that Helen Epstein doesn't even dare to try.

Instead, she gives us a life only obliquely on trial, featuring a succession of witnesses who, with varying affection and dismay, point the way to a verdict outside the reductive realms of guilt and innocence. Papp feasted on contradiction: Says Bernard Gersten—the best friend fired from his second-in-command job at the Festival "like some road company Trotsky" (his words)—Papp was "often reversing principles that he had loudly proclaimed earlier." One day Papp might announce that "the main figure in the theater is the actor," but on another he reminds everyone that "in this theater, I'm the creative impulse." One of his strongest partisans is Ellen Holly, an actress who enjoyed her work under Papp—which doesn't prevent her from the exquisite observation that he was "almost frivolously capable of betrayal."

Born Joe Papirofsky in Brooklyn, Papp moved from shame of being a Jew to early cover behind his changed name and finally to late-life pride in his religious heritage. Even at Eastern District High School he is identified by Bina Rothfield, his copresident of the Dramatic Society, as "adorable, very cute...but totally self-involved...not careful about whom he hurt." Papp was married four times, not counting his liaison with the mother of the daughter whom he met for the first time when she was 34. When he learned that one son, Tony, was gay, he assumed instantly that his essential absence must have been the cause—once again demonstrating that a little learning, such as pop psychology, is a dangerous thing. He liked to think that if not for World War II, he wouldn't have been in the theater.

In example after example, Epstein demonstrates clearly that Papp was the eternal autodidact in unexamined conflict with his own miscasting. Never quite addressing her subtitle, "An American Life," Epstein surely suggests that Papp was always an outsider clawing his way to the top of whatever identity would have him. It takes no ghost from the grave to tell us that more than anything, he abandoned or betrayed his friends and colleagues because he was a busy-holic, familiar in the world of presidents, CEOs and artistic directors, poorly prepared for the craft or art in his charge but determined to let nothing stand in the way of his need for power.

Better the theater, perhaps, than the nation or Wall Street. Destructive as he could be, Papp was oddly like that great vandal and builder who became his nemesis–that same Robert Moses who stood so formidably in his way as he fought for Free Shakespeare in Central Park. Even as he hurt recklessly, he also became the only postwar Off Broadwayite to catapult himself into the big time on Broadway while turning the profits of *A Chorus Line* back to an institution that prided itself on opening its door to Poor Theatre stalwarts such as Joseph Chaikin and Mabou Mines. Certainly, he kept his Lafayette Street headquarters humming with talent, even though many artists found themselves passing through a door that was always swinging both ways.

Toward the unthinkable end, he was asked "what he viewed as his most important accomplishment in life." His reply is astonishing only because Shakespeare doesn't figure in it: "Producing David Rabe's plays. And my marriage to Gail." For Rabe, however, this must be bittersweet news. Epstein tells us that he never forgave Papp for the shabby way he produced *In the Boom Boom Room,* a ghastly experience Papp punctuated with an obscene midnight phone call to Clive Barnes at the *New York Times.* "In the end," says Rabe, "we failed each other at the point of our deepest connection–over the plays.... You *had* to be willing to walk, to say no, to risk alienating him when necessary and I didn't do it."

An American life indeed. Few of us are lucky enough to find renown simply because we're the right monster for the historical moment; for all the fame, it must be horrendous to endure the strain of continual cover-up, hiding oneself behind a new name and consuming institution. It's an un-American story, however, in one salutary sense: Papp never took much money for his work, forced only toward the end to concede that he deserved something like security. There are few resolutions: in illness, he found his son, dying before him from AIDS, and he also found pleasure in bird-watching at his home in Katonah. But just as it was too late for his restless instincts to find true sensibility, it was also too late for him to offer reliable good taste. Epstein admits that what Irving Howe wrote of Joe Papirofsky's favorite writer, Michael Gold, "would be used by theater critics to describe" Papp's productions, so why not confirm her prophecy?

"He was a hater of refinements of thought," wrote Howe, "partly because he could not distinguish them from refinements of manners.... The writing that Gold accepted and announced was notable for a naive arrogance, a sweaty earnestness, an utter lack of literary awareness or modulation." No more accurate reflection of that naive arrogance could be found than the list of people Papp approached to succeed him, starting with actor Meryl Streep, moving on to directors Jerry Zaks and Mike Nichols, then—at last—to JoAnne Akalaitis, though he nonetheless went behind her back by offering the job to Robert Marx at the same time. Was he serious? Well, yes—in his way. Only later did Akalaitis discover that he was offering her $30,000 even as others on the staff were pulling down six figures. Like the protagonist in Antonioni's *L'avventura*, an architect who deliberately spills ink over his own drawing, Papp was finally no more serious about Akalaitis than he had been about Rabe—or Shakespeare, for that matter. He rarely loved wisely, and he didn't rule well. It says something about the rest of us in our equally American lives that he was nonetheless the only national theater leader we've ever had.

(December 1994)

Did Dinosaurs Dream

Imagine a nation prepared to coerce its millionaires into supporting rehearsals and productions of new plays. The method would be simple: in the event of a court case of any kind, the overpropertied citizen could save face with a jury by declaring how much he has spent as a patron of the drama, thus proving that he was both a patriot and a democrat. He would recall to the jury that he had been appointed as chief funder for a play at last season's drama festival. To illustrate his magnanimity, he would point out that his contribution represented at least 6,000 days' work at the going minimum wage—in short, that he had been a big spender. With any luck, the jury, grateful that its ritual entertainment had been so munificently protected, would vote an acquittal, the democracy none the worse for getting the best out of its most criminal class.

What was good enough for Athens, guaranteeing reasonably productive rehearsal conditions for Aeschylus and Euripides, ought to be good enough for us. My social utopia—exacting heavy tithes and guilt from the rich—is certainly titillated by the Athenian model, even as I'm forced to recall that this was an isolated example of beneficence in a society otherwise engaged in plunder, slavery, and other disgusting sports, such as holding poets up to ridicule. My theatrical utopia, therefore, has to be constructed from kinder, gentler models. Which don't exist.

Daydreaming, as I often do, about the time machine that transports me into a shareholding membership of the King's Men—learning my lines as they slide off the pen of my colleague, Will—I have to remind myself not only of lousy plumbing but of the exhausting rows about pleasing that cunning king: wiser, perhaps, than Newt and Jesse, but probably not much kinder. Utopia, if it were possible, would be even better than the Globe, combining the best of each monstrous civilization —Handel writing entr'acte music for Shakespeare's plays; Mozart sharing mathematic wisdom with Leonardo; Schubert enjoying a long life, devoted lovers, and heaping plates of trout; Wagner opening up his perfect theater to Mozart's perfect operas; Gordon Craig confining himself to mysterious design while not dreaming of conceptual directing; Shaw and Yeats, smarter than everyone else, yes, but not to be seduced by dictators; Eliot and Pound discovering that they're Jewish. Economists, accountants, and lawyers would be banished forever, along with nation-states, the bomb, the Internet, and the barbaric diction—nouns turned into verbs, "-ize" endings, and all the muddling neologisms (along with the users friendly to them)—that are all "downsizing" us to mewling and puking death.

Just as I can envy Believers, comforted by a utopian afterlife on their way to the inevitable dust, so do I envy Optimists, who, despite the evidence, insist on possibility. Not long ago, I was reading a remarkable review by Edward Said of Eric Hobsbawm's *Ages of Extremes: The Short Twentieth Century, 1914–1991,* in which Said tells the story of Hobsbawm's Part Three, called "The Landslide," evidently an account of "the twenty years after 1973 . . . a world which lost its bearings and slid into instability and crisis," the crisis including such high points as "the re-division of the world into rich and poor states; the rise of ethnic hatred and xenophobic nationalism . . . politics as the art of evasion, and politicians as assuagers rather than leaders; the unprecedented importance of the media as a worldwide force; the rule of transnational corporations . . . the collapse (as he says earlier) of most things—the world economy, socialism, the artistic avant-garde." This, says Said, agreeing with Hobsbawm for a moment, is a picture of the human race, "now clearly undergoing 'a renaissance of barbarism.'" Yet for all that, he concludes his review with the following query: "I would still want to ask whether there aren't greater resources of hope in history than the appalling record our century seems to allow, and whether even the large number of lost causes strewn about does not in fact provide some occasion for a stiffening of will and a sharpening of the cold steel of energetic advocacy."

A friend of mine tells a tale of his Borscht Belt days, when the host at a party toasted the performers with the following wish: "May the bristles on your artistic brush remain forever stiff." I'm willing to echo that sentiment in support of Said's stiffening will and even the apathetic advocacy of anyone prepared to think and act while chewing gum. Said has to be right when he concludes with the observation that "the 20th century after all is a great age of resistance, and that has not completely been silenced." And it's useful that he reminds us earlier of Hobsbawm's "melancholy conclusion" that history "is no help to prophecy." It may be a toss-up over whether Said or Hobsbawm is making the greater or lesser claim to cautionary optimism, but I know, for myself, that I'm not prepared to go gaga over ideological promises of any kind: better to be left behind than to be left or right.

In the middle of the bad news, by the way, Said reports on Hobsbawm's observation that the novel has had a "surprising renaissance . . . in places like Russia, Latin America, and parts of Asia and Africa . . . an exception to the general eclipse of the major traditional aesthetic genres." Yet, even if this is so, what fun and enlightenment can there be for those of us laboring in the vineyard of the other genres? The novel, bless it, is a strange and private place, not fighting to be done on the dole of the downsizers. If I can't take much encouragement from Said's desperate grasp at rhetorical straws, it may be that I'm merely acknowledging what we all know in the middle of the night in the middle of anywhere we happen to be seeking sleep and solace—namely, that this is the century and the history we've got; if we're approaching the seventh age, then we can't fail to notice that battles once fought are being staged again; the ghastliness of history is indeed repeating itself, not as farce but as tragedy.

With the best will in the world, our theaters aren't up to any of it, once again as much a part of the problem as any solution. Of course, I try to re-create that visionary utopia in one way or another every day, delighted by the technology that can bring me a Schubert lied or a Mozart aria at the push of a button. I even try to make a new theater, not out of dreams alone, but out of hard work and a confrontation with necessary bureaucratic devils. But I'm not a dreamer anymore. Utopias, whether tribal fiefdoms or theater companies, are almost always captured by scoundrels. I'm glad that scoundrel Brecht wrote some of the plays he wrote, particularly the ones that show him in a sharply defined struggle with himself. For the most part, like Jerzy Grotowski, I read him now for fantasy. For reality—which is to say, truth by way of the solace to be found in meditative intelligence—I know by now that I shall always be reading Beckett. As he said to one of his friends some days before his death, "If I fall down, don't pick me up." The only utopian dream to capture my belief is the one that tells me to go until I drop.

I'm grateful to my teacher, Bernard Knox, for the reminders about Greek patronage, found in his article "A Duty to Art," in the March–April 1995 issue of *Civilization Magazine,* published by the Library of Congress; Edward Said's review of E. J. Hobsbawm's book appeared in the *London Review of Books,* March 9, 1995.

(June 1995)

Jerzy Grotowski

I can see from a quick scan of my critical scribbles that, like many at the time (the sixties), I took Grotowski at his word: for me, he was one of "a handful of practical dreamers—Martha Graham, the Becks, Stanislavsky, Brecht—who have succeeded in this century against the pressures of a culture insensitive to the real process of work." By 1981, with *The Constant Prince, Apocalypsis cum figuris,* and *Akropolis* only a fleeting memory, I summoned the heresy of a different memory, something I referred to as his "Catholic moan and sadomasochistic urge."

That heresy had stuck in my throat all alone, I suspect, but could be released when it became clear that Grotowski's deliberate moves into something "beyond theater," as I think he put it, had quite plainly left theater out of the equation. The word *paratheatrical* kept coming up to describe what he'd been doing in one laboratory or another, but with titles such as *The Mountain of Flame, The Way,* or *Vigil,* the trail of incense hovered over what looked to be more like therapy than art. Somebody reported that far from singing the song, "the song was singing me," an unforced, touching sentiment, surely, but not one that connects all the dots so insistently laid out by Grotowski in his signature work.

What happened to those dots? I suspect he was simply—or not so simply—running away from the high cost of celebrity and hero worship. That, at the least, is what he found in the West. In Poland he was able for a twelve-year moment to seize the right, from both state and church, to turn their various oppressions into a theatrical intensity that had never been seen before in such harsh darkness and blinding light. With utmost precision, he made the long stretch of rehearsal time his perfect friend—in a barely hidden sense, even his lover. The actors, more physically inspired than any I've seen before or since, were never literally sexual, but their cruel, hair-raising assaults on space were so awash with energy and thrust as to suggest orgy anyway. Maybe Grotowski had uncovered the secret of the Black Mass and was quite understandably running from the unholy terror he kept releasing in theatrical endeavor.

One other odd memory survives: his chameleon presence. When first seen here, he was masked by dark glasses, and in his rumpled, overweight disguise, he looked like the last person to inspire those gorgeous acting athletes. Some years later, he returned pencil-thin, as always whiter than other Occidentals, not exactly an athlete, of course, but possibly more comfortable in his frame. One admirer declared in later years that he looked like a Dürer. What I see in his most recent photograph is the image of old man Ibsen, obdurate, private, everlastingly alone. In the mid-eighties, he had made *Peer Gynt* the springboard for an exercise. He wanted us to know, however, that "it was nothing major, nothing important, and should be ignored." A true artist to the end, refusing what he knows he cannot do — or be.

(February 1999)

Endgames

Legacies and Their Discontents

Oh, please, ye gods and hurricanos, bring back the Cold War! Surely, even thirty years ago, it was kinder to our digestive slime than are its telegenic successors—ethnic cleansing, nationalistic terrorism, the manipulation of markets and currencies, primordial racism and xenophobia everywhere, everybody fighting every two-bit, bystanding sucker instead of the corporate thieves scooting off with the boodle. And then—oh gods can't you spare us?—there's the elected leadership: Bill the satyr who never knew a friend he couldn't betray, Boris the besotted bear, Tony "Blur" (I can't do better than what the British have already coined), and Gerhard Schröder, not shrewder or different from his predecessor, Old King Kohl, monarch of building sites, the very image of what it is to live off the fat of the land—and other people's labor.

Not that their predecessors were eloquent testimony to higher values. It may be only that with screens dominating both work and play, with entertainment the name of everybody's game, the leaders, like the entertainment, are automatically as present to the eye as they are absent to the mind. All that can be said for the camera is that, even as it can be made to tell a few lies, it can't hide everything. What we see is definitely what we get. Would I care so much, however, if I didn't spy the presence of all those political absences in the theater now with us?

How dumb theater has become, a clone of the media dopiness it ought to be using as daily instruction in what not to do. Please understand, I don't claim the authority I once could call upon when I went eagerly to theater (part of my job) three or four nights a week. Now I'm the public at last: I pay for entrance, and consequently I select the doors I might risk entering. So, for a start, my record is clean—almost—on the collected works of Andrew Lloyd Webber. After being dragged to *Cats* in London years ago, I haven't risked a return for more punishment. Nor am I keenly curious about helicopters onstage. For that matter, I don't give a damn about most musicals these days, since, as a lover of singers from Melchior to Merman, I haven't yet acquired a taste for the amplified voice. Further: I would make a Faustian bargain with whatever god is available that in return for the elimination of Sound Design from all our theaters, I would write a month's worth of positive reviews for whatever situation comedies producers would be inflicting upon the stage. (Harmless fun: nobody would believe me anyway.) Then I would beg Shakespeare pretenders, most of them conceptual directors, to take a short course in everything from blank verse to history, perhaps even in reading the texts themselves before embarking upon their crabbed little updates.

It cannot be that I'm spending my cranky gene on technology or the easy target of those few directors in every country who treat theater as their personal playpen, replete with all those new technological toys. The truth always has to be that, apart from the past having its own crimes to hide, the present isn't destined to be worse. Yes, the theater is organized now around the usual suspects: imitative repertories, imitative acting styles, and imitative playwriting, all including one-potato, two-potato, three-potato casts imitating the spoiled-brat lives of couch potatoes everywhere. And yes, it's all too automatically easy to lament the triumph of spectacle, as if we never knew that a Lion King would be more popular than a Lear King.

The looming fallacy, with us even thirty years ago, is to imagine that dramatic literature can be as central to those in hot pursuit of dollars as it is to those who take it not as distraction but as a Book of Instruction in the way we might lead our lives. Drama has always been compelled to reinvent itself, and even when not far from the same ploy as T.V. perpetuates today—playing to the gallery—only at odd moments and from odd characters has it recovered its lonely, eloquent voice. The nineteenth century bore all the hallmarks of a hundred-year war against that eloquence. Don't get me wrong: Dion Boucicault was a daredevil, taletelling melodramatist, often funny to boot, and even the fabled well-made plays—imitations run riot—had their charms. But it remained for Ibsen, Strindberg, Chekhov, and Shaw to rescue the European century from total dramatic disgrace. (Yes, I know about the Russians before them, and I even know that Russia is partly in Europe, but for the public at large—read those contemporary reviews in London and Paris—theater

was meant to be forgettable.) Thanks again to Ibsen, Chekhov, and company, our own fast-departing century has a better record, one that into
the sixties presented a heady mix of (mostly) Boulevard frivolity and,
often enough, Real Drama. By which I mean the other usual suspects:
you know who they are, and for once I'll even give a reluctant wave to
the heroic efforts of Eugene O'Neill, as much a part of the problem,
finally, as he was of the solution, an antistylist with the tinniest of ears
who nonetheless persisted against the prevailing demand to keep complexity and darkness out of our theaters.

We floated from the fifties to the sixties in an "entertainment" capital
that had no trouble welcoming the latest Tennessee Williams play or
whatever the French thought was serious those years (Giraudoux,
Anouilh, even Beckett and Ionesco) and eventually the young Peter
Brook directing Anouilh, then Dürrenmatt with the Lunts, the last pure
stage stars on Broadway, and finally, to sensational effect, Brook again,
with Peter Weiss's *Marat/Sade.* All of which is only sociological summary,
failing to account for wondrous battles over the Method vs. the Brits, or
the distinct emergence of experimental styles, from the Living to the
Open Theater. Our unchartable generation didn't know it was supposed
to choose between screwball movies and living theater: we loved the film
noir, the play black, and anything that touched us where we lived.
Shakespeare's language didn't send us yawning to our dictionaries, partly
because it didn't hurt if the occasional movie star, such as Katharine Hep-
burn, put herself into Rosalind's tights or Portia's robes.

We were not above complaining, however, that the sixties were not
half so glamorous as the thirties. We missed the Group Theatre and the
Mercury; we had been sorry to see Orson Welles off to Hollywood even
as we were the first to see *Citizen Kane* ten times (I was ten) and curse
RKO for wrecking *The Magnificent Ambersons.* The surviving First Ladies
of the theater (why were there no First Gentlemen?) didn't in the final
reckoning look so good: Katharine Cornell barging down Cleopatra's
Nile, baritone drawls in full sail, as if hosting an extremely dignified
debutante's ball; Helen Hayes mooning and swooning through Joshua
Logan's *The Wisteria Trees,* his Deep South adaptation of *The Cherry
Orchard,* still another job not well done and not worth doing. And then

there was the deliciously plummy comic Hermione Gingold, congratulating us in a musical revue on "that magnificent statue of Judith Anderson in the harbor"—and thus providing a useful reminder of how pompously self-important so much of Broadway looked.

No harm in pricking the High Culture balloon at any time. And if I'm mixing up decades, I assure you it's deliberate. The profit and loss columns in my accounting for the nineties had better reflect from the start that theater is both Fox and Hedgehog: it knows many things, but structurally, it is always the mirror held up to one big thing—not quite nature, hardly that, since nature would allow for free forms, unplanned delights, and even unimagined plagues. If not nature, then, something not so elusive, but banal to define: in the face of "dumbing down" in this decade, we're condemned to the same attritional struggle, keeping alive a spirit of inquiry perhaps more common to the poem or novel and much harder to maintain in such a gregariously social genre.

So where do we appear to be now within that prevailing structure? For one startling moment, we should pause to acknowledge that experimental theater, if it ever truly existed—and in the sixties we thought it did —is no longer with us in any particular disguise. I use the word *startling* as my own signal that nothing startles any more: only at the Metropolitan Opera, for example, could a Robert Wilson version of *Lohengrin,* its stately freeze-frames clearing remarkable space for Wagner's ecstatic musical foursquare march to the heavens—only at the sheltered old Met could any of these Rothko quotations arouse the chorus of boos heard opening night, apparently organized by a claque but very much an encouragement to the buzzards lying in wait for anything they haven't seen or imagined before. Surely, with Wilson at the same drawing board more or less successfully for more than thirty years, this can only be a rehearsed form of *startle.* Lucky conservatives are so laggard about the new, they don't even know that moons ago it passed into the old.

But not old hat. If experiment as such has enjoyed its minute of fame, it's partly because it has moved like the global economy itself into regions of extravagant cost. Disney, after all, is on the new, antiseptically clean 42nd Street for the obvious reason that some smart boomers woke up one morning to discover that making our streets safe for stretch limos is a good investment: presto-changeo, once again there's no business like Show Business, especially as brought to you by Big Business. That some of it may be an upmarket version of what looked equally beautiful in the past (as it is evidently with Julie Taymor) should come as no surprise. If property is theft, so is theater: the only measure is why and how well it's being done. So *A Chorus Line,* as I once observed, lifts one scene from the Open Theater's *Mutation Show*—unattributed because there's no copyright on images, which is surely just as well. (I knew the jig was up years ago when, after attending a Happening in a Soho loft, a Mabou Mines' stage manager said huffily in the elevator that the poor sod painter had stolen one of Mabou's images. So much for the purity of the experimental ideal.)

For the rest, not being a quantity surveyor, I'm not prepared to offer statistical proof that theater today is more mundane and boring than it was in the 1960s. Yet it is. Perhaps it's just too well washed and scrubbed. Who can fail to notice how efficient it is? Everything moves in the theater these days except my heart—thousands of light cues, a million instruments, sound booming up your kazoo, overtures of one sort or another before every act, platforms and trestles sliding from here to there in ghostly unison. I doubt that Brecht's revolving stage for Courage's travels would make the slightest comparable effect today. (And who could figure out a silent scream in a theater world addicted to noise?) *Peter Pan* on the Olivier stage at the National Theatre revolves, spins, lowers itself, rises, and literally slides a house and a mounded island from one side to another. The kids love it, and why not? They believe in Tinker Bell, but there's a reasonable chance they won't believe in the alternative magic that theater can deliver, if allowed.

Not always, but too often, what will be missing for them will be the charge brought to the stage by great actors left to themselves. Do I need to explain and illustrate? It may be that arguing with history is like arguing with El Niño. With the gradual disappearance of great actors trained to inhabit stage space with their Olympian talents—voices slicing the air like machetes, bodies submitting to their own designs, gargantuan appetites for the Big Scene, and even a capacity to throttle down to the small, the intimate—there will be only the most elusive ancestral memory for what once was and might be. Film, bless it, doesn't fill the bill, though it's unmatchable for unscripted surprise of a different kind from what the stage can do at its most spontaneous—the splendid, mountainous eyebrow of Spencer Tracy or Jack Nicholson, for example. Sometimes, too, an actor often flaccid on stage, such as Anthony Hopkins, has a field day with those quirks, accents, or glances that suddenly turn him into a virtuoso of buried feelings. For the most part, even when great stage actors take to film, they're never releasing the deep architecture of their true intensities, mostly because, in film, they're not the boss.

I've yet to see Judi Dench in *Mrs. Brown,* but on the evidence of her stage performance in David Hare's *Amy's View,* I know without a doubt that the Oscar this year should have been hers, even though I know equally that Helen Hunt, the only American nominated and as gifted an emotional seismograph as film will allow, was predestined to win because the Hollywood vote is fundamentally a vote for their own pay-packets next year. What is it that Dench at her best does onstage? Some of her arsenal is simple enough: she listens, she breathes, she waits, she pokes at the flower arrangements while listening even more to the voices around her. Hare gives her the best passage in the play when, as an aging actress, she describes what it is to seize the moment, the stage. The description is the demonstration itself, as full, rounded, darkly burnished as anything you could hope to see or hear this side of lieder or chamber music. It's quite definitely ancestral, a throwback to what was more common once, almost an homage to an art that surely can't be dying. But that, of course, is what Hare's play purports to engage: a drama about the actress and her loathsome son-in-law, a T.V. producer-mogul who argues that the stage should simply lie down and finally die. Hare, as is his sub-Shavian wont, tries to be fair to both bastions, but like Strauss letting the music in *Capriccio* win over the words, he gives the last word—and image, Dench in her grimy white makeup just after a matinee—to the actor and the ancient art she's so formidably guarding.

It isn't a play that measures up to its leading actor. Hare, like so many of his contemporaries—David Mamet springs instantly to mind—is by now a compulsive master of his own tricksiness, pulling strings every step of the way, trapping characters in murky talkfest arguments from which the only escape is likely to be still another argument leading to the final black- or fade-out, which, after all, must be reached, if only to keep up the pretense that something momentous has been happening. Maybe it's the processing of words that's beginning to take its toll: Mamet, for instance, seems glued to presenting rapid-fire talkers in most of his plays, often sporting eerie echoes from Warner Brothers' stock company in the thirties. Cagney and Bogart would be at home inside his dialogue, so it's scarcely surprising that he's been showing signs of greater comfort in the movies he's writing and directing. For the stage, however, in this year's *The Old Neighborhood,* he's offering living proof that less is less. Three short skits hanging by threads, one from another, making for three brief expositions and precious little development, and you have the emotional equivalent of afternoon soaps getting uppity about their social standing. Mamet would be hyped by reviewers if he recycled his tax returns, but deep down there's no deep down there: his plays seem to have melted from spreadsheets rather than from an imagination that's actively arguing with itself anymore.

What can be said about reviewing in the nineties—a particularly depressing phenomenon I've come to think we deserve? With all lack of respect, most of it is exhausted, in part from editors offering less space but mostly because there's not much deep down there, also. It's a job, ya know, so what else can be done? At the head of the class is the chattering *New Yorker* (admittedly another easy target), flying in John Lahr from month to month, himself now converted to a new form of criticism in which interviews with principals merge without a hiccup into reviews. Three or four years ago, I started keeping "book" on his movements and sneaky little complicities with hype and publicity, but after a time threw out the evidence, noticing that it never stopped coming on strong anyway: the evidence, I realized, will always be there. Lahr picks out some genuine talent, whether Ingmar Bergman moving from Stockholm to the Brooklyn Academy of Music or Natasha Richardson as Anna Christie on Broadway. But it's still a weird distortion of the hard, analytic role he ought to be playing, reducing the act of criticism to a barely hidden cover for press agentry. Even a hip reader wouldn't be likely to know that when Lahr reviewed the Toronto production of *Ragtime* a year before its New York opening, he may have been nudged there by his publisher, an investor in the show. No doubt that his editor, the vulgar reductionist Tina Brown, thinks it's fun to scoop other journals with hyperbolic blowjobs of shows months (and even a year) before their New York appearance. Lost in all this is the not-much-understood-let-alone-respected job of simply being a witness to stage history.

The larger corruption is that most reviewers are riding the same bandwagons, almost as if they're afraid to file a dissent when all the others are screaming hallelujahs to the latest nonevent. The old complaint was that reviewing took special pleasure in denunciation. Now, instead, while there may be unison about poor, hapless *Capeman,* there's also far more bewildering affirmation, as if popular theater were actually producing mighty new works, the nineties being crowned officially as a golden age. Nothing can find its audience these days without advance notice that the millennium has arrived before the millennium. It ain't easy to be heard above the din, so it's only natural, I suppose, that otherwise literate friends begin to talk in sound bites.

We keep hearing that we're mean-spirited snobs who simply don't want to be entertained like everybody else. But let's not be bullied into any debate over "elitism," not only because the word simply refers to the best, but mainly because the debate hijacks even more space for the stupids who own and operate most of the airwaves and theaters everywhere. If James Cameron is really "king of the world," as he proclaimed at the Oscar ceremony celebrating his *Titanic*—itself a rip-off of better such accounts in books and movies years ago—what time is the next swan to a better world? He's inescapable, naturally, and he's right in the usual ghastly way. But there's more of him than us, so surely there's no need to cede any more territory to him than he already possesses. It's odd how aggressive and mean those populists become. Not content with cash, annuities, and mere power, they still look behind them to make sure that no upstart elitist is threatening their box-office returns. If only.

It's a phony war, diverting attention from the groundwork—a lifetime's labor—that is always there to be done if you give a damn about measuring up to past ideas, present reconstructions, the full show of history addressed, challenged, and reimagined for the sake of making an available and noble art vivid and even threatening once again. In the sixties, American actors were either unprepared, especially for the big sustained energies and hefty vocalises needed for the heavyweights, or they were locked into their sweat-soaked personal expression—mumblers for the most part, unable to think of anything but their close-ups. Soon enough, repairs were made on the acting front, sending hundreds of variations on the same themes in the same packages. This was the U.S. catching up with London and its own clone-regionals: British actors working their way from the definitive Fleance to the umpteenth Treplev seemed to be afflicted by what we used to call the "Old Vic Knee," that reliable placement of leg on step, the hand slapped heartily on top of the bend; American actors could be said to be suffering for decades now from Regional Bleat—loud, clear (at last), but empty to the core.

Not all, of course. But the same can be said for any of my selective overviews. What's distressing about the tricks played by time, inertia, and the damage that's the traveling companion of contingency anyway, is that so many of the survivors are not necessarily the fittest. Our sociological progress, surely, is more than a Good Thing: crossing the gendering and the races is just about the best event (selfishly) that could have happened to a theater art otherwise plagued by the literal and the so-called real—as if actors truly are those characters, or even as if those characters come to us with some kind of fixed biography along with their original colors and genders. But even when such salutary improvements—raising the stakes, pushing down more walls, more barriers—have to be acknowledged, the loss in eccentricities and difference is strange to behold, as if everyone is trying to be like everyone else.

Sometimes, of course, the crimes against theatrical nature are even stranger than that loss. For some unaccountable reason, Alec Baldwin and Angela Bassett wanted to playact the Macbeths this year, bringing yet another stillborn Shakespeare to the New York Shakespeare Festival, scene of more "Bard-icides" than can be usefully counted. No doubt good intentions should be rewarded, and word on the street has it that Baldwin is not only a good fella committed to good causes, but also that he's one of the few screen images willing to face the stage reckoning; that said, however, there's no reckoning worth making on such slouch and lurch as cover for the freewheeling zero buzzing in the collective heads of stars and director (that usual suspect for directorial ditsiness, George C. Wolfe). Why do they bother, especially since it's clear that it's only the violence they understand:

big drum background, lightning flashes, real rain, slash, lunge, and burn, the biggest casualties poetry and the human mind?

I could go on, and you know it: a plus here, a minus there, wondering if that's all that's left, a structureless structure, building blocks for the kids on the block, a theater on the margins, yes, but pushed even further to the edge, mattering less even to those who make it.

So I go on—just a little. To cleanse *Macbeth* from my system there was Cheek by Jowl's *Much Ado About Nothing* in a fleeting visit to BAM, still another Declan Donnellan arrangement marked by smart elisions, a wickedly apt suggestion that the text may actually be about something, and a deliriously high-stepping gift for the poetic gab. Under Donnellan, the update slides effortlessly into illuminating the truth, even if it's not so new to see the British Raj exposing itself as assholedom run amok. That said, the occasion would be even more reassuring if it didn't also mark the moment when Donnellan is putting his company to pasture, at least for a sabbatical time. Like so many today, and even in the 1960s, he's going it alone, perhaps an ever-recurring theme, an open admission that theater can't quite stay together when everything else is falling apart.

If I have to reach for my own form of millennial observation, I'll admit that when that Berlin Wall came down in 1989 we were gulled into thinking for an instant that all the standing structures in our various worlds would suddenly relax into the real business of being alive: making us wiser, helping those less privileged than we have been, turning more and more people onto the fun of knowing more, of learning, doing, teaching, reading, loving, and relaxing. A delusional moment, certainly, but from it I still take a lesson or two. Where theater is concerned—and that's why I'm on this planet—there's only hope in the few not yet bludgeoned into resignation as a way of life. Pockets of resistance are always appearing in the nineties, even if they're compelled to be visible and audible only to those prepared to seek, to see, to listen.

Have I left the sixties to speak for themselves? I hope so, if only because I can live well enough without nostalgia, thank you very much, and I prefer to look to the moment even as I peer out from beneath the covers to see what lies ahead. It was almost uplifting the other night to see Ionesco's *The Chairs* on Broadway, of all places, one jot of evidence that a wheel can

indeed come full circle, and in this case return with a superbly celebra-
tional vengeance, no longer the Absurd, but Reality incarnate. The trick?
Only two great actors in their prime—Geraldine McEwan and Richard
Briers, veterans of Shakespeare, farce, and a thousand other traditions,
chewing up the ample scenery, upstaging the Sound Designer at every
turn, proving once again, as if we didn't know it already, that acting as it
happens only on the stage is indeed the shortest distance from fantasy to
reality: a one-way street to the bottom of our souls.

(June 1998)

The Critic Vanishes

The latest nemesis, then, is nostalgia, precisely what was biting at my heels
when accounting, in 1998, for our legacies and their discontents. In 1999,
Broadway trooped dutifully behind London's lockstep armies, producing
new productions of three mid-century plays: Eugene O'Neill's *The Iceman
Cometh,* Arthur Miller's *Death of a Salesman,* and Tennessee Williams's *Not
About Nightingales,* the latter the only surprise—apprentice work from
Williams's files, never before produced. As usual, the carefully staged
drumbeats signaled universal acclamation, as if plays and actors alike were
beyond compare, the premise behind the hype that theater, like any
respectable Bordeaux, simply gets richer—more "nose"—as the years pass
by. It's a comforting fallacy, especially when, as in the case of *Iceman,* you're
about to reach deep into your pocket for a hundred smackeroonies.

Placing myself at a safe distance from nostalgia is by no means
designed as a vote against the past. If anything theater, more than music
or painting, is in constant thrall to the new, its classics safely embalmed on
specialist reading lists: it takes no ghost to notice that Freud's Oedipus is
better known than Sophocles', while Christopher Marlowe is now likely
to be known mainly as a dishy supporting player in a larkish Oscar-win-
ning fiction about Shakespeare. My theater, if I had one, would be only
too thrilled to resurrect *Tamburlaine the Great,* or even Goethe's *Faust,* for
pity's sake, surely as important to theater as Beethoven's Ninth is to
music. The past is our laboratory and our playground, yet our profession
and our audience remain barely literate in it. Where music has spent the

past half-century in hypnotic and belated obsession with Mahler, performing and recording him in numbers Tchaikovsky would envy, theater keeps Arthur Schnitzler out of sight, forgetting, or perhaps never knowing, that in Mahler's Vienna, Schnitzler was his literary equivalent, breaking molds and hearts in much the same way.

Nostalgia, in any case, is not truly about the past: rather, it's one of several instruments available—like birthday parties, anniversaries, and millennial hysterics—to help us forget that the greatest and only show on earth is the long haul from cradle to coffin that can't be stopped by anyone, not even for ready money. *Iceman* and *Salesman,* both pumped up with bombast about illusions, are theater's gesture to the nation's need for ritual now and then, like one of those ten-hanky state funerals guaranteed to cover the sins in the national past. Displacing grief denied in the home, they're hat-trick illusions, their playwrights too whipped by the unyielding strain for eloquence to notice that professional victims, drowning in self-pity, have no more connection to tragic vision than Sprite has to Sauterne.

Notice I use "hat-trick" as synonym rather than O'Neill's "pipe-dream," repeated shamelessly as evidence that O'Neill can never escape the charge that he's always been a stranger to language. Not that I'd want to hear multiple "hat-tricks" either: what's so awful about the play is its insistence on talking…and talking…when it has so little say. Hickey makes his entrance eighty minutes into the first act, and yet there are still two more acts to go. What's worse is that, star-power notwithstanding (this time Kevin Spacey, a loose-limbed charmer skimming fearlessly over the surrounding monotonies), Hickey turns out not to be the protagonist at all. Having done the deed before his entrance, what finally matters is how Larry Slade will act upon the news. Hickey is touched by O'Neill's saving grace—his ancestral, barnstorming nineteenth-century attraction to the big gesture—but only a writer bewitched by his own confusions could so strenuously evade the consequential dramatic richness in the character still with everything at stake. Think of Lear abandoned on the heath by his playwright while Edmund natters for the rest of the play about his grievance.

Mary McCarthy, in a 1946 review of *Iceman* that should have wiped the play forever from the pseudocultural map, reports that "*pipe-dream* recurs with a crankish and verbally impoverished tastelessness about two hundred times during the play." Bully for her, troubling to count or exaggerate: what's more striking is her unmasking of how this well-made play, like so many of its more manicured cousins, strays so far from one observable reality or another even as it pretends to be in a location we can all recognize. O'Neill's derelicts, as she puts it, never show the "terror of drink." They lay down their heads on tables, but they're never "visibly drunk or hungover — no obscurity of thought, no dark innuendoes, no flashes of hatred." The play's realism spreads itself across the stage only as "mood or décor," each character released only to a single, persistent trait — grouchiness, Englishness, Boerishness. In perhaps her most devastating observation, these "non-verbal, inarticulate" monologists "arrive not at despair but at a strange, blank nihilism."

(I cite McCarthy, incidentally, for two driving reasons, not because I share her views all the time [she's obtuse, even dumb, about Williams]: first, her sentences are so much more fluent and targeted than O'Neill's, and second, she's a critic free of sentimentality — i.e., nostalgia — in every word she writes, including *and* and *but*.)

I don't want to drift into the "-isms" quagmire, but McCarthy's comments compel me to sigh once again over "realism" as the black hole into which so much dramatic possibility has fallen. One need not pick a quarrel with the genre's honorable origins or associations, especially the late nineteenth-century geniuses who couldn't help investing every "real" event and character, every cross-conversation, with the layered density and mysterious half-lights in a Rembrandt oil. What never occurred to Ibsen, Strindberg, or Chekhov is that drama might emerge from rooms full of characters whose verbosity is matched only by the paucity of their vocabulary.

Hickey drones, Willie is a beached wail. I'd like to respond otherwise, since I still harbor gratitude to Arthur Miller, Elia Kazan, Jo Mielziner, and especially Lee J. Cobb for their inadvertent assistance at my real birth in 1949. Beached myself in Yale's freshman year, I was made to know forcibly that as a token marginal — Jewish, unathletic, short, and no possible candidate for future American leadership — I had better find some ambitions in double-quick time. My father had shoved me into heavy doses of chemistry, atomic physics, logic, and calculus. Later, he loomed in my memory as a master of manipulative dramaturgy, condemning his leading character to—what?—blankness, failure, a nihilistic decision to snuff himself out.

Inserted into this charming scenario, and only too much aware that there are no third acts for Americans, was my first visit to Broadway's *Death of a Salesman,* followed by subsequent clandestine side trips to second acts featuring Willies such as Thomas Mitchell, Gene Lockhart, and Albert Dekker. Already the glow was fading, though I wouldn't admit it, nor could I name the reasons. Had I the cash or self-respect (more important) to do so, I might have jumped the Atlantic in my sophomore year to catch Paul Muni's Willie, probably moved, though no doubt baffled, as I was later, by Muni's sour comment that he could never figure out where Miller's prose was giving way to Miller's poetry, or the other way around. I'd been rescued, yes, from paternally determined fate, but I still needed time to discover that first love usually sows seeds for first betrayal. For years I could carry myself on the ambition to repeat the Cobb experience, not available from the other actors, and—as I came to think during the next twenty years—not likely to be available ever again because that sizable, organ-voiced Cobb performance had lumbered down from the Book of Job, Miller's words and arrangements mere pretexts for Cobb's version of all God's outlaws.

It's only a low-grade contradiction to admit that, despite evidence of a mind now closed to *Salesman,* my heart still skips a half-beat whenever facing Willie in new outings by actors such as Dustin Hoffman and Brian Dennehy, especially in their scenes with the latest Biff. Willie's halting steps toward discovering the boy's love are mapped by Miller with a surer hand than he has managed anywhere else. Suddenly, it doesn't matter that we've been imprisoned in an airless, dumb-luck universe where Woman plays drudge while Man plays Peter Pan. Miller is tapping into an almost invisible, primordial source, something at once savage and delicate, lying in an outer darkness too terrifying for most of us to face.

These scenes keep the play on performance rails for me: revelation, so hard to find in the daily grind, is more than welcome in a play. Even so, it's easy to jump off the nostalgia train when considering that the route to those authentic passages will be dominated by the avuncular preacher-engineer running it. A better memory, not likely for revival, would be

Rosalyn Drexler's *Room 17-C,* her wicked 1985 deconstruction of *Salesman* in which all destinies are liberated into an Alice-Wonderland where Linda can finally warn Willie not to kill himself because "it'll be anticlimactic," one of the most eloquent lines of dramatic criticism I've ever heard.

Tennessee Williams's *Not About Nightingales* is not literally a nostalgic return from the past, since it had been safely buried by its author soon after its rejection more than sixty years ago. Well known as a prebreakfast writer and a lunchtime critic, Williams used to toss his newest pages into the trash from where they were rescued by his friend of the day. Without these rescues, Amanda Wingfield and Blanche DuBois may have disappeared forever into that great memory play in the sky, even though there's equal evidence that the Bird—as he was known by friends such as Gore Vidal—was happy enough to see his chicks returned to the nest for revision.

That said, there are few clues in *Nightingale* that *The Glass Menagerie* or *A Streetcar Named Desire* might be lying in wait for their creator's liberation from the models he had been encouraged to use in his University of Iowa playwriting classes. These included regular assignments to produce short plays based on newspaper stories, clearly connected to the rage at the time for the "living newspaper." The exercises gave him the freedom to imagine formal techniques outside the realm of neatly arranged kitchens and living rooms: a spread of public events over dozens of episodes, strong lighting contrasts, voice-over announcements, chants, mood music, and even caption titles to prepare the scenes, all in aid of broadcasting the playwright's indignation about major social abuses.

Soon after pleasing his teacher, Edward C. Mabie (formerly a leader of the Federal Theatre Project), with early efforts, he fell out of favor on the submission of two scripts: the first, a contribution to a collaborative documentary about socialized medicine, the second a "tragic" love story, his response to an assignment to write an autobiographical play. According to Allean Hale, editor of the *Nightingales* text, Mabie "tore up" the medical play because it was such "a searing indictment" of doctors. He may not have recognized that this, too, was autobiographically inspired, Williams's earliest public reaction to his sister's frontal lobotomy.

The love story, *Summer Storm,* may well have been a dutiful response to the assignment, but ending as it did with "the heroine stripping to the buff," it shocked Mabie and the class into silence – an early sign that Williams was drifting away from the rule books. "Mabie," says Hale, "did not further Tom's application to pursue a graduate degree at Iowa," in retrospect, the push he needed into the merciful discovery of his own voice.

It was one thing to get kicked out of the Iowa system, another to kick the system out of himself. Within a month after picking up his bachelor's degree, his eye fell on a news story about the Klondike Massacre, the literal roasting alive of striking convicts in a high-security Pennsylvania prison. In what must have been white heat itself, Williams drafted *Hell*, describing it as "an expressionist drama based on the prison atrocity in Philadelphia County." In a matter of weeks, this became *Not About Nightingales*, the best, he thought, of his four long plays. His confidence, however, did not sustain him: soon, in his journal, he was calling it "pretty cheap stuff." And then a month later, as Hale reports, "it seemed incredibly bad, and he felt quite desperate." By the end of what could have been his first graduate semester, he decided to put the third draft away, "unsure," says Hale, "whether it was very good or very bad."

Am I alone in my knee-jerk regard for Williams's privacy? In the absence of word from the other side that his confidence in *Nightingales* has been restored, there's no reason to assume that he would grant permission for its first production. Charting a playwright's innocent beginnings in his archives makes perfect scholarly sense; producing them in London and New York theaters, however, looks like carelessness; and giving them over to Trevor Nunn's gargantuan appetite for flashy directorial display turns out to be a mode guaranteed to wrench *Nightingales* cruelly out of context. This is graverobbing, not revival, nostalgia turned on its head into another form of lie – the past dressed up to look and feel like the present. Just as directors argued in Congress against colorizing their black-and-white movies, so too might dead playwrights argue that there oughta be a law against tarting up their buried children, to say nothing of leaving them in peace.

But there I go again, resurrecting my ancient quarrels with directors who can't resist colonial usurpation of other people's visions. The irony in this instance is that *Nightingales* reads more like movie than play, "a film noir," in Hale's words, almost an inevitable development from a young man in the habit of escaping to black-and-white movies every night. All the more reason, if it had to be done at all, for a production not given to technicolor. Nunn releases the ear-splitting screams of prison whistles almost as often as O'Neill spouts "pipe-dream." And since it's modern times, most of his actors assault our ears with seriously abused voices. Williams has yet to find nuance of his own, so to claim, as Hale does with uncommon generosity that, in "dialogue and characterization," he's already "surpassing" the model of Wallace Beery's 1935 prison movie *The Big House* is to say not very much indeed. Hale is a skilled archival detective inclined to turn miniscule clues about the future Williams into heavy-breathing significances: she calls *Nightingale's* plaintive, Priscilla Lane heroine "flirtatious," but it's a leap-and-a-half to link this quality, as Hale does, to Blanche du Bois. So far as I can recall, flirting is an action, part of Rosalind's armory when seducing Orlando, for example, and not a notable sign of playwright-at-work. Director, scholar, producers—all of them—have been flirting with reflected glory from a not so glorious play.

Unlike our vulture culturists, Williams kept moving on, sometimes even embarrassed with his past, finding lines such as "I've always depended on the kindness of strangers" as the occasion for one of his great, hacking guffaws. Ten years after the *Nightingales* exercise, he has *Menagerie* and *Streetcar* safely behind him as well, his mastery of line and lyric perfectly intact. Would he wish to give his millennial final word to a pre-articulate John Garfield clone who tears up "Ode to a Nightingale," identifying it to Ms. Lane as "a little piece of verbal embroidery by a guy named Keats"? Or would he take this occasion as an opportunity to summon up his last guffaw?

The late John Dexter, a British director noted for planning his work with actors in much the same way as Alfred Hitchcock anticipated shot after shot on a storyboard, was once exasperated by a group of actors luxuriating in subterranean levels of energy, turning his blocking into the theatrical equivalent of a shamelessly lugubrious wake. Unable to contain his frustration any longer, he suddenly erupted into the following request:

"Why don't you act"—and here he made the most of a hastily invented Pinter pause—"Why don't you act better?"

Perhaps that is as much as I want to ask of theater anymore: Act better. Or to raise the stakes: Act more like an event fit only for the stage. Shakespeare did well enough with the resources of the day, and even as we embellish him with the latest technologies, he's still back there echoing his *Henry V* Chorus: "On your imaginary forces work."

But this does not mean that, as audience, we are alone in the endeavor. The Chorus is asking us to give way to the actors, to allow them to populate the space with detail:

> And let us, ciphers to this great accompt,
> On your imaginary forces work.

Note the humble stance—"ciphers"—which for an instant reflects only on actors but quickly embraces the rest of us, busily surviving in our own great reckonings. Shakespeare's humility here can barely disguise his pride. Not so secretly, he knows his stage, with its "flat, unraised spirits," can "dare" to bring forth "the great object" of a kingdom—"two mighty monarchies," in fact. And in the end, it will be our thoughts, joined to the dramatist's limitless powers, that will refine the most amazing conflicts into parings containable in "an hour-glass." His business is to rearrange time and space, and in so doing, the ciphers will play their part.

Yet if play and players are—for me—still the thing, they don't need me to take up arms on their behalf. They go their way quite properly with no thanks to prophets or programs anywhere, and if they must share space with Big Brother technologies, the best of them will make themselves felt anyway. In the millennium's dying fall, it might appear that theater has lost its hold, crowded out by the prevailing infotainment networks, websites, and other assorted bombardments from capitalism's momentary victory over common good sense. But as the original maker of illusions—not pipe-dreams—more informative than mundane realities, it can still find forms yet undreamt.

Some of us will not be there to see them. This is cold fact. The warm truth, however, is that theater, even working below its purer levels, always casts light on how fragile we are: every act is ephemeral; like it or not, we have our entrances and our exits. With the latter in mind, I'm arguing against nostalgic returns and obsessive rewrites of the past because I'm arguing with myself about my own memory plays—or the way memory plays with my vision, my life. An exit now from dramatic criticism, however, need not be a fond farewell to life, though that, too, must surely come. It means slowing down the search for the perfect theatrical wave, consolidating all the memories into material for new ideas, fresh endeavors. It means—one final nod to Mr. Beckett—giving up and going on.

(October 1999)

Index